AN UNCHARTED JOURNEY

BERTHA C. REYNOLDS

Bertha C. Reynolds

AN
UNCHARTED
JOURNEY

FIFTY YEARS OF GROWTH IN SOCIAL WORK

NASW PRESS

National Association of Social Workers, Inc.
7981 Eastern Avenue, Silver Spring, MD 20910

Richard L. Edwards, ACSW, *President*
Mark G. Battle, ACSW, *Executive Director*

*To young social workers who are facing realities and shaping our
profession with courage and creative energy*

Other books by Bertha C. Reynolds
Learning and Teaching in the Practice of Social Work
Fifth edition, National Association of Social Workers

Between Client and Community; A Study in Responsibility
Third edition, National Association of Social Workers

Social Work and Social Living: Explorations in Philosophy & Practice
Second edition, National Association of Social Workers

Copyright © 1963 by Bertha C. Reynolds

An Uncharted Journey
First edition by Citadel Press, New York, 1964.
Second edition by Practitioners Press, Hebron, Conn. for the
Bertha C. Reynolds Centennial Committee with the permission of
Rachel Levine, Executrix, Publishing Rights, Bertha C. Reynolds Estate
Third edition by the NASW Press, 1991

Reynolds, Bertha Capen, 1885–1978
    An uncharted journey: fifty years of growth in social work /
Bertha C. Reynolds.
      p. cm.
    Reprint. Originally published: New York : Citadel Press, 1963.
    Includes bibliographical references and index.
    ISBN 0-87101-193-X
    1. Reynolds, Bertha Capen, 1885–1978. 2. Social workers—United
States—Biography. I. Title.
HV28.R48A3 1991
361.3'2'092—dc20
    [B]   90-28265
                                                                               CIP

CONTENTS

Part One: BEFORE GREAT CHANGE

1   EMBARKATION   13
2   SOCIAL RESPONSIBILITY   23
3   FIRST PRACTICE   45

Part Two: A PSYCHOLOGICAL REVOLUTION

4   EVERYONE IS A LITTLE QUEER   57
5   THE TWIG IS BENT—A TREE INCLINED   71
6   DRAWING OUT AND LEADING FORTH   85
7   CLINICS AND RESEARCH   98
8   POISED FOR ADVANCE   116

Part Three: ECONOMIC EARTHQUAKE

9   THE SOLID EARTH IS SHAKEN   135
10   VITALITY   153
11   RETHINKING   170

Part Four: ADVENTURES IN EDUCATION

12   NEW DIRECTION   189
13   LEADERS AND TEACHERS   197
14   TEACHER ON WHEELS   210

Part Five: WAR CLOUDS AND SMOG

15   PAUSE IN TRANSIT   231
16   KEEP 'EM SAILING   243
17   THE SMOG THICKENS   260
18   EDDIES OF CONTROVERSY   279

Part Six: HARBOR

19   TIME TO REFLECT   295
20   WE HOLD THESE TRUTHS   311

Notes   325
Index   347

ACKNOWLEDGMENTS

Acknowledgment is gratefully made to the following for permission to quote from books and periodicals of which they are the publishers: The Commonwealth Fund; the Department of Mental Health of the Commonwealth of Massachusetts; Family Service Association of America; Holt, Rinehart and Winston, Inc.; National Association of Social Workers; National Conference on Social Welfare; National Travelers Aid Association; and Russell Sage Foundation. Specific credit for quoted material will be found in the Notes section of this book.

FOREWORD

Bertha Capen Reynolds (1885–1978) was one in a generation of intellectually restless women that included Jane Addams, Edith Abbott, and Dorothy Day. These women were looking to move beyond traditional domestic roles to careers that could give a respectable but vigorous air to their feminine and religious impulses to do good works.

Social work gave Reynolds's missionary spirit a scientific base with which to convert the traditions of charity and reform into paid professional work. This spirit of reform, combined with a deep personal striving for independence, was part of a more general movement led by Reynolds and like-minded women who were molding the traditionally female professions of social work, teaching, and health care. Christopher Lasch, in *The New Radicalism in America 1889–1963*, saw in these women a rebellion against the circumscribed norms and values of their middle-class milieu.

Unable to confront both her urgent quest for autonomy and her alienation from everything connected with the constraints of a lifeless Puritan upbringing, Reynolds plunged into the kind of "nervous prostration" common to other educated women of her time. Jane Addams, writing of her own neurasthenic sufferings, described similar conflicts—the yearning for adventure and the desire to truly experience life while at the same time feeling fear in the face of that experience.

For Reynolds, conflict and contradiction were familiar companions from the earliest days of her religiously conditioned New England upbringing. She was descended from Mayflower passengers who brought with them values of thrift, self-sufficiency, and service to God and country. But the young Bertha, growing up on a subsistence farm with her widowed mother, brother, and other family members, associated these values with the family's austere, reduced circumstances. In fact, paradoxes and controversies marked Reynolds's life and are the salient theme of her professional autobiography. She was a Marxist with strong religious beliefs, a Freudian rigorously trained in psychiatric social work who had an unwavering commitment to unionism and revolutionary social change, and a shy and contemplative intellectual who vociferously took principled and often unpopular stands.

At the beginning of her "uncharted journey," Reynolds presents herself as a maverick. Although it is true that she had radical ideas, the image of maverick, or dissenter, does not do justice to her role as loyal critic. Reynolds's contributions were not just those of an "unbranded outsider," but of one who carefully directed her critique toward broadening the knowledge base of social work. In challenging the boundaries of social work theory, Reynolds sought to include the study of political economy and Marxist theory. However, in the reactionary political climate of the McCarthy era, social work's institutional boundaries contracted, and Reynolds found herself excluded from mainstream professional circles.

Reynolds's working life began in 1914 when two phenomena converged: the entrance of women into the professions of teaching, social work, and nursing and the professionalization of the helping role of social work. In 1915, Abraham Flexner challenged social work's claim to professional status because, he said, it lacked the transmissible body of knowledge or method to qualify it as a profession. Shortly after publication of the "Flexner Report," Mary Richmond formulated a theory and method of investigation, diagnosis, and treatment modeled after the medical profession that could be transmitted through professional training. Reynolds hoped that she could be trained in this scientific casework method while working with children and families at the Boston Children's Aid Society.

Psychoanalytic concepts had filtered down to an elite group of social workers, predating their general acceptance by the social work profession in the mid-1920s. Reynolds was in the vanguard of most developments in the field, and she was among the first group of social workers at the Smith College formal training program in psychiatric social work. But she felt ambivalent about the psychiatric approach to social work. On the one hand, she was attracted to Freudian theory because it met her intellectual needs and provided her with a science of human behavior. On the other hand, she objected to the medical model of social work practice because of its tendency to locate pathology within the individual. Instead, Reynolds began viewing behavior as an adaptive response to the transactions between the person and the social system in his or her environment.

After World War I, as America sought to deal with returning shell-shocked soldiers and their families, the country became interested in psychiatry and the cause and treatment of mental illness. By arming itself with a scientific knowledge base, social work believed it could claim legitimate status with other professions. Increasingly, casework was being shaped by Freudian theory. While most social caseworkers were forming diagnostic treatment plans to "cure" the individual, Reynolds began to develop a philosophy of practice that addressed itself to the natural forces of life adjustment and growth.

During the Great Depression, in the face of massive economic deterioration, social work was embroiled in a professional crisis. Helpless to deal with the overwhelming extremes of poverty and the social dislocation engendered by the depression, social work had retreated to an emphasis on counseling, with the government taking over the role of reformer and service provider through the proliferation of New Deal public assistance and economic recovery plans and projects. During these years, Reynolds turned toward political activism and left-wing political ideology for a philosophy of social work practice. Along with younger rank-and-file workers, she strove for the unionization of social work and direct struggle for social change.

Reynolds wanted to revolutionize the relationships through which both social worker and client were bound to the system of social service delivery. She sought to empower clients by relocating social work "at the crossroads of everyday life" and by placing the client in control of services. In seeking to empower social workers, Reynolds challenged the structure of the profession by broadening the intellectual base of the field through the creation of interdisciplinary advanced training for the leadership of the profession and by working to unionize social workers. To this end she designed a curriculum, the so-called Plan D, to broaden and restructure social work's intellectual foundations.

Reynolds designed Plan D as an advanced post–master's degree training program at the Smith College School for Social Work, where Reynolds had been Associate Director since the mid-1920s. This program embodied her response to the challenges posed to social work by the depression. By including course work on economic principles applied to social work practice, political theory, and group theory, in addition to personality theory, Reynolds gave the profession's future leaders a sound interdisciplinary education that could serve as the foundation of a critique of society. After three years, however, the director of the school withdrew his support of Plan D, and Reynolds left Smith in 1938.

After working as a casework supervisor for the National Maritime Union, it seems that Reynolds was subject to an unofficial blacklisting; after 1947 she failed to find a job in her field. In keeping with her character, she turned this adversity into opportunity and used the time to write two books and numerous articles and manuscripts about religion, ethics, and Marxism; social and political issues; and social work theory and practice.

In the dedication to *Social Work and Social Living,* Reynolds wrote, "This book is dedicated to an unbreakable tie with the interests of humanity." Reynolds placed social work firmly within the framework of collective relationships, regarding the client–social worker relationship as an alliance rather than a mechanism of social control. For social workers today, this paradigm is of major importance. As new generations enter the field, social work continues to seek its function and role within a changing society. In times of widespread depersonalization, poverty, racial and class strife, and moral decline, society is confronted with seemingly insoluble problems. Faced with a clientele bound to social work delivery systems by cycles of crime, teenage pregnancy, and vulnerability to abuse, the profession finds itself impelled in the direction of social control. In this profession, dedicated to individual change and social responsibility, we lack the strategies or knowledge to bridge practice and theory to social action.

Reynolds's work provides a humanistic model, one that promotes an alliance among social worker, client, and wider social and political movements. In recent times social work has revived its interest in the contemporary relevance of Reynolds's contribution to practice and social welfare issues. In 1985, centennial celebrations were held at Smith and at the American Orthopsychiatric Conference in New York. That same year saw the founding of the Bertha Capen Reynolds Society. In the progressive tradition of Reynolds, the society is a supportive network for social workers committed to humanistic practice aimed at both individual and social change.

Reynolds based much of her work on an ethical stand summed up in the motto, "people come first." It is to this motto that the profession must now turn in using Reynolds's legacy for guidance through difficult and uncharted territory.

Sharon Freedberg, DSW
Assistant Professor
Lehman College of the City University of New York
Social Work Program

ORIGINAL FOREWORD

There is a certain fascination in contemplating what the world looks like to an ant hurrying about its business in a forest of meadow grass. While we humans assume that we know all that is important, missing meantime the teeming life of the soil of the meadow, it is an adventure to let our imagination range about as if we were indeed ants.

An Uncharted Journey might be called an ant's-eye view of a period of history, for some forty years after 1914, when the changes affecting human life on our planet were so staggering as to defy analysis—and we are still in the midst of them. If we have been accustomed to think that technical progress will solve most of the problems of human existence, which have been identified heretofore with scarcity of the means to maintain life, we have been badly frightened to perceive that technical progress may well destroy life before men ever learn to live with their inventions and each other in peace. A part of mankind has always exploited and wasted the natural wealth of the earth and of human labor. Men have always been afraid of those who might want the same resources they claimed and have become accordingly, as they had the power, aggressive and cruel. The world has now gone into panic lest there will soon be too many people on this earth, and, at the same time, into terror of atomic self-destruction until there is no one left. This has been a period of frantic search for understanding of our past and present to give some guidance for the future. Latterly, a despair-

7

ing note has crept into the brave words of our philosophers : We don't know. We can only hope that humanity will survive to keep trying to understand its own life.

The New England woman whose ant-like journey we are to consider, was caught up in a procession of social explorers whose aim was to try to ameliorate the human struggle for existence at points where it seemed to be failing. The whole period was full of the turmoil of wars and devastation, of want and suffering—even that which related not to lack of physical necessities so much as to hunger of the spirit. It may seem a paradox that in the presence of mass misery, of which the world was more conscious than ever before, a profession dealing with individuals one by one should come to a striking development. On second thoughts, it is not strange, for men and nations often respond to mass misery with fear, and turn, in their sense of helplessness, to limited solutions that are indubitably important to those immediately concerned. So social casework came to dominate other forms of social work in this period, and to absorb much of the turn toward scientific thinking in the professional education of social workers.

The story of social work in these years is indeed one of growth toward a scientific outlook, out of a narrow Puritan conception of "doing good." The young profession moved from a search for the causes of poverty to a vision of understanding people that, it was hoped, would eventually remedy most of the evils that pile up in slums, hospitals and courts, and even in wars among nations. This hope was shattered by the Great Depression, which made evident that psychological readjustment can not solve utterly devastating evils like finding no place in the world for one's energies, no means of livelihood, no goal in living except to prepare to be blown to bits for the profit of faceless greed. After the Depression experience a scientific approach had to face the question whether individual psychology was the last stop for scientific progress. Was there no science of society? Must chance and chaos rule in the interrelations of men and nations which are definitive for the future of mankind?

The woman who tells her story here had a need to make sense of things and a maverick mind that was not satisfied in a fenced-in place. She became a controversial figure in social work over such questions as the relationship between treatment of individuals and a search for understanding of social forces; the attitudes of the profession toward organization of people to better their own condition as against being recipients of social services; the question of public social welfare as against privately supported philanthropy. The story is one of controversies, befitting a time of social upheaval and personal confusion.

Why should this story be told? The writer was at first dubious of its general relevance, impressed by its ant-like limitations. It was one person's view in one time and place. However, the combination of autobiography and limited history of a significant period did have potential meaning for others. So the story came into being. Those who knew social work in other of its many phases during the same period may not recognize the picture as the activity in which they took part; neither will some psychiatric social workers see in it the beginnings of what they practice today. Nevertheless, in its synthesis of events and personal struggles, it becomes a history of ideas as they grew and of how one person grew with them.

That single person would not have begun the task alone, and could not have persisted in it without the faith and encouragement of a group of friends who wish to be nameless, even though their work for greater human happiness will never let them die. These seers of the future have never faltered in their belief that this story of a limited time and person has something to say to a new world in birth.

You may not agree with all the ideas which became the mainspring of life to the one who lived the story. They could not be left out, or the story would become a dance of ghosts. They could not be adequately set forth when confusion is so great even about the facts which underlie the writer's world

view and social imperatives. However, the book is here, and
mainly because of an upspringing faith in people. Men and
women, you among them, are crossing every barrier today,
to mingle their laughter and tears, their vital energies, in a
struggle for survival of all that makes man human. The need
is one, and it is compelling. The goal is one—that children
to come will have an abundant life in a just and rational and
warmly fraternal world. Beside these imperatives differences
melt, and common striving brings resurgent hope.

AN UNCHARTED JOURNEY

CHAPTER I

EMBARKATION

One April evening in 1914 is memorable because it brought a new and exciting sense of belonging to social work in Boston. It was Play Night for the Monday Evening Club,[1] and the little theatre at Elizabeth Peabody House was crowded. The play was *Simple Simon and the Social Workers: A Social Diagnosis in Three Acts,* and the cast consisted of social workers and physicians, playing themselves and Mother Goose characters. I was a member of the chorus and had special reasons for being glad to be there.

Looking at the program of the play, *Simple Simon,* which lies before me, I feel like a youngster at a hole in the fence which allows him a glimpse of what goes on at the carnival. Are we getting a slightly illicit revelation of the inwardness of social work in 1914, which could never have been expressed in conscious terms at the time?

Whether or not we are entitled to it, this is what we see: Starting from the episode of Simon's encounter with the Pieman, the social workers assume that there is something wrong with a boy who tries to get a pie for nothing. They rush him first to the Massachusetts General Hospital for a physical examination, and then in turn to the Associated Charities, the Psychopathic Hospital, a police station, and the Juvenile Court, posing the question of what they are to do with him. In all these places, and in a series of hilarious episodes, Simon simply refuses to talk, and only by an excessive knee jerk that knocks over a doctor at the Psychopathic Hospital clinic does he show any responsiveness at all. In the end, the doctors characteristically reserve diagnosis until science shall tell them *why* Simon behaves as he does. The social workers give him up, but observe in passing that they have not seen so many of them together since the Chelsea fire. The climax is reached as the curtain is about to fall, when Mother Goose wanders on to the stage, and Simon breaks his silence to shout to her, "Mother Goose! Mother Goose! They think I'm a c-c-c-case!"

The program adds a final chorus as follows: "Now all ye who are inclined through hunger, cheek or curiosity to taste free of charge a baker's wares, remember he is somewhat liable to be crusty and heavy with cares. When hungry people beg for bread, we seldom pass them by, but human generosity is taxed to the utmost when they ask for pie. Ah, Simon!"

Conscious effort is required today to relate this Play Night to the conditions prevailing in the spring of 1914. Not until August of that year was the world to know what a global war was like. That experience would even reach into quiet Boston and stop the production in 1915 of an Alice-in-Wonderland skit which was to have graced a second Play Night. Life was too grim for too many people, they said, for such levity to be in good taste. Not yet had people become accustomed to living on the brink of war.

On the local scene, Boston was proud of its social conscience reflected in the number of its philanthropic agencies. Not less than fifteen were represented in the attempt to study Simple Simon. Especially new and prideful were the Psychopathic Hospital and the Juvenile Court. Social diagnosis was the central theme of the play, but Mary Richmond's book of that name was not published until 1917. It was possible for Miss Richmond[2] to use the words *case* and *casework* without guilt (with the substitution of *client* for *case* when referring to a person), but in 1914 social workers were laughing at themselves, through Simple Simon, for their scruples about it. A whole group of words, *psychiatry* (some pronounced it "sickiatry"), *psychiatrist,* and *psychiatric* had been coined but were not in general use. In the playbill, the later-to-be-famous men who examined Simon were listed as "physicians from the Psychopathic Hospital."[3]

The Binet-Simon tests were new and enthusiastically used. Somehow they seemed to offer hope of new solutions for constantly recurring problems. However, once they established that many people who were wrestling with life problems they could not master were really only children, and many children who were failing would never grow up mentally, what was a social agency to do but consider such people unhelpable? There would never be institutions enough to hold all who were diagnosed as needing them, and children who should never have been born could not be mercifully escorted out of this world. Social workers struggled with much the same problems as before, but nevertheless psychology was a magic word in those days.

The final chorus strikes social workers of today with something of a shock. What is it, in its flavor, that is repellent? Is it that hunger is grouped with cheek and curiosity as if all three were personal characteristics? Of a different order of beings? One senses that asking for anything free is not quite nice, but to ask for pie is worse than for bread.

Trying to place ourselves in the atmosphere of the chorus, one gets a feeling that its point of view is closer to that of potential givers (whose patience might be tried) than to that of a hungry boy, whom, in our goodness of heart, we "seldom" pass by. If the chorus is chanting a moral for the play, to whom is it addressed? Apparently not to those who have pies and limited patience nor to social workers who are responsible for doing something about folks who bother those who are "crusty and heavy with cares." The admonition is to those who ask too much when they have not the means to pay.

The choice of dramatic episode is interesting in relation to a period when economic problems were the distinguishing concern of social work. This is an economic problem identified

as a personal one and becomes exciting and laughable as it ex-
poses the inability of social workers to deal with it. The conclusion is startlingly realistic for that day—and for much
later: that medical psychology was too undeveloped to help
much, and that a client, even without brains, can thwart all the
experts if he chooses not to reveal himself.

If I was now embarked on a journey that was to last almost
a lifetime, it was by no easy route that I had reached that
starting point. I had graduated from Smith College in 1908,
with a B.A. degree, a Phi Beta Kappa key and a determination
to serve the world. I had little idea how I could do this and
earn a living, for, to my knowledge, if one did not teach there
were few other paid occupations open to college women. Four
years later, I enrolled in the Boston School for Social Workers
with far less confidence in myself but, by now, with a sure
knowledge that there was a profession for helping troubled
people, if I could only qualify for it. In what vocational wan-
derings had I lost my way in the meantime?

I had spent the first year as housekeeper in the family farmhouse in Stoughton, Massachusetts. The family consisted of
my mother who was a successful teacher of a "steamer class"
of newly arrived immigrant children in the Boston public school
system, my brother who operated the one-man fifty-acre farm,
and a blind sister of my mother. I wanted to give Mother a
year of freedom from unreliable housekeepers before I set off
for a career in which she was sure I would be of no use to the
family.

The following year I obtained a teaching position with a
"missionary flavor" in the high school department of Atlanta
University in Georgia, where white and Negro teachers shared
a restricted life on the dark side of the color line. The salary
was $350 a year, minus the cost of travel south, and perhaps
that helped to persuade me that I was a missionary. This experience in teaching, for which I was in no way prepared,
brought the impact of the hard facts of exploitation and injus-

tice and the terror of violence. It was also a rich introduction to wonderful people of both races who were devoting their lives to education in the South. One of the faculty was Dr. W.E.B. Du Bois, then a young teacher of history, soon to go to New York to become Director of Publicity and Research for the newly-formed National Association for the Advancement of Colored People.

In the spring of the second year in Atlanta, I broke down completely with the sinister diagnosis, now unknown, of "nervous prostration." The usual recommendation for this condition was complete rest, which could well result in permanent invalidism. Fortunately for me, I was in no position to take it. For the record, other prescriptions were large doses of Epsom salts to clear the system and a tonic (to combat symptoms of neuritis) of which red pepper was an ingredient. The existence of vitamins was unknown. I had read about psychotherapy in college courses in psychology, but only in bizarre records of hysterical patients. For another year I lived at home, did some housework and raised chickens for pin money. I faced a hopeless future, for I was convinced that my active working days were over.

Enter a social worker! Miss Jane McCready from the Ellis Memorial Neighborhood Centre in Boston, was a school visitor where my mother taught. She said there was help for my condition. Dr. James J. Putnam, who had sponsored a recent visit of Dr. Sigmund Freud to this country, had told her to bring to him anyone she thought he could help. She said that a "dislocated consciousness" could be as serious as a dislocated arm but was equally curable. I had little confidence, but would try anything.

Four interviews with Dr. Putnam changed my outlook on life and restored me to the living world. Dr. Putnam gave me confidence that I had the latent strength to do whatever I most wanted to do, and he highly recommended a course in the School for Social Workers. I would have several months in which to complete my convalescence before the School would open in the fall. By that time fairly good physical health had been established, although depression and dread were lurking around the corners. When the going was hard, I learned to live a few hours at a time.

Before I entered the School, I had my first glimpse of social work in action. I had been introduced to an Atlanta graduate who worked in the Social Service Department of the Massachusetts General Hospital. She invited me to visit her there for a day and observe. I saw desks surrounded by white-covered hospital screens placed along the side of a large open corridor, and women in white coats interviewing patients who waited on long settees to see them. I saw on their desks books I would be eager to read, such as a study of mental deficiency! Could one *learn* as well as work? Sometimes these workers went to other desks and conferred. To my unsophisticated eyes, social work consisted of *talk*, which was, after all, not too tiring an activity. One reassuring comment from a social worker stuck in my mind. "Considering all the time you spend in meetings, the working day is not too long." When I read at home the reports they gave me of the early years in medical social service at that hospital, I was deeply stirred. If I could only do something as wonderful as that!

Also, that summer I was privileged to spend a week at the Ellis Memorial Camp in Sharon, where I was accepted as a person who could drive nails and put up clothing hooks in the dormitory—thanks to my experience with chicken coops. I am sure some of my prejudices were worn down in contact with delightful children from one of Boston's worst neighborhoods.

In my admission interview at the Boston School I stated, with apprehension, that I had had a nervous breakdown and recovered. I remember that Miss Zilpha Smith said that recovery was quite possible. Academically, I had some prerequisites: a major in psychology, as it was then offered; and some contact with scientific method. I had had no economics and very little sociology. As to health and social experience, my difficulties with both began in the first weeks of life.

I was born in Brockton, Massachusetts, into the family of

an organ maker and tuner who was soon to die of tuberculosis. By the time of my birth, two older children had died of infections, unrecognized as tubercular. Old diaries reveal that the family resolved not to become fond of this child who would die anyway. Of course they changed their minds, but I believe that this fact, together with a too-early weaning and resulting nutritional difficulties, fixed an impression on even so young a child that acceptance could never be taken for granted. It had, in fact, to be *earned,* as I must have sensed when the birth of my brother occurred eighteen months later. This event added the care of a delicate child to my mother's anxieties over a sick husband, and while I spent much time at my grandmother's nearby, I was soon entrusted with some care of the baby.

When I was two, my father died. For a whole year I missed him and often asked why he did not come to see us if he *wanted* to. "Couldn't he borrow a wagon and come?" There is no doubt that in my father's last year I was many times taken away from him when I wanted to stay, and Mother must have had to be the depriving force.

So, with no base in a secure parental relationship and with sibling rivalry well concealed in helpfulness, I began a childhood on Grandfather Capen's farm in Stoughton, Massachusetts. Mother, Brother and I had one half of the old house, while grandparents, an aunt and an uncle occupied the other. We had plenty of time to play but no playmates except each other, since there were no near neighbors. Mother taught us at home because we were considered too delicate for the rigors of a District School with an unsupervised noon recess. We began school life with other children at ages twelve and ten, when Mother secured a teaching position and we moved to Peabody, Massachusetts. Scholastically, we were ahead of our grade but in social experience were learning the know-how that most children acquire at age six.

All my life I had wanted friends and envied girls I saw in town walking arm in arm. Now I had friends, but after a year we moved, then moved again into Boston, and found ourselves in neighborhoods of alien culture, at long distance from church which was our only source of social life. To my disappointment, after grade school, the Girls' High School was chosen for me. Boys were endlessly fascinating creatures so far seen only in cages, so to speak, in church or schoolroom, and I had hoped for a high school offering some extracurricular activities. At Girls' High there were none, except for the school paper on which I held a minor post.

I did not want to be a teacher like Mother and hoped for some occupation which would leave evenings free for social life. Going to college meant preparing to teach in those days. However, Mother's aunt, Miss Bessie T. Capen, principal of a famous preparatory school for girls in Northampton, generously offered a year at her school to finish college preparation and then a four-year course at Smith College if I wanted it. I was doubtful about it, but how could I refuse an opportunity to which few in our social rank could ever aspire?

At the Capen School, I had almost nothing in common with the other students, most of whom were not wealthy, but far above my social status. My Methodist upbringing made me refuse as sinful the recreations that filled their lives. I used my leisure for solitary walks and reading. During the four years at Smith College, I continued to live at Capen School. I could now find friends with whom I was comfortable but, for the most part, among girls who lived off campus. Though I saw little of campus activities, those were happy years.

I do not remember that much of this history of social experience was elicited in my admission interview at the Boston School for Social Workers, but I could hardly have seemed like a person marked for success in social relationships. In addition, I carried with me a rich crop of prejudices from my rural New England background. We farm folk looked upon industrial workers in the town as an unthrifty lot who would vote at town meetings for improvements for which owners of land had to pay increased taxes without receiving corresponding benefits.

To us, town people were generally the source of depredations and disorderly conduct. If they were foreigners or Catholics, so much the worse. My stay in Atlanta had brought to my sympathetic feeling for Negro people more confusion of emotions than balanced clarity. I shiver now when I think to what a narrow arc of human relationships my prejudices would have condemned me had they been left undisturbed.

At the end of the year's study at the Boston School, I was asked if I would consider a second year's specialization in child welfare on a scholarship. I felt unable to do so financially and also thought I needed more to get into direct practice at that time. I was thrilled to be offered three jobs in children's agencies. The one that appealed to me most was a newly created position in the Boston Children's Aid Society, that of intake secretary.

In a memorable interview, the General Secretary, Mr. J. Prentice Murphy, described the anxiety with which people in trouble approached an agency which might or might not help them. It would make a vast difference to them, he said, what kind of welcome they received at the door, how they were listened to and understood, and how they were introduced either to the worker who would make a more detailed study of their case or to alternative resources in other agencies. The skill in interviewing would consist in drawing out just enough to know where to steer them for the service they needed, but not letting their eagerness to talk to the first person they met deprive them of a worthwhile contact with their visitor later.

I had two questions about the job which only experience could answer. How could I judge how far to go in getting close to people who were to work with someone else? How, if I were as sympathetic as seemed desirable, could I bear to see them go on to others or to tell them the painful truth that we could not help them? Nevertheless, I was happy to be the agency's welcoming hand and to be in the working world as part of a great undertaking—to give to unhappy children a real chance.

As I thought over that interview, a motto came to me that might fittingly hang over my new desk:

SPEAKING THE TRUTH IN LOVE[4]

The motto was never lettered nor hung and was forgotten for years, yet I think its choice was profoundly connected both with my stage of growth at that time and what I have hoped most to achieve throughout my life. Dr. Putnam had showed me that I had lived with a shell around me, never letting my real self shine through the crust of what other people expected of me. Prentice Murphy gave me a vision of what helpfulness to people could be, facing with them the truth about themselves and their situation, obscured though it might be by illusions based upon fear, frustration and hatred. These things could not be faced if they were presented harshly, without love. What is true? What is compassionate and loving? Could one have a better guide in the complexities of a new profession?

By April, 1914, I had been working almost a year and was to receive in June the B.S. degree which Simmons College awarded after a year of successful practice following the year of graduate study at the Boston School. In that period, there must have been many occasions when the social workers of Boston foregathered and I was among them—notably at the supper meetings of the Monday Evening Club. I do not know why it took the release afforded by participation in a Play Night to give me that wonderful feeling that after more than five years of vocational wandering I had at last arrived in a profession I was proud to call my own.

CHAPTER 2

SOCIAL RESPONSIBILITY

If the social workers who tried to get a diagnosis for Simple Simon were not quite sure for which service they were socially responsible, their young profession was very sure that their community required them to do more than just help those who were directed to their door. A brief survey of the annual reports of the period shows that by 1910 the Associated Charities, for instance, had a department for the care and study of homeless men. It had formed a committee on problems of alcoholism, composed of representative citizens including physicians. It had made a study of nonsupporting husbands and pointed up the need for legislation to protect their families from suffering. By 1911 the Associated Charities found its work vitalized by co-operation with medical social service and took added interest in health factors in cases of poverty. It shared community concern about prison reform. The new diagnostic category, "defective delinquent," pointed to a need for custodial care of certain cases. Co-operation with the Massachusetts Commission on Child Labor secured a law prohibiting employment of boys under twenty-one in night work as messengers. The General Secretary was on a committee to investigate employment agencies. Reporting on housing violations was made part of the work of staff and volunteers as they went into the tenements. The Associated Charities followed closely the operation of the new law to aid mothers with dependent children and was much concerned about recreation facilities in its neighborhoods. During the same period, settlements were active in city districts

23

to secure recreation and health care. The medical social service departments of hospitals aided greatly in the campaign of the Anti-Tuberculosis Association.[1]

One of Miss Richmond's papers[2] speaks of a wave of reform which swept over the United States between 1905 and 1914. The "muckraking" exposures of corruption in the large cities had made gradual methods of social betterment seem futile. Enthusiastic theories, stemming especially from sociological studies in the colleges, made *prevention* the watchword, far-reaching legislation the means, and abolition of poverty the foreseeable goal of social effort. The pioneers in the Charity Organization movement, who had tried for years to educate their public to the efficacy of case-by-case methods in the redemption of families and neighborhoods, found their work regarded as obsolete by a younger generation upon whom they had counted to develop their methods further. It was in the air that fair wages, established by law, would do away with poverty. Given social justice, the poor would be as well able to manage their own affairs as anyone else. Philanthropy was outmoded. The voice of organized social work could only counter, as Miss Richmond did, that there was a retail as well as a wholesale method of reform and that the first was essential to the second.[3]

It was in this period that a political party, Theodore Roosevelt's "Bull Moose" party, actually placed in its platform for the election of 1912 a social program which had been presented at the National Conference of Charities and Correction which met in Cleveland that year.[4]

A Committee on Standards of Living and Labor[5] presented to the Conference a report which states: "There are essential elements in a normal standard of living, below which society cannot allow any of its members to live without injuring the public welfare. . . . Industry therefore must submit to such public regulation as will make it a means of life and health, not of death or inefficiency. . . . The community can cause to be formulated minimum occupational standards below which work is carried on only at a human deficit."[6] The standards were comprised under the heads of a living wage; the eight-hour day; the six-day week; minimizing of night work for all and its prohibition for minors, with assurance of a rest period of eight hours for all women; safety and health through inspection, regulation and prohibition of poisonous articles in industrial processes; housing, in fulfillment of "the right to a home"; prohibition of child labor; regulation of seasonal employment; regulation of women's work, including protection at the time of childbirth; and social insurance to provide compensation for accidents, trade diseases, old age and unemployment.[7]

This program had to wait for twenty years, filled with unremitting effort on the part of social reformers, before a substantial part of it was incorporated in legislation under the "New Deal" of another Roosevelt. Its implementation had to wait until labor won the right to organize and to demand reforms and could secure at least a minimum of government backing. Not yet has it been fully realized.

In the bleak winter of 1912 an event occurred which etched itself deeply into Massachusetts history, even though it seemed to have little impact upon social work. It was the great strike at Lawrence,[8] one of a chain of textile cities lying along the Merrimac river. The giant woolen mills, protected by a high tariff from foreign competition, employed some 30,000 workers, mostly foreign-born, speaking at least forty-five languages and dialects, and unorganized except for a few skilled crafts. A new state law had reduced the working week for women and children under eighteen from fifty-six to fifty-four hours, that is, to a nine-hour day, six days a week. To these hours, for most of the women, should be added many hours over cookstove and washtub, with little time out even for childbearing. The woolen companies fought the law, and now increased the speed of the looms, or the number of looms per worker, to compensate for reduced time. The average wage for the unskilled was six dollars a week.

The strike started with a cry, "Short pay! Short pay!" which

echoed from loom to loom and mill to mill when a cut in wages
was evident on the first payday in January. In a matter of hours
the mills were emptied and surrounded by a mass picket line,
the first in Bay State history. Some 25,000 workers were involved. They faced starvation, but they said, "Better to starve
fighting than to starve working!" A whole city of small shop-
keepers was as penniless as the millworkers.

The A.F. of L.[9] would have nothing to do with the strike,
though its craft-union workers were idled by it. It was the
I.W.W.[10] which sent organizers, raised money for food, explained the issues in dozens of dialects to women unaccustomed
to any kind of united action, and helped the strikers to run the
strike committees themselves. The workers sang on the picket
lines in the bitter cold, and observers saw them show a queer
kind of happiness in the solidarity they felt with workers in
other cities who sent help. No longer were they despised foreigners but men and women learning how to speak, to debate,
even to produce shows and to decide policies.

In that distressed city there were soup kitchens to be kept
going; shelter had to be found for the homeless. The sick and
those injured on the picket lines had to be cared for. As the
weeks dragged on, groups of pale and hungry children were
organized to be sent to workers' homes in other cities until the
emergency should be over. In all this, were social workers contributing their skills and resources as they would have done in a
flood or fire disaster? We have no such record.[11] But the work
was done, an incredible amount of it, by the strikers themselves
and such labor organizations as sent aid.

The strikers fought police violence (even directed against the
children leaving the railroad station for placement) and over-
came provocation and charges which resulted in the jailing of
their leaders. The turning point of the strike came when Victor
Berger, Socialist Congressman from Milwaukee, demanded a
Congressional investigation of the causes of the strike, and
child workers among others went to Washington with their pay
envelopes to testify.

The strike was won in March, with a wage increase of from five percent to thirty percent, the lowest-paid workers receiving the greater proportionate amount. There were certain benefits besides wage increases which aided other millworkers in later, less hard-fought, strikes. That same year Massachusetts passed a minimum-wage law, the first in any state, but soon to be followed by laws in eight others. In two years thirty-five states had passed laws providing for workmen's compensation for industrial accidents.

If the young profession of social work did not extend its sense of social responsibility to situations in which people in desperate cases seized the initiative on their own behalf, chose their own leaders, and disrupted the life of a city to win obviously needed gains, it was no more confused than were government officials, police, and ordinary citizens. It was, in short, a part of the self-contradictory life of its time. It had both good impulses and fears, a sense of rightness and of self-protection. On the whole, it could be counted on for some success with the retail method of improving the chances of a good life for human beings and for some excursions into carefully considered legislation under well-selected sponsorship.

Because the picture of social agencies has changed so much since the period before 1914, I take time here to describe briefly what the agencies of Boston were like in those days. They can be grouped into four major categories:

1. Family service organizations such as the Associated Charities.
2. Settlements and neighborhood centers.
3. Child-placing agencies.
4. Hospital social service departments.

THE ASSOCIATED CHARITIES

The Associated Charities was the Boston incarnation of the Charity Organization Movement. Transplanted to the United States from cities like London and Glasgow where whole districts were in perpetual poverty, Charity Organization in the new world found little hereditary pauperism, but wave after wave of uprooted people coming from Europe to the eastern seaboard and wave after wave of migrants moving west for better opportunities as the frontier advanced. There was no mind-set here for a conception of more-than-temporary need nor for the possibility that work might not exist for all who were able and willing to work.

In Boston, the Associated Charities had carried out the principles of the Charity Organization Movement: study and diagnosis before action; charitable relief a last resort and related to an adequate plan for family rehabilitation; and organization of people with an impulse to help the disadvantaged into a corps of volunteer visitors, trained and guided by a few paid and experienced workers. The "friendly visitors," each responsible for only one or two poor families, were the key to the personal influence upon which the Associated Charities based its hopes not only of rehabilitation of families and neighborhoods but of creating a social consciousness in the city which would work for reforms. In the thirty years of its existence in Boston, the Associated Charities had played a major part in creating the responsiveness to human need for which the city was famous.

The Associated Charities operated through sixteen district offices, each in close contact with its neighborhood, and each guided by a District Conference composed of leading citizens of the area and of volunteer visitors. The District Secretary was a bridge between the Conference and the city-wide giving public, on the one hand, and the district on the other. She had to keep straight what might otherwise be "a tangle of good intent."[12] She had to be an educator for staff and volunteers in the principles of philanthropic work which she had learned herself by apprentice training in the agency. The educational work of the Associated Charities had, indeed, been the source of trained staff for responsible positions in other cities throughout the United States. If money was needed for a family, the

District Secretary had to raise it herself, case by case, from trust funds established in the city for special purposes or from benevolent individuals (known in the jargon as B.I.'s).

A major contribution of the Associated Charities to the social work of Boston was the organization of the Bureau of Registration, which later became the Confidential Exchange of Information. This card index of all applicants to social agencies was not meant to be primarily a means of preventing duplication of charitable gifts to the same family by agencies unaware of each others' action. It was a means of confidential communication among agencies already interested in a family, so that they might not advise at cross purposes and demoralize instead of helping. As Miss Richmond said, "Conceive of twenty doctors dosing the same case at the same time, without consultation and each in his own way. Our medical code of ethics forbids such a state of things, but its results could be no more disastrous among the sick than were our charitable practices among the poor."[13] The Exchange was used in 1913 by practically all of the professional social agencies of the city.

SETTLEMENTS

The settlements, of which there were some sixteen co-operating in the Boston Social Union by 1910, had some of the same traditions from England as the Charity Organization Movement, but beamed their activities to areas of need other than lack of food and shelter. Their three watchwords were health, vocation, and recreation. They wanted to bring together the privileged and the underprivileged for *sharing,* as they would say, rather than giving, some of the finer things of life. There were music, drama, art, and dancing clubs and classes open to the neighborhoods. In the college settlements, students of local colleges, or alumni from elsewhere who were free to do so, could live for a time and participate in the life of poor neighborhoods. There was organization of the neighborhoods for action to secure needed improvements from the city, and there was organized participation of neighborhood groups in combating bad housing, centers of moral contagion, and alcoholism.

A list of activities of South End House is probably typical. This house, approaching its twentieth anniversary, had set out to raise the health level of its area, comprising a factory and lodging house district. Beginning with the youngest children, it had established stations for distribution of pure milk at cost, later turning these over to a specialized agency. It had classes for pregnant mothers and mothers of infants before the city did this work. It pressed the city for medical examination of school children who showed signs of "undervitalization." It supplied visitors to schools where neighborhood conditions were demoralizing. It organized a league to protect children from vice. It organized lodginghouse keepers to develop standards which would qualify their houses for recommendation in the Room Registry of South End House. It maintained a New Hampshire vacation house, organized a Music School, and participated in the experiment of a State Hospital for Inebriates at Foxboro. Its staff were active in city politics for good government and especially for control of alcoholism, vice, and vagrancy.

The settlements were interested in many of the same reforms that concerned the charities of Boston, but from the angle of organized neighborhoods acting for themselves rather than helping family units of people in need. Their different outlook was later expressed to me in this way: "You caseworkers see people only when they are in trouble and at their worst. We live with them in good times or bad, and see them at their best. It makes our attitude different. We encourage them to take social action and help them to do it effectively. We abhor charity, and so do they."

CHILD-CARING AGENCIES

By 1913 there were ten child-caring agencies operating in Boston, most of them the outgrowth of children's institutions which were now placing children in foster homes. By far the largest was the tax-supported agency, the Division of State Minor Wards of the Massachusetts State Board of Charity, which had in its care some 6,000 children. These were committed to the guardianship of the State because of neglect, dependency, or delinquency and were returned to relatives when investigation showed that conditions suitable for them could be established. The Massachusetts Society for the Prevention of Cruelty to Children, a private protective agency, worked closely with the Division, the courts, and the private child-placing societies. The State Board of Charity also had a protective function for all children in the State through its licensing of boarding homes, regulation of adoptions, and inspection of incorporated charities. The child-placing agencies had agreed upon a division of the State into districts from which each would accept applications. This did not preclude certain agencies from special services for certain problems, such as the Children's Mission finding homes for children needing long-time medical care or the Children's Aid specializing in work with unmarried mothers.

The history of the Boston Children's Aid Society, dating from 1863, reveals a social vision which made it a leader in children's work throughout the United States. First, a few boys, aged seven to twelve, were taken from bad homes, or even from the streets and the jails, to a temporary farm home for a few months' training and then were placed in foster families, if return to their own relatives was impossible. The same plan was successful with girls also, but could not begin to reach the numbers of children needing such care. In the year 1871, the courts dealt with 1,233 children between the ages of six and fifteen. I have heard a pioneer probation worker say that the children confined in jails were so small that officials said they needed to cover the cells with chicken wire to keep them in.

In 1884, the B.C.A.S. engaged Charles W. Birtwell to be an "outdoor" city worker, to find right in the slum neighborhoods, as well as in the courts and jails, the children the Society might help and to find them earlier. As a part of his work in the city,

Mr. Birtwell initiated a unique service called the Home Library
Association which was still very active in 1913. In poor homes
in city neighborhoods, libraries of children's books, each in an
attractive bookcase, were placed and changed from time to time.
The selected home and the child librarian were honored, and
around these libraries volunteer visitors held weekly story hours,
health talks or planned recreation. Volunteers reviewed books
to be purchased. It was before the days of children's work in
Branch Libraries and was different from settlement clubs. Mr.
Birtwell continued his work of farsighted and practical pioneer-
ing until his resignation in 1911, when J. Prentice Murphy
continued the great tradition. By this time the B.C.A.S. was a
fully developed child-placing agency without an institution,
employing a staff of some twenty people.[14]

The children's agencies shared with the Associated Charities
its principles of thorough diagnosis before social treatment and
of fitting the social prescription in every case to the needs of
the persons involved. Looking back, it seems that the enthusiasm for foster placement, which was at its height in that period,
overestimated what a change of environment could do for a
forlorn child and failed to understand the degree to which
such a child would take with him into a new setting the very
conflicts that had seared his soul in the old. The children's
workers of that day believed strongly in the unique value of
the skills they had developed through the years by apprentice
training and felt that their specialty could be learned in no other
way than in actual practice.

HOSPITAL SOCIAL SERVICE

Social service, as it began in the Massachusetts General
Hospital in the fall of 1905,[15] was only "permitted" a place for
a desk in the corner of a corridor. By 1912 it had grown to a
row of desks in the same corridor and had opened a new epoch
by having certain of its workers attached to three clinics, the
Nerve, Children's and Orthopedic services, as an integral part
of the Out-Patient Department. Its work was still largely done

by volunteer visitors and some students from the Boston School for Social Workers, directed by a small group of paid workers. Since 1908, the social work had been guided by a Supervisory Committee, of which Dr. Richard C. Cabot was chairman, and which represented the out-patient medical staff, "expert social workers," the Visiting Ladies' Committee, and the hospital administration. It had begun to formulate a system of training for its work which was unlike either nursing or social work, yet had features of both.

Hospital social service was inevitable in view of the obvious waste of curing patients of diseases which were the product of their living conditions, sending them back to the same conditions, and then receiving them again, sick with the same illnesses. Obviously, also, doctors could not take time to know those life conditions or to do anything about them. There was not even time for the painstaking re-education of patients and families that would insure that medical recommendations were carried out. A staff with mobility had to be in circulation between the out-patient clinics and the homes of patients and the medical and social resources of the community. These, the medical social service didn't aim to duplicate but to co-ordinate in the interest of the patient.

The Massachusetts General Hospital, which served suburban and rural communities throughout the State, helped to develop medical and social resources in places that did not have them. It fostered anti-tuberculosis classes where patients lived. For two areas of need, it developed new forms of social work.

One was named in the report "Sex Problems." Whereas the children's societies had dealt with unmarried pregnant girls, beginning at the point of application for a plan for the coming baby, a hospital met the girls at the point of diagnosis of pregnancy with the advantage of a medical setting. An understanding and skilled worker could help the girl face her situation soundly, before attitudes of despair, recklessness, or defiance had hardened. There were also girls equally exposed to the danger of pregnancy and only thankful to be told that they had escaped it, but needing understanding help just the same. Furthermore, the stigma attached to venereal disease at that time complicated both hospital care and emotional adjustments, even among married women who had no guilt to justify the scorn with which they were often treated. Social service was difficult in all these cases, but it helped to improve community attitudes and resources.

The other innovation was work for psychoneurotic patients, organized by Dr. James J. Putnam and Dr. Richard C. Cabot in 1907. The thought at first was that these conditions originated in family problems which needed to be understood and that these patients required long hours of talking which a busy doctor could not afford. The means of therapy were described as explanation, encouragement, re-education, and suggestion, all compounded with essential warmth of friendship. By the third annual report, a class in clay modelling was proving a valuable resource for recreation as well as re-education of psychoneurotic patients in social attitudes. Vacation living for two weeks in New Hampshire, in a group led by a social worker was also tried with success, and, in some cases, placing in boarding homes. The key to rehabilitation of these patients, Dr. James Putnam said in his Third Report, was the personality of the worker, her ability to appeal to the patient's intelligence, confidence, and courage. Nothing could be done without a relationship of mutual respect between social worker and patient. Everything depended on re-education of mental attitudes, especially toward strengthening the patient's ideal of himself, his finding a goal in life, and some sense of his social relationships to others.

The social service department of the Massachusetts General Hospital had, by 1912, inspired the founding of other departments in hospitals throughout the country and was frequently called on to give advice or to train workers for these new ventures. It had brought to the medical staff a concept of the patient as a whole person, not just a bunch of symptoms, and a person in the midst of a family situation. It had stimulated research into methods of combating tuberculosis, study of causes of psychoneuroses and industrial diseases, and had vitalized work in social hygiene. It co-operated with agencies of all sorts in its stated effort "to abolish ourselves," and yet found itself more and more necessary as a distributing center between the patient's needs and available resources. As a link between two professions working for the same patients, it was invaluable.

All of the four groups of agencies believed strongly that volunteer service was essential to their work. Professional workers had come to fill an important place, to guide and to educate, but could not replace the personal touch and the link with the general community which volunteers contributed to an agency. The child-placing societies, which seemed superficially to have moved farthest toward professional service because of their development of technical skills, were most dependent on the volunteer service of foster parents.

No one of the agencies in neighborhood work, child-placing, or hospital social service found the Charity Organization formula directly applicable to their field, yet each was as fully dedicated as was the Associated Charities to the responsible, case by case method of dealing with the problems of disadvantaged people. If there was to be professional education for social work, it would have to take account of the mind-set of this philosophy, as well as the difficulties of putting it into practice.

When Mary E. Richmond, as early as 1897, read a paper at the National Conference of Charities and Correction on "The Need of a Training School in Applied Philanthropy," she deplored the fact that the profession to which able and dedicated young people were willing to offer their lives could provide them with no means of securing training for the skilled service it demanded. The profession did not even have a name more descriptive than "applied philanthropy" and had no professional standards nor more than a fragmentary literature. It had

become a bundle of specialties too soon without well thought-
out reasons for being specialties. Was there no body of common knowledge that could be taught? Must we remain, she
asked, in the stage of development which, in the history of
medicine, countenanced barbers bleeding patients and pulling
teeth while druggists' apprentices made diagnoses? Miss Richmond recognized the crude practices surviving after twenty
years of organized charitable work, but insisted that these could
be overcome if only a definite professional standard could be
set by regulated professional education. That standard should
include professional ideals, habits of thought, and a philosophy
of life.[16]

Such an education would involve full-time study to master
the sciences and underlying principles. Apprentice training
could only teach how-to-do in one set of local conditions. Miss
Richmond's plan was for a two-year course, beginning with
general principles and adding specialized training in a second
year. There should also be provision for short courses for special
students and courses for volunteers.

Miss Richmond added, "We should search the country over
for the right man to organize it. We need a university-trained
man who is now engaged in charitable work, and who has had
wide, practical experience in it. There are a few such men."[17]

Miss Richmond expected that her "rough sketch of a plan"
would only be realized "far in the future." Instead, the New
York School of Philanthropy was organized the very next year,
under the auspices of the New York Charity Organization
Society, and it was only six years later that the Boston School
came to be the first to be sponsored by two institutions of higher
learning,[18] and the first to be a full-time professional school
from the beginning.

Dr. Jeffrey R. Brackett, who was called from Baltimore to
Boston in 1904 to head the new School for Social Workers,
was eminently the rare person Miss Richmond had described.[19]
After his graduation from Harvard, Jeffrey Brackett had spent
a year in study and travel in Europe and four years at Johns

Hopkins University, where he received his Ph.D. degree in History and Political Science. Continuing with the University as instructor, Dr. Brackett spent fifteen years in close association with the Charity Organization Society of Baltimore, of which Miss Richmond was General Secretary during most of the period. He was drawn into public service in connection with an economic depression and the Baltimore fire disaster. He had participated in apprentice training for social work in Baltimore, New York, and Boston, and had taught in the summer session of the New York School and in late afternoon and evening classes at the New York Charity Organization Society. In 1903, Dr. Brackett had been elected president of the National Conference of Charities and Correction, which was then a leading educational force in this field. He had written a book, *Supervision and Education in Charity*. He had come to believe as strongly as did Miss Richmond in the principles of professional training which she had set forth.

Four circumstances combined to make Boston the site chosen for a professional school. It had an unusual body of interested people to back the school and help raise money for it; the city had excellent social agencies experienced in training students; it had Simmons College[20] interested in careers for women for which a vocational education could be offered; and, not least of all, Boston contributed a rare woman to be Assistant to the Director in the person of Miss Zilpha Drew Smith, former General Secretary of the Associated Charities. No better introduction to Miss Smith can be given than Miss Richmond's dedication of *Social Diagnosis* to her: "*To Zilpha Drew Smith whose steady faith in the possibilities of social case work has been the inspiration of this book and of its author.*"

When Dr. Brackett agreed to come to Boston in 1904 he insisted upon certain principles. The School should train workers for the whole field of social work, public agencies as well as the private organizations that had so far dominated the scene, for the specialties as well as organized charity, and for community organization as well as agency practice. His

choice for a name, Training School for Social Workers, reveals
important facets of his thinking. He felt that *training* suggested
the strong emphasis upon practice which was desired. His conception of social work, a name for the profession which Dr.
Brackett claimed to have originated, was given to students in
his introductory lectures each year as follows: Helpfulness to
people is not confined to any profession or to all of them.
Neighborly kindness has always existed. How is professional
helpfulness different? It is *work*—that is, people devote
themselves to this art not as dilettantes but as to a vocation,
responsible for knowing what they do, and, as far as it is
humanly possible, for good results in human welfare. It is
social because it involves going where needy people are and
getting close to them, and keeping close, also, to the whole
community that is contributing to, and affected by, whatever we
do to help.

In seemingly small details, Dr. Brackett steered the new
school to establish sound principles. It should be a graduate
school, with the concession to the Simmons curriculum that for
Simmons students the fourth year leading to the B.S. degree
should be taken at the School, and the preprofessional courses
in social work and field work in the preceding three years should
be given by the School faculty.[21] Graduates of other colleges
could earn the B.S. degree in one postgraduate year, but the
degree was not actually given until the candidate had added to
the year at the School an academic year of practice in a job
under supervision.

Dr. Brackett insisted that the lectures should be given in
the mornings. This caused dissatisfaction among employed
workers who were accustomed to devote the "tired leavings" of
busy days to piecemeal education. Dr. Brackett contended that
professional education was important enough to the agencies
so that they should allow adequate time for it. Students must
be serious enough to devote either full time (with academic
credit) or, for special courses, substantial blocks of time. The

case method of teaching was largely used, for which schools of law and medicine had set a precedent.

To agencies that wanted special courses to train *their* workers, Dr. Brackett replied that the School could not become a bundle of apprentice programs. It must teach specifics but all in relation to the whole of social work and the whole of community life. It had little professional literature from which to teach but used thoroughly the periodicals, pamphlets, and reports which existed, and the writings of the early pioneers. A rather large collection of these came to the School in the donation of the Philanthropic Library of the Boston Children's Aid Society.

Dr. Brackett's concept of education was that beyond developing technical experts, professional training should prepare the whole person for a professional outlook and a sound philosophy of values. He tried to show in his lectures the relation of social work to community interests like health and recreation, schools, churches, and industries. He brought labor conciliators and a representative of the Consumers' League to the School to show how labor relations are an interest of the whole community.

The School kept in close touch with the field of social work by systematic scheduling of visiting lecturers from every type of community agency and by observation trips to see social resources like parks and playgrounds, housing projects, factories, and government facilities. Dr. Brackett saw Miss Smith and himself as co-ordinators of theory and practice. They required of the students written reports on lectures, reading, observation trips, and field work and took time to go over these in conference with students. Field practice ranked high in importance. In 1912-13 when I was at the School, field work was allotted twelve hours a week, divided between two agencies, one of which was to be the Associated Charities. I believe each agency had in turn, in the two semesters, a concentration of the major part of the time, while the one not in concentration kept the student in touch with the work by conference attendance and a little visiting.

The students who enrolled in the first classes averaged nearly thirty years of age, and half of them were to use their training as volunteers. The introduction of paid workers into philanthropy was still recent enough to have affected the psychology of its practice only slightly.[22] Paid workers were responsible for supervising and training volunteers, while the latter made many of the direct contacts with clients. As late as 1907 it was noted that women were paid much less than men in social work and that salaries were kept down by the public impression that it was a "luxury" occupation which should not be paid at all. In the same period, men of the type who would go into the ministry or the Y. M. C. A. were thought to be deterred from entering social work by a belief that it dealt only with abnormal people. Dr. Brackett's answer was that in its preventive aspects social work dealt with all kinds of people. Despite public misunderstanding, by October 1912 the School was enrolling a class of fifty full-time students. The second year was then offered experimentally to a few students in organizing charity, in medical social service, and probation.

When I attended the School in its tenth year it had survived financial difficulties and criticisms which seem quaint to us today. One was that there was no need of education for doing good, if one had a kind heart and common sense; another that education spoiled natural qualities and created a bureaucratic coldness; a third that a school preparing workers for *service* to the poor was superfluous since all the money given for philanthropy should go directly to the needy and not be wasted on "administration." Some people maintained that social work divorced from religious teaching was useless. Dr. Brackett's lectures dealt with these criticisms and more, representing community attitudes which young social workers would meet constantly. He devoted much time to the English Poor Laws, an illuminating record of six hundred years of perverted and blundering charity, and to the Baltimore fire disaster which illustrated how a whole community could be organized to meet sudden need. Students were organized to advise with the School

on curriculum, and their comments, delivered about 1907, cause
a flicker of amusement today. They said that despite Dr.
Brackett's co-ordination almost all the visiting lecturers began
with the English Poor Laws and that the Baltimore fire *should*
burn itself out after awhile.

My twelve hours of field work per week were divided between a district office of the Associated Charities and the Boston
Society for the Care of Girls, a child-placing agency transformed from the old Boston Female Asylum. The long-un-
painted, rotting, frame tenements of South Boston were my
introduction to the places where poor people had to live. I had
never seen poor people before, except in Atlanta, where it was
natural to associate the board shacks in the Negro districts
with race discrimination. Here, one had to come to terms with
a queer feeling in oneself that people who were poor, just
by being so, became a different kind of human being. I remember my surprise on an early visit to a tenement to find the
woman preparing haddock for her husband's supper, much as I
would do at home. Had I expected her to be sitting in rags
munching a crust of bread?

My field work at the B. S. C. G. must have been more exten-
sive than taking an adolescent girl to lunch on her visit to the
city, but I can remember little about it. The staff conferences
on Monday mornings, however, cling in my memory, possibly
because of doubts which were never faced. Two of the girls
in foster care, whose names came up frequently, were from a
family of motherless children of whom I had previous knowledge. I could hardly escape wondering if, had my mother died,
I would have been the object of such scrutiny of my little pec-
cadilloes on the part of a body of strange ladies.

The case conferences at the A. C. must also have stirred some
doubts beneath the surface of my acceptance of all that went
on. A group of people connected with the district, a doctor, a
lawyer perhaps, a businessman or two, together with several
volunteer visitors from more favored parts of the city, met
with the District Secretary to consider cases and make policy

decisions. One widow's family would be voted a pension if the District Secretary could raise the money. If another did not do better with housekeeping and care of the children, a grant would be withdrawn, and they could go to the Overseers.[23] I remember the sentences, "Let them stew in their own juice," and "Hadn't we better break up this family rather than subsidize such bad conditions?" I do not believe these were typical attitudes, and they may have come from one man in the group and have been remembered only because they were shocking. I do know that the finely human District Secretary worried sometimes that decisions might be affected by the moods of conference members, and I know she told me that she was exhausted on conference days because she tried to lead without seeming to do so.

Throughout the course at the School and in experience in the agencies, I often heard it said that after diagnosis comes a plan of treatment based upon it. Who makes the diagnosis and the plan? The answer was, "Of course, it is the client's plan. No plan is possible unless the client participates in making it." This statement, however, somehow seemed to have the flavor of an afterthought. The frequency with which the label "un-co-operative" was applied to clients seemed to indicate that a desirable correspondence of plans was not always obtained. Much of the skill of a social worker seemed to be involved in persuasion to secure acceptance of "best laid schemes" which went "aft agley." I am sure that I sensed this only partially, but unfaced doubts probably made me remember instances of it.

My year at the Boston School gave me mainly (and this was very important) a new outlook on social work as a professional service, not a sentimental "doing good." It was taking social responsibility for the outcome of what one did, as far as this could be foreseen. Kindness to people, which gave one the pleasure of seeing faces light up, was not enough and was not kindness if it produced more beggars, more deserting fathers, more exploited children. It was Miss Zilpha Smith whose penetrating questions in every discussion of case situations brought out the hidden aspects of what looked to a novice like simple need and response-by-giving. She would ask: Was a budget adequate for health? Was relief for an undernourished family whose father worked for low wages actually subsidizing an industry and helping it to keep down wages? Was a runaway youngster being robbed of any place to play? Was a bad neighborhood condition being looked into for the sake of other families living there? I found her disturbing sometimes and bless her for it now.

Looking back through years jammed with conflict, the values of social work, in this period before the great changes that came with World War I, seem unbelievably coherent and stable, viable enough to last for many generations. Certain presuppositions, however, would not be as comfortably lived with today.

One was acceptance of a class structure in America, or is it that today we are less frank to admit it? No one could fail to see that there were many poor, even in this fortunate part of the world. Events like the Lawrence Strike brought close to home how wide the gap had become between the comfortable and the six-dollars-a-week workers or between those who were secure and the unemployed who stood in shivering lines during depression crises. One notes in the writings of Mary Richmond,[24] for instance, anxiety that communications be kept open between the privileged and the unfortunate—as much for the sake of the privileged as the others. The springs of benevolence must not dry up. For fear of this, Miss Richmond regarded public assistance and the wave of legislation for mothers' pensions with distrust, as she also feared their abandonment of methods of personal differentiation among those in need.[25]

If there was to be an open road between rich and poor, upon what reason for contact could it be built when they no longer lived in adjacent neighborhoods or even in the same communities? Certainly the experience of the Charity Organization Movement (in revolt against the mistakes of the harsh Poor Laws and the excesses of indiscriminate charity) had shown

that giving material relief alone was not conducive to the rehabilitation of the unfortunate. A personal touch was needed,
but *for* something. For what? For education and character
improvement in the poor, personally? It was the only reason
anyone could think of and carried a certain solace when, in
sight of unaccustomed misery, one could believe that the victims
were somehow deficient in knowledge or character, and given
these, their problems would be solved. The assumptions of superiority in the givers were not fully faced. They did feel an
obligation to share what better ways of living came out of their
more favorable conditions of life. Education for social work,
then, was beamed to the people of the more comfortable classes
who, as volunteers or paid workers, took *noblesse oblige* seriously enough to prepare to make a career of intelligent benefi-
cence.

In general, social workers who attended professional schools
were educated to follow the vision which Miss Richmond so
eloquently expressed in her papers, a great crusade for human
betterment in which case-by-case personal contact with people
in poor circumstances would not only raise individual families
to a higher level but would furnish data for far-reaching reforms. The favored classes, learning to know their poor neighbors personally, could never thereafter be indifferent to the
causes of poverty, disease, and crime, or fail to support needful reforms. To do our work well at this point of intersection
of social classes and of economic levels was to play an important part in the future of our country. So the School in Boston
taught, and so we believed.

CHAPTER 3

FIRST PRACTICE

The Boston Children's Aid Society occupied the top floor of the Charity Building on Hawkins Street, up long flights of stairs which delivered clients and workers at its door breathless. The staff was a family group to an extent which today might cause a lifting of professional eyebrows. We did not call each other by first names, but, like proper Bostonians, compromised with use of the initials with which we signed our records. Thus I shall introduce a few beloved figures:

There was JPM, general secretary, with the black hair and blue eyes of his Scotch-Irish ancestry and the springy step and twisted smile of a true lover of warm comradeship and the good story. He used to ask all the workers in turn to his home for dinner and an evening of good fellowship, and his wife, IGM, who sometimes worked in the office, was as relaxed and entertaining as he.

There were two who boasted twenty-five years of service under Charles W. Birtwell. EPD was lovable and nervous, a woman of immense energy which sometimes interfered with the doings of others. JPM said she squashed some young workers and others "climbed right over the desks and locked horns with her." Unfortunately, I was in the former class. SCL was a veteran probation officer whose bent spine was said to be the result of endless bicycle-riding in pursuit of wayward boys. He was always rushing in and out, barely making trains.

Then there was JEK, a little Englishwoman who seemed

made of wire springs, devoted to her unmarried mothers and their babies. When her disordered desk became impossible, she moved to another one. And I can not forget MSD, big of frame and heart, whose voice I can still hear booming out, "Isn't life interesting?"

My job was to lubricate the office works for all of them, as well as for distraught clients who sat at my desk by the door, surrounded by screens so that their tears need not be seen by curious eyes. It was the only desk with privacy except JPM's cubicle in a back corner. The waiting space around the switchboard was often bedlam, for there were no playrooms then in which to sequester lively youngsters.

The first lessons I remember learning in casework were connected with disciplined thinking. Asking questions was not easy for me because I had been brought up by the rule: "It isn't polite to ask questions. If people want you to know anything they will tell you." Here, I must not lose myself in what they were telling to the extent of forgetting what it was needful to know. After emerging from a few interviews in red-faced ignorance of the address where an applicant could be reached or of just who was taking care of the baby now, I began to learn a control of thought processes that was new to me. Dictating records was another exercise in remembering and sorting what information was relevant.

That it takes knowledge to determine relevance was forcibly demonstrated to me when, after a year at intake, I became a placing-out visitor. Dr. William Healy and Dr. Augusta Bronner had moved from their outstanding work in the Juvenile Court in Chicago to direct a new clinic in Boston dedicated to the memory of a beloved children's judge, Harvey H. Baker. I had read their newly published book, *The Individual Delinquent,* and had been impressed that practically anything might be significant in a child's early life. When I prepared a summary of my first case for the Judge Baker Clinic, I, therefore, omitted not the slightest sneeze I could capture in the record. I remember how Dr. Healy snorted when I handed it to him and how he told me he wouldn't read it until I had really made a summary.

Ignorance of the motivations of behavior was common to all of us in those days. If we had a naive faith that a good home would cure the lack of one in the case of every unhappy child, we were often disappointed and left wondering how we had failed to secure a home that was *right* for this child. We were not aware that painful experiences may live on in the unconscious and be as productive of conflict in a new environment as in the old. We did not know that children do not "forget" as easily as they seem to do. I can not recall without bitter shame the case of Donald, the eight-year-old son of a refined but alcoholic mother, who had episodes of stealing in one foster home after another. I felt that something drastic had to be done to stop his losing good homes for this behavior and so agreed to a teacher's suggestion that, since the last occurrence was at school and other children had been suspected, he should be exposed before the other pupils. I learned a lesson from the failure of this procedure, but did not know till years later that we were probably dealing with a child who expressed in this way an irrepressible conflict about his mother.

Work with unmarried mothers followed in those days certain principles designed to avoid creating more social problems. How-to-do in this kind of case involved trying to locate the putative father to secure some financial support if possible. We did not countenance forced marriages and assumed that it was best that the mother keep her baby if it was at all possible. It was firmly believed by most social workers that if she did not, being relieved by adoption or otherwise of the baby's care, she would probably make a habit of illegitimate pregnancies. JPM was strongly for individual treatment and against the assumption that domestic work with the baby was a standard solution. He thought the undue strain upon an immature girl was as likely to produce unfortunate further alliances as was relieving her entirely of responsibility.

I did not realize at the time how far-reaching was JPM's

vision and compassionate understanding. Now, as I review the
Annual Reports of the Boston Children's Aid Society from
1911 to 1918, I am amazed at the breadth of his concern. In
one place he says, "We cannot as a community longer continue
to pick out certain types of cases. We must receive and treat
every type."[1] He notes that fixed rules are unwise; that there
should be research to discover means of prevention of the ills
we treat. The number of children per visitor should be reduced
to forty or even thirty. In another place he says, "To interpret
and inspire are among a social worker's most important duties,
and she can do neither if crowded by daily tasks."[2] He expresses concern for the quality of work done by the Overseers
of the Poor and in the Division of Aid To Mothers With
Dependent Children, which was then foundering for lack of
adequate staff.[3] In the 1918 Report, JPM was hailing the
establishment of the League for Preventive Work which was to
study problems of alcoholism and set up a Dietetic Bureau to
advise social agencies on food. He urged that Boston agencies
establish a Council. During this period, the B.C.A.S. had
pioneered in finding and subsidizing special foster homes in the
city that could take an arrested child at any hour of the day or
night, so that no child need go to the City Detention Home. The
B.C.A.S. also joined with other children's agencies in establishing a clinic in one of the hospitals where children under study
and in care could have thorough health examinations.

The weekly staff meetings at B.C.A.S. were in themselves a
rare educational opportunity. Whatever the administrative problems that had to be discussed with the staff, I think never a
meeting passed without some consideration of world events or
of the philosophy behind our work. Whatever the subject, it was
played upon by JPM's mellow and keen human understanding
and his irrepressible sense of humor. One of these talks was his
estimate on the outbreak of world war, that the gradual
progress of civilization might be set back for years, but that,
while millions of ordinary folk went about their work as usual,
changes of vast import to them would be wrought. On another

occasion, discussing the Red Cross Home Service, JPM predicted that social casework would have to change some of its attitudes and methods, for the public conscience would not tolerate toward families of its servicemen the condescension that had too often marred work for "the poor." Some of us, years later, agreed that it took us about ten years to grow up to what JPM gave us in those staff meetings, but that, in the meantime, we had remembered them.

Another educational experience, which came after I had been Home-Finding Visitor for perhaps a year, was my first attempt to write for publication. The New York School of Social Work undertook to publish a series of monographs on child welfare, for which it planned to collect some of the rich experience then buried in the files of children's agencies. Volume I, Number 1, was to cover the selection of foster homes for children, and the principles and methods followed by the Boston Children's Aid Society, with illustrative cases. The New York School sent Miss Georgia Ralph to help organize our material. At that time Miss Mary Doran (MSD) was supervisor of Home-Finding, and I was her assistant. We shared the writing, Miss Doran covering the application forms, references, and standards, and I, the visits to prospective foster homes and how one evaluates what one sees and establishes a relationship with the foster mother as a volunteer worker for the Society. Then Miss Doran closed the seventy-four-page monograph with an account of how homes were approved or disapproved, how records of homes were kept, and how homes were used. The monograph was published in 1919. Because certain paragraphs sum up what I had been learning about casework, as well as about home-finding, I include here these excerpts:

"Considering the visit as a means of estimating a family's possibilities, there are two conflicting yet supplementary purposes with which a visitor goes into a home. First of all she tries to see the home in the picture it presents at any given time, *as a whole,* just as it is. The object is to slip in with the least possible disturbance of the family life, to get on such terms with the members in little friendly ways that they feel free to be themselves, and then to let the currents of family life go on as usual, while the visitor, uncritically almost, enjoys it all from the family's point of view. Only so is it possible to get sympathetically just what living in that town and house, going to that church, working and playing in those ways, all really mean to the family itself. . . . . Another attitude of mind gets its best innings when, after going away from this little picture of family life, one interprets the facts and impressions gained. Unfortunately for simplicity's sake, these two attitudes can not take turns in this fashion. All the while that the visitor is temporarily living the family's life, the interpretive mind must be registering guide posts and exploring roads that promise to lead to points of significance. When the work is new, the visitor is mostly led by the family; experience makes it more and more possible to direct the conversation at the same time that one lives in it. . . .[4]

"Nothing can be done until friendly relations are established with the family. The ice is never broken twice in the same way. There are the open-armed, the diffident, the aloof, the reserved to meet—all with different lines of least resistance to a friendly approach. Nothing is worth more to a visitor, barring the gift of insight, than a circle of personal interests and experiences of her own wide enough so that she can open up conversation in ways that will tap the springs of interest of all sorts of people. After there is a full flowing tide of talk, the order of approach to what is wanted follows only the sequence of ideas.[5]

"The new volunteer for home service for children learns partly by what she is told of the work and more by what she sees of the methods by which the Society is making her acquaintance. This argues strongly for procedure in investigation which is ethically as fine as the methods which we want the foster mother to use in her dealings with the Society and with the children. We want to find in her reliability and frankness, and we must approach her with no unworthy subterfuges. We can not approach families as people to be *used* only for our purposes and expect them to have an unselfish regard for the children. We want people to respect our judgment even when they differ, and we must respect theirs. . . .

"Most families need, in addition, to know definitely about the work of the Society. Those who have lived sheltered and happy lives have no background of knowledge of the world out of which the children come. They need a background both for their encouragement in meeting the problems that must inevitably come if they take a child and for their appreciation of the real bigness of the task they are undertaking. Many people think that taking a child to board is as easy as getting a canary and would be a fine resource when they want to retire from real work. They do not understand that they are being called to travel the rocky road which fathers and mothers find wearisome with their own children, and this, moreover, with children already handicapped by birth and environment. If they understood all, but few persons probably would undertake the work; but they can be helped to a realization that it is a big thing demanding the best that is in them, and the rest can be unfolded gradually as problems arise. After love for a child has come many things will be easier."[6]

Altogether, I was extremely fortunate that my first five years in social work were spent in the B.C.A.S., filling positions in turn in intake, as visitor of placed-out children, and homefinding visitor. There were hardships to be sure. Among these I did not count the low salary ($720 a year, rising to $960), for I felt I would be glad to pay, if I could, for the privilege of working in that setting. However, travel for home visits was often exhausting, for there were no office automobiles, and one spent sometimes as much as eight hours in being transported to make one two-hour visit. I remember I took myself in hand on the first day of such travels, consumed as I was with anxiety lest I miss connections at the next junction. "Now see here! You won't last if you don't stop trying to push trolley cars and trains. Just ride them and see what happens." Meals were often sketchy, and one could map the towns of Massachusetts accord-

ing to their ability to produce a decent lunch. One never knew
if an evening out could be anticipated or whether one would be
stranded in some railroad station with a concert ticket in one's
purse. Nevertheless, the rewards were large in terms of human
contacts with children and foster parents and in the sense one
had of increasing the sum of human happiness.

The children's agencies of that time were on the growing edge
of social work in its reaching out for more understanding of
human behavior. We read the new books as they appeared and
discussed them. One unique opportunity was offered in the late
winter of 1918, when "the first course in social psychiatry ever
given in the world" was launched at the Boston Psychopathic
Hospital by its Director, Dr. Elmer E. Southard, and Chief
Social Worker, Miss Mary C. Jarrett. I joined the group for
some six weeks of late afternoon lectures and discussions.

The Boston Psychopathic Hospital had been opened in 1912
under Dr. Southard's direction as "a diagnostic station for the
study of mental defects or possibly mental disease, without the
ponderous shackles of legal commitment."[7] Dr. Southard believed that diseases of the mind should be studied as diseases
of the body as a whole, and that an out-patient department
where patients could come voluntarily for treatment was essential to a state hospital system. Miss Mary C. Jarrett was
brought from the B.C.A.S. to head the social service department.

Our course was a series of rambling talks in which Dr.
Southard thought aloud about psychiatry and social work and
how each discipline could use the other. I remember some an-
noyance at his obvious lack of preparation and his humorous
sallies which looked like lack of respect for his subject and for
us, the social workers hungry for knowledge, who sat before
him. We had no idea of the greatness of this man of genius,
whom to know was a memory to cherish all one's life.

When he died of sudden pneumonia two years later, his life
was summarized, but not contained, in these facts about him :[8]
Dr. Southard's profession was neuropathology, which he taught

at the Harvard Medical School from 1904 until his death. He was pathologist at Danvers State Hospital from 1906 to 1909, contributing to research many papers of outstanding value. He could spend fourteen years in the microscopic study of the brain tissues of idiots to determine "the minimum brain machinery with which speech and thought processes get performed,"[9] and at the same time broaden neuropathology to include studies of classification and many allied subjects, such as physical changes in old age, causes of delinquency, industrial mental hygiene. Every conceivable problem came to his clinics at the Psychopathic Hospital, and none was alien to his interest or ruled out by his classifications. On the side, he was an ardent student of grammar in many languages (related to his interest in classification), a champion amateur chess player, and a philosopher devoted to Professors James and Royce at Harvard, attending their seminars (and sometimes leading them) until his death. He was a prolific writer of scientific papers, a brilliant teacher, an unselfish developer of research in others, and a leader in planning research for years ahead. "His idea of a holiday was to go to New York and shut himself up in a library where he could get in fifteen hours of reading uninterrupted."[10]

Dr. Richard Cabot lists four new ideas which were Dr. Southard's contribution to the ferment of the war years:[11]

1. The idea of a neuropsychiatrist to study not the nervous system alone but "the whole human being in all his relations and aspects."

2. The psychiatric social worker and social psychiatry to break down the narrow specialization that had grown up in medicine, and bring social facts into consideration.

3. The diagnostic scheme of the Kingdom of Evils (of which we shall hear more).

4. Orderly exclusion in diagnosis. An exhaustive search of all known alternatives, beginning with the best known and most curable and proceeding to the more obscure.

None of these ideas was wholly new, but Dr. Southard lent to them, from his enthusiasm and the brilliance of his mind, a new quality that made them more immediately useful to more people than before.

Perhaps the following will explain why we did not fully appreciate Dr. Southard in our brief course in 1918:

> Jubilation at the birth of a new truth seems more characteristic of him than any single trait that I know. He was not soberly pleased with a new idea. His mind gamboled and capered about it with radiant delight. He played with it, turned it upside down and inside out, tossed it up and caught it again. Sometimes (alas!) he did this before an audience discovered the new idea there before their eyes (though quite invisible to them), and proceeded to play a game with it in celebration of its birth . . . his audience was apt to think he was laughing at *them* instead of at his new-born idea.[12]

Dr. Southard's life philosophy could be summed up in these words of Dr. Cabot:

"Never to take a passive, an oppressed, a down-hearted, or disappointed attitude was a principle with him. Passivity, he held, is disease; activity is health. Every setback, every misfortune set him scheming anew. In fact, as one of his close friends said, 'Surely he must have turned his own death to some advantage.' "[13]

Of course we were unaware, in that winter of 1918, that Dr. Southard's new ideas, with which he played so joyously, would start a movement of immense consequence to life in the world and particularly to medicine, and to our young profession.

Sometimes a day in one's life stands out uniquely as a day of decision. June 8, 1918 began like any other day with a walk to work along the ridge of Beacon Hill and down its congested north slope to Hawkins Street. One letter in the morning mail changed the direction of my life. It was an announcement from Dr. Elmer E. Southard and Miss Mary C. Jarrett of the opening of a summer course at Smith College to contribute to the war effort by training workers for the rehabilitation of "shell-shocked" soldiers. The course was to begin on July first, just three weeks away!

I knew at once that, if I enrolled, it must be with a serious intention of using the training and that I must go to it free of any commitments to the B.C.A.S. Considering what that association had meant to me in personal satisfactions as well as a means of professional growth, the decision was one of the utmost seriousness. I spent the noon hour in the dimness of St. Paul's Cathedral to think and pray alone. That evening I sought consultation with another social worker, one engaged in psychiatric work.

Two earlier decisions of great moment had prepared me for facing this one. The first was in my second year at Smith College. I had not wanted to teach, yet here I was preparing to teach Latin because there seemed no other career open to me as a woman. Under stress of a religious sense of vocation, I decided that, come what might, I must prepare for missionary service. I changed my curriculum and faced family disapproval with a new sense of personal responsibility for my own life.

The second earlier decision was not important in itself, but it had established a principle on which all later decisions were to be based. In the winter of 1917 I had been offered a job as visitor in the Home-Finding Department of the B.C.A.S., to work with Miss Mary Doran. I did not want to leave my group of children in foster care. I loved them and enjoyed seeing them grow in their new homes. I enjoyed sharing with foster mothers their perplexities while they were making such growth possible. Why, then, should I change?

I was alone in the B.C.A.S. office serving my turn at Saturday afternoon duty, and I carried on an uninterrupted debate with myself. The agency badly needed a home-finder. That was evident in the scarcity of good homes on which all work with children depended. I had shown the needed qualities, and the agency wanted me for this responsible job. As I watched the pigeons wheeling in the gray sky I thought of the battle fields of France, of the wounded in hospitals, and of those who would never come back. I said to myself, "What right have I to take less than the greatest amount of responsibility I am capable of carrying, when others give so much more than their personal enjoyment—their health and their very lives?" The decision to do the home-finding job clicked and seemed right.

Now on this June day of 1918, the pull toward taking the new course in psychiatric work was to fit myself to carry greater responsibilities. It was also, I am sure, an unconscious urge to learn more for myself, so as to solve the many problems which four interviews with Dr. Putnam had by no means settled. Of what, however, would the new responsibilities consist? I could have little idea, except that I would be dealing with disturbed people and assisting in the application of remedies as yet quite unknown to me.

The urgency which drove me to consult, that evening, a stranger whose name I have now forgotten was fear of my own background of nervous illness. No doubt I wanted psychiatric study the more because of this, but also feared change the more. Might I lose the precious adjustment I already had? I had even been reared with the superstition that too much study of psychology could cause a mental break. What would it do to me to work in constant contact with mental abnormalities?

I can remember little of that consultation, except that, if reassurance was guarded, there was at least no warning to keep away from psychiatric work. I emerged with a conviction that any risk I was taking was about the same as that of anyone else and that the opportunity was worth the risk.

That same evening, with a sense of making an irrevocable leap and with regret at being able to give no more than three weeks' notice, I sat down to write JPM, resigning my job at B.C.A.S.

CHAPTER 4

EVERYONE IS A LITTLE QUEER

The sixty-odd women who assembled on the campus of Smith College in July, 1918, were fired with enthusiasm to know and to serve their country. Many came directly from college; some from teaching, nursing, or publishing; a few from experience in social work. The new training school was directed by Professor F. Stuart Chapin of the Sociology Department of the college. Dr. Edith R. Spaulding co-ordinated the courses in psychiatry, and Miss Mary C. Jarrett, the teaching of social work. Both assembled a large number of lecturers, expert in various fields of medicine and social work, and they wove the content of teaching into a surprisingly unified whole.

Each student was required to produce a comprehensive social-psychiatric case history, preferably of herself, and a survey of some research problem. Before the summer was over, plans were made to extend the course by six months of practice in some hospital or social agency.[1] I was given advance credit for the field practice because of five years' experience in social work.

In that war summer no one knew that by November people all over the world would be dancing in the streets to celebrate the end of hostilities. Everyone expected a continuation of the large number of casualties, including nervous and mental breakdowns, which the armies overseas had suffered. The students were eager for duty in army hospitals.

There were lectures in psychiatry or social work for four hours every morning and frequently also in the evenings. Two

afternoons each week we attended observation clinics at
Northampton State Hospital, where we saw patients suffering
from all the conditions about which we were studying. The
rest of the time, and for some students this was far into the
night, we read psychoanalytic literature. Since I insisted on
thinking, I limited my reading to what I thought I could absorb.

The lectures in psychiatry followed Dr. Southard's classification of mental conditions into eleven major groups, suggesting
an approach to diagnosis through orderly exclusion, beginning
with the disease categories which were best known, or best tested
by laboratory methods, and ending with the least well defined.[2]

It was understood early in the course that there was nothing
about a shell that caused a certain kind of "shock." The strains
of civilian life which produced the eleven varieties of diseased
reaction were operative also in battle conditions, with added
incidence of fear of annihilation or injury. Some who broke
under the strain of war would sooner or later have broken at
home. Those who seemed to go to pieces suddenly could have
been seen to be cracking up for days before a shell exploded
near them. One lecturer told us that the stretcher bearers at the
front used to lay bets on who would break next, and with
surprising accuracy.

We became accustomed to thinking of psychiatry as a key
to unlock all the mysteries of personality in all kinds of circumstances. Circumstances became less important to us than the
kinds of people exposed to them. Why, it was asked, did one
man in a trench raked with shell fire, sleepless and underfed for
days, develop a nervous collapse while others in the same trench
had stomach cramps, rheumatism, or no symptoms at all? A
personal history of each might be expected to show significant
differences in their reactions to strain.

We learned about the working of the subconscious, and many
things in everyday life became clear to us. We saw fears displaced from childhood, jealousy displaced from other persons,
hostility disguised as solicitude. desire as fear, and wish as

certainty. We watched each other's slips of the tongue with glee and lived in a world where nothing was quite as it seemed and was frequently the opposite. We learned that the normal could best be understood through study of the abnormal, just because, in states of disease, inhibitions are lost and the workings of the mental mechanism can be seen, as are the works of a clock when its back is removed. No wonder we felt that we had been fooled by appearances all our lives and that we now had the key to wisdom in human relations. We were rather proud of our own abnormalities now that we understood about them. It may be significant that the alumnae paper which began to be published during the following winter was entitled *The Social Syndrome* (a collection of symptoms)!

I can remember three distinct impressions from the summer at Smith, which was an amazing whirl of feasts of new ideas for hungry minds. One was a feeling of relief and self-confidence. If mental abnormalities were only exaggerations of mechanisms found in everyone, why should I feel especially marked by a predisposition to nervous illness? The fact that I could recover was in itself reassuring.

Secondly, there was, of course, much in psychoanalytic literature that was new and could be shocking to a woman reared in the extreme of Victorian prudery. Dr. Putnam had taught me to be frank with myself about sex, but such ideas as penis-envy or the castration-complex did not seem more than remotely applicable to social work as I knew it. However, I said to myself, "I will put it all on a shelf in my mental cupboard, and when I find in practice any facts that need such hypotheses to explain them, I will take down what is appropriate." Some years later I recalled this and noted that almost all of what I learned had been taken down and used in some fashion.

The third reaction came over me as I walked along the campus one day—a sense of unreality in all we were doing. How we dealt *in words* with what were bitter realities to those who lived them! While we tested each other with the tongue-twisting sentences designed to reveal the slurring of speech characteristic of general paresis, what did we really know of this disease which then doomed its victims in from two to five years after the first appearance of symptoms? What did it mean to have an infection twenty-five to thirty years in the past, known or unknown, treated or untreated; to live a normal life all those years, then to be stricken, behave strangely, waste the family's money, sicken and die? What did it mean to a patient with recurring attacks of mania and depression never to know what sudden change would come, to find despair utterly real one day and exuberant hilarity the only way to live the next—and one's family disagreeing with the estimate both ways? Life would be broken up by repeated hospitalizations, with cures only temporary at best. Still less could we know what a "split personality" meant to friends who saw a dear one retreat from the world into silliness, or violent behavior, or bitter delusions of persecution, not normally felt but endlessly elaborated. Only practice could remove the dream-like quality of this hothouse experience with the most baffling of human ills.

In the midst of this tidal wave of new insights, we analyzed cases in our social seminars by Dr. Southard's classification in *The Kingdom of Evils.*[3] Dr. Southard emphasized strongly that this classification was *not* a form for collection of data but only for its interpretation, for diagnosis and a guide to treatment. He spoke with admiration of Miss Richmond's *Social Diagnosis* as a model for gathering information. He noted, however, that fully half of the cases described in that book would be considered psychiatric cases by a psychiatrist. The revolutionary idea in this course was to shift the focus of attention from the family as a unit, and an economic unit primarily, to the individual as a person. His economic state would be important to diagnosis only *after* the conditions within himself had been appraised and his ability to act within the legal structure. Dr. Southard thought that the rapid advances in technology and industry brought almost into the foreseeable future the abolition of poverty, except where there was personal disability.

In reviewing the volume[4] written by Dr. Southard and Miss

Jarrett and published after his death, I find it still sparkling with Dr. Southard's brilliant intellect and rich in his philosophy and insights (whether or not one agrees with them). Why did not this scheme of classification take hold as social work moved rapidly to adopt the psychiatric point of view? I think there were at least two reasons: one was that, in spite of Dr. Southard's warning, people who were interested in *The Kingdom of Evils* tended to use it not only to interpret data but to collect it. In this use, it would soon seem rigid and clumsy. It became habitual to think of ruling out first the physical and mental condition of the patient, and that might seem to be enough. Also, the use of a focussed diagnostic scheme belongs to a stage of mastery of use of data which social work did not have for a long time. The early stages of the application of a new scientific outlook are experimental and rambling, gathering data before one can see its meaning and only focussing much later. Working under the direction of psychiatrists, as we were to be, we social workers found psychiatry itself in the same unfocussed state. So we were to have a decade of voluminous histories of patients with only sporadic mastery of what to do with the information.

The revolutionary content of what we learned in that summer at Smith stayed with us, if the classifications did not. We thought in terms of patients as individuals. We social workers were most concerned, as the psychiatrists were, with what went on inside the patient. It was also our job to know what, in his family, community life, and war service, had contributed to his illness. We were eager to help get the patient back to normal living, but to do so mainly by restoring him to himself, when, as a whole person, we liked to believe that he could cope with his life conditions in his own way.

Our concentration on therapy, rather than on the social accompaniments of the patient's illness, was brought out when the class was eagerly awaiting the assignments for six months of field practice. When the announcement was finally made in August, those who could not be accomodated in army hospitals or Red Cross units, but were sent to the New York Charity

Organization Society, were bitterly disappointed. "We did not come here to learn social work but psychotherapy," they said.

Miss Jarrett had a serious talk with the class before we left Northampton. She said the future of our new discipline held two possibilities: we could think of ourselves as assistants in psychotherapy, working under the direction of psychiatrists much as psychiatric nurses or psychotherapeutic aides do; or we could develop a profession in our own right, bringing into psychotherapy the *social* outlook and skills which would require our thinking for ourselves (not mainly following orders) and would place us alongside the psychiatrist as another different but allied professional. She said we might not have a choice in a given situation how we would be used, but it would be much better for our professional future if we were aware of how we wanted to be used.

One solemn warning was given to us as we set out, conscious of having new insights granted only to a few. We had had, we were told, more hours of lectures in psychiatry than were given in most medical schools. We should *never* speak of Freud or air our psychiatric knowledge in front of doctors, at least not until we were assured of a sympathetic hearing, and then only with becoming modesty. In spite of this warning, some of us occasionally fell into this barbed-wire fence—to our sorrow.

September, 1918, was the time of my initiation into the real lives of mental patients and their families. It was my fortune, as it had been at B.C.A.S., not to be a pioneer but a follower of pioneers, close enough to see something of the problems that had largely been solved.

Miss Hannah Curtis had been the first social worker at Danvers State Hospital. She had gone there from social service with tubercular patients at the Massachusetts General Hospital, to be a taker of "eugenic" histories. The Hospital, by the time I went there, had a large file of records of "repeating families" from the coast towns and the Merrimac Valley. (The daughter of one of these families once remarked while she was a patient at the Hospital, "Everybody in our family is up here now except Mother and the kitty.") Miss Curtis told me how one day the Superintendent of the Hospital asked her to stop gathering genealogical data and get for him the social facts in a puzzling case. What she brought back was so illuminating that he said to her, "Don't you ever do anything else." From that day the Hospital staff learned how to use and appreciate social service.

In her five years of service before she took the position of Supervisor of Social Service for all the Massachusetts State Hospitals, Miss Curtis established certain principles. The social worker was to be free to be a friend to all patients and their families and a link to communities which had a tradition of distrust and fear of hospitals for the insane. For this reason the social worker should not be asked to return patients to the Hospital when they became disturbed while on visit in the communities. A hospital car with a supervisor and attendant would be sent if that was necessary. The social worker should not be a bill collector. A state financial agent discussed with families how much they could pay. The social service car should not be conspicuously marked as from the Hospital, lest families feel embarrassed by having it stand at their door (though, of course, the state license plate would identify the car to the initiated). The social worker was to work directly under the medical staff and be regarded as a fellow-professional, living on an upper floor of the administration building where the staff had apartments and eating in the doctors' dining room. These details, important in the hierarchy of a hospital, gave social service status and dignity.

Miss Curtis had already organized the social service department (still consisting of only one worker) into three distinct areas of work: 1) *Histories* (a) taken in the community when families did not come to the Hospital to give them to the doctors, (b) investigations in the community to clear up doubtful points for diagnosis, such as: Was the patient deluded or speaking the truth about home conditions? Was a family lying to get rid of a patient? (c) investigations in medico-legal cases upon which

might be determined a diagnosis fixing the patient's responsibility for a crime; 2) *After-care*. When patients were allowed
to leave the Hospital on visit for a year before final discharge
the social worker was responsible for (a) investigations to see
if home conditions were suitable for a visit, (b) education of
the family in care of the patient, (c) help in employment or
other adjustment problems; 3) *Supervision* of some thirty
chronic patients who had been placed in boarding homes in the
surrounding communities. Miss Curtis had changed this long-
established supervision from a medical inspection which upset
both patients and foster families to a friendly visit that maintained good relations with the Hospital and used its facilities
when needed. All of this work had been developed under Super-
intendents Dr. George M. Kline[5] and Dr. John B. MacDonald
whose support and understanding made it possible. Those of us
who followed Miss Curtis in social service (and others did
follow in all the hospitals of the State Department of Mental
Diseases) had the inestimable advantage of her wise counsel in
her position as State Supervisor.

In September, 1918, the great influenza epidemic swept the
United States. Danvers State Hospital was not greatly affected
except that perhaps more of the old people among the patients
died than would have passed away in any other period of equal
length, and the existing shortage of nurses and attendants was
made more critical. We were quarantined to visitors, in or out,
almost as soon as I arrived. That made trips to the communities
impossible for several weeks. I used the time to study records,
and volunteered to help in ward duty for a few days. There was
not much that I could do, except to help back into bed restless or
agitated old ladies who kept getting up and looking for the way
home. (I was not, of course, assigned to wards where more
acute and difficult cases were living.) Nevertheless, just to have
one more person on a ward was help enough—for instance, to
allow a student nurse to go to class who could not otherwise be
spared. It gave me valuable experience with the tediousness of
life in the chronic wards, the long hours the nurses had (twelve

hours with time out for meals and two hours for class or rest), and the frustrations of not being able to reach patients with persuasion or comfort.

Danvers State Hospital had been a pioneer in its rejection of any form of mechanical restraint of disturbed patients. Only hydrotherapeutic baths and packs were allowed, and only on a doctor's prescription. Sedatives were used sparingly, and also on prescription. Electric shock therapy and tranquilizing drugs were far in the future. Dr. MacDonald, the Superintendent, was a Canadian originally from the Glengarry country, warm-hearted, conscientious, devoted to the interests of the patients. The tone he gave to the whole hospital was both stimulating and kind. Social workers sensed this from the staff conferences at eight o'clock every morning which we were supposed to attend when outside work permitted.[6] We learned not only from hearing discussions of diagnoses and of after-care plans but from incidents like this: An old man in a wheel chair told the doctors he did not know where he was, but he supposed it was some kind of a hotel. He was worried that he could not pay his bill, "and all my life I've paid for everything I got." Dr. MacDonald leaned over to him and said, "I'm the proprietor of this hotel, and you shall stay here as long as you want and it won't cost you a cent." The old man's face lighted up as his hand shot out to grasp the doctor's. "It's a good offer, and I'll take it," he said.

A first task was to learn to drive the hospital Ford car, which was accomplished by driving 100 miles and certifying to the fact (at that time the qualification for a license in Massachusetts). Since my teacher, most of the time, was a patient who could not have a license, although he had been an expert with machines of all sorts, the 100 miles had to be accumulated by driving around the grounds and included no experience in traffic. With my teacher's words in my ears, "If anything is going to happen it will happen mighty quick," I drove with trepidation, especially in the river cities like Lawrence and Lowell where traffic concentrated on bridges. It might be said that I drove with the back of my neck and the pit of my stomach. The car, which had a habit of staying out nights with the garage boys, also showed inexplicable freaks of temperament. But I can think of no more exhilarating experience than driving up and down the dipping hills of the Newburyport Turnpike on a beautiful morning in spring or fall.

The community contacts were endlessly interesting. We saw the life of people in the fishing villages and the granite-cutting towns of Cape Ann; textile cities like Lowell and Lawrence, still full of ghostly memories of strikes, past and present; leather-tanning cities like Salem and Peabody; or shoe cities like Haverhill and Lynn. We saw rural places where our boarding patients lived and suburbs of Boston like Malden and Everett. We saw a cross-section of America, mostly working folk whose devotion to their unresponsive sick patients, sometimes through the years of a lifetime, almost surpassed belief. There were also instances of unbelievable meanness and cruelty, which it was the business of social service to unearth. People tormented their sick ones deliberately sometimes, and drove them into mental illness or got rid of troublesome people who might tell too much. In one such case, the patient, a woman, held her lips shut and controlled her boiling emotions until she was almost diagnosed a schizophrenic from the "marked lack of feeling" evident in her examination. It took a delicate, probing investigation in the community to establish the whole story of a refined woman's entanglement, the complicity of a respected citizen in the town, and her final despairing threats which might mean exposure for him. After she was released from the hospital as "not insane," it was not entirely orthodox that social service should be extended to her, but we did contrive contacts to help her through a most difficult period of readjustment in the community.

Yes, there were unusual people to be helped, and there were great numbers of inadequate people to be given the small amount of moral support which was possible and which might make the difference between their living fairly well in the community and being taken out of it at public expense. I did not find the work depressing. In fact, I said once that I met much the same kinds of people as in the general community, only here the deviating individuals were recognized and given care, instead of struggling along alone or making life miserable for other people. Not having too much expectation that the advanced conditions could improve, what gains they did make were hailed with a sense of real accomplishment.

Although the job at Danvers was isolated in some respects, quartered in a hospital set on a hilltop surrounded by rural villages, it was not without professional contacts. The cities outside of Boston had social agencies of some sort, often very good ones, and we served them and used them co-operatively, in the interest of their clients and our patients. We became a recognized part of the social resources of the district.

An important point in practice concerned social service records. Miss Curtis had established the principle that the social record of the patient should be included in the folder of the medical record so that every busy doctor would have the social facts immediately available. Dr. MacDonald was concerned, however, about the possibility that medical records might be subpoenaed in court cases and break the confidentiality in which some social information had been given. He ruled, therefore, that social records were not to be considered part of the *official* record of the patient but were to be clipped separately within the medical folder. Protection of the confidential nature of social records was not, however, any more certain than in other situations. There is, in fact, a special hazard where two professions meet. Doctors who would protect confidences on medical matters with a sure self-discipline periodically blurted out to a patient, "But your wife said. . . . ," while social workers at a staff conference sat frozen with horror. No amount of warning in red type in a record would entirely preclude this danger, and we learned to avoid direct quotes in delicate situations.

One of the things I learned at the hospital was a focussed method of recording visits. Busy doctors would read only what

was to the point and arranged to attract the eye. Case histories
followed a topical outline, and investigations were organized by
headings showing the points to be cleared up, the testimony of
each informant, some indication of the informant's opportunity
to know, and his general reliability. It was the running notes on
after-care visits which had been most likely to be rambling with
no heading except the meaningless "visited." I felt that the
system the doctors used in their ward notes was much better
and adopted it.[7] I later found it very useful in training students
to accurate thinking.

First, the paragraph was headed by a concise, underlined
statement giving the most important facts derived from the
visit. Next to this heading was a brief statement of the time,
place, and circumstances of the visit, who was seen, and anything else bearing on the authenticity of the report. Finally, if
more detail was neded to explain or elaborate the heading, it
was contained in a brief, running narrative in the body of the
paragraph.

How did the social psychiatry we learned at Smith flourish
in the setting of state hospital practice? For the most part, there
was no conflict. Diagnoses were flexible as we heard them discussed and voted on at staff meetings. Treatment was largely
by the controlled environment of the hospital, giving to the
patient, exhausted and frustrated by his inability to cope with his
responsibilities in the community, a chance to recuperate. Often
regular living and freedom from responsibility did assist nature
and at least ameliorate his condition. Occupational therapy was
a large factor, not only in the workroom where needlework,
pottery, weaving, and other crafts were taught, but in the work
of the greenhouse and gardens, and around the buildings.

We social workers, proceeding with due caution, found most
of the medical staff skeptical of Freud's theories but with a rich
fund of practical experience in dealing with mental patients. To
give patients, even those who were deluded, a listening ear, to
gain their confidence, to help them in minor adjustments where

their own powers of adjustment were impaired, were good practices by any theory.

The prevailing attitude in the hospital was to see the patients as people, like other people. If they were handicapped, their relatives often seemed more so. Their peculiarities seemed only exaggerated forms of those found in everyday life, and a surprising number improved enough to return to their communities under some protection. It was believed that the hopeless patients in back wards need not have reached that deteriorated state if psychiatry had been as advanced when they first became ill as it was in the postwar period. Even more would that be true now, with the medical discoveries of the last forty years in fever and shock therapies, antibiotic drugs, tranquilizing drugs, and psychotherapy.

I was happier at Danvers than ever in my life before. This job had everything: interesting and challenging work, to which was added in the last year an opportunity to train a student in field work for the Smith College School; beautiful surroundings in the country; recognition for what I did; companionship of both sexes among the social workers, the medical staff, and their families; social life in the hospital and outside on picnics and trips to Boston for an occasional show—all this made life in lodginghouse rooms in Boston look drab. The salary of $100 a month plus full maintenance was enough to provide savings as well as help to my family if they had been willing to take it. Why, then, did I ever leave Danvers?

When I was asked that question by the aunt of a friend of mine, my answer was, "Because I was too comfortable." The old lady remarked after she had recovered her breath, "Well, I've spent my life trying to find a place that was comfortable enough to stay in. What a reason for *not* staying!"

After some four years at the hospital, however, I had begun to feel that perhaps I had learned and given as much as I could there. I had always intended to go back to work with children. A clinical psychologist whom I consulted phrased it in this way, "You want to cast a longer shadow in the world than you can if you work always with mentally disabled people." That about said it.

It was at the National Conference of Social Work in 1922, the first I attended, that I heard about the new demonstration clinics being set up by the Commonwealth Fund. I asked about them further and left my name for information about openings in that program. Talking it over with Dr. MacDonald, I told him I would not leave during the academic year when we would have students in training, but might want to be released in summer if an opportunity arose. He was fine about it, as about everything. In June of 1923, the chance came. I was transferred to the Division of Mental Hygiene, still under the Department of Mental Diseases, to work in new clinics for the habit-training of preschool children.

CHAPTER 5

THE TWIG IS BENT—A TREE INCLINED

The Mental Hygiene Movement, which had been burgeoning from the pioneer beginning initiated by Clifford W. Beers after his experience as a mental patient, was entering a new phase after World War I.[1] Not only better care and rehabilitation of the mentally sick but *prevention* was the watchword. America was sick of conflict and afraid of it.[2] Return to normal living seemed to depend not only on removal of sources of disturbance but on such treatment of psychopathic individuals and groups as would eradicate their menace to society. Better than building ever more efficient psychopathic hospitals was the mental hygiene of childhood, to cut off at the source the appalling waste of juvenile delinquency, mental disease, and crime.

The Commonwealth Fund and other foundations were interested in experimental child guidance clinics. Two were begun in turn in Minneapolis and Cleveland. Massachusetts set up a Division of Mental Hygiene in its Department of Mental Diseases. Dr. Douglas Thom, the director, had a brilliant idea. A state department could not hope for the funds available to the demonstration clinics of the Commonwealth Fund. It had to reach impressive numbers of people and produce results visible to legislative committees. Why not attack the problem of juvenile delinquency still earlier than the age when children came to the attention of schools, neighborhoods, and courts? Why not go into the homes of preschool children when the habits were forming which would probably pattern the life of the child? If these

71

clinics were set up in medical centers where well-baby clinics had already become an accepted facility, could not these young children and their parents be guided toward health instead of maladjustment? The cost would be minimal, using existing hospital clinics in the afternoon hours, and several clinics could be served by a staff consisting of a psychiatrist, a psychologist for intelligence testing, and a social worker for histories and contacts with the parents in the homes. It would be an educational service, carrying mental hygiene concepts into neighborhoods not likely to be reached by lectures or child-care magazines.

This was the rationale of the new clinic movement which I joined. We began work from an office in the east wing of the State House, overlooking Boston Common, and we went out to what were called Habit Clinics in the North End of Boston, East Boston, Roxbury, and, later, the West End. Dr. Thom had already experimented in a privately financed clinic, which was continuing, and he felt ready to expand the movement into other cities of the state, such as Lowell and Lawrence, as fast as community interest could be developed.

The idea had great possibilities, and there could be no doubt that lack of early training in good living habits was a factor in much of the maladjustment found in later life. Clinic histories could trace, for instance, the beginnings of neuroses or delinquency in the child whose world has been his oyster, and who reacts violently to the deprivation involved in any sort of control, or the child who gains power over his environment by exploiting bodily processes: enuresis, vomiting, food fads, or the child whose fears and tempers make the family his slave. We wanted to reach also the child who withdraws and is not noticed because he is so good.

The parents of small children who lived in poor neighborhoods and were burdened with many economic problems were not usually, we found, much inclined to seek help for their difficulties with such young children. "He's so little," we often heard and "When he gets older he'll have more sense." Some parents were immigrants who brought child-rearing patterns from quite different cultures. A child who would normally be "spoiled" and taken care of by dozens of adoring relatives in a peasant village in Italy might become much more a nuisance in a congested tenement with no safe place to play outside, but the parents would have no understanding of the idea of taking him to a clinic as if he were sick. If he reacted to his frustrations by temper tantrums, so did they! Or, in the Jewish neighborhoods where poverty and hard work and frustrated ambitions made many sick, solicitude for a child who was fretful and refused food might bring the parents to clinic, but reasoning could not make them stop increasing the child's tensions by their concern.

We had, in a sense, to go after our cases. The medical centers which offered us space for our clinics made a good link with community health facilities and with interested pediatricians. We had to make our own tools, so we wrote leaflets on child-training which were translated into several languages. I remember two of these were: "Is your child afraid of the dark?" and "Do you wish your child would obey you?" They were written in short sentences and often in question and answer form. Whenever there was opportunity, we gave talks to groups of workers with young children.

The necessity of selling a new idea called for quick and visible results. If parents were to be interested to come for advice (of which they probably got a plentiful supply from relatives and friends), they must get advice in a definite form which they could apply and from which they could benefit. So we began by attacking problems which happened to be a nuisance or an intolerable burden to the parents themselves, like enuresis, temper tantrums, vomiting. So, also, by chance or by choice, we slipped into a pattern of an authoritative approach.

Our attempts to develop incentives for good behavior led sometimes to amusing results. In enuresis cases, for instance, we tried giving the children gold stars to be pasted on a chart for every "dry night." A chart full of stars gained a reward of a cake of soap and a wash cloth. There followed epidemics of enuresis in large families which had had only one case before. Children who liked to come to clinic to play with the toys, undid their good records for control of tantrums when it came time to go home without the toys to which they had become attached.

During the first year, I was absorbed by the interest of the new movement but overwhelmed by the hopelessness of many of the situations we faced. I had been satisfied with small gains in cases of full-blown mental illness, but I thought that in preventive work with small children we could expect a much larger ratio of success. Instead, we found children being started wrong in life, because their parents and grandparents had not been caught young enough, and there was little we could do about it. In a study of 400 Habit Clinic children[3] made at the end of two years, we found, for instance, that 80% of the children failed to get what a home should give, not only in physical necessities but in home training in conduct, in some of the culture of their group, in some self-expression in play, and some social contacts with children of their own age. Only 13% suffered from poverty that we could identify, but most from spiritual poverty, friction between parents, irresponsible parents, ignorance (in more than half the cases), and mental or nervous instability in the parents. Of the children, 32% showed some physical disability, such as enlarged tonsils and adenoids or poor physical condition, 6% tested mentally deficient, 13% more were estimated to have poor personalities for social living. On the whole, the children were more normal than we would expect, considering their abnormal surroundings.

Looking back, I can see in myself a growing dissatisfaction with what we were doing. I thought Dr. Thom's theories were sound, but the trouble was in the way they were applied. If the advice given to parents seemed more and more unimaginative, mechanical, and even punitive to parent or child or both, I thought it need not be so. In fact, I was assured by the social worker in the private clinic that Dr. Thom himself conducted, that fine results were obtained and parents were most appreciative. Only now, years later, does it become clear to me that

persons and theories interact in establishing habits of practice—
our habits, if you please.[4] If much of our work was based on a
power struggle between parent and child, and our role became
more and more to advise the parent how to win, the program
attracted, for that very reason, persons to whom it was important to win in a contest. Being in a position to give authoritative advice could only channel success into securing acceptance
of it. In turn, the parents, who responded to instructions and
had the self-discipline necessary to carry them out, must have
been frequently those who also craved control and had only
lacked the latest methods and the backing of experts to rein-
force what were essentially their own ideas.

It is of course unfair to apply to work done from 1923 to
1925 standards which were not fully developed until nearly a
decade later. We had little knowledge of the essential dynamic
of parental love in moulding a child's responses to training nor
of the blighting effect on a child of parental rejection. We tried
to help parents to impose correct forms of behavior upon a child
from the *outside,* rather than from the inner springs of feeling
which are decisive for them both. Thus a hostile mother might
secure obedience by more consistency in training than she had
been able to evolve but, at the same time, plant the seeds of later
neurosis in her submissive child.

It seems now that we thought too much in terms of cutting
off the secondary gains of bad behavior. One of the new things
in mental hygiene at that time had been a greater awareness of
the delays in recovery from illness which were due to the patient's clinging to the satisfactions of being ill and cared for
solicitously. Similarly, we urged mothers to ask what the child
got out of temper tantrums, staying awake at night, screaming
for mother to stay with him? We then advised mothers to give
no such advantage. "Let him alone, and he will change his behavior when he finds he gets nothing by it." We thought then
that mothers were too undisciplined themselves to carry out a
sound program of training their children. That may have been
true, but I also wonder if they did not sometimes sense instinc-

tively what we overlooked—that they might be dealing with a really frightened child crying in the dark or a child actually frustrated to the point of frenzy with whom they were genuinely unfitted to deal.

Comparing my doubts about this program now with those I had had about the family casework of the prewar period, I see some similarities. Organized charitable work with families had tended to find deficiencies in character which had contributed to failures in self-maintenance. We found deficiencies in the qualities necessary for child-rearing. Now, having shifted attention from economic success to meeting standards of behavior which we considered healthy, we distributed blame when we did not see all the roots of behavior nor realize that it could not be modified by easy didactic methods. In other words, we were as free (and mistaken) with our so-called scientific advice as our ancestors in social work had been with moral precepts, and we resembled them more than we knew.

Nevertheless, the raw materials of life-situations were before us, and we gathered them up into our histories and gradually learned to understand them. Students were placed with us by the Smith College School, and they learned, I am sure, despite my anxiety lest they learn the wrong things. We were all baffled by our ignorance as we touched life in intimate ways in our contacts with families. Most of all we lacked understanding of the cultures of Europe from which most of these families came and of what it meant to live in the crowded insecurity of those city neighborhoods.

At the end of the first year in the clinics, I was asked to give a paper on "The Mental Hygiene of Young Children"[5] at the National Conference of Social Work, held that year in Toronto. Here is what I wrote, and what I would not change today:

"A word as to the point of view of a psychiatric social worker in a habit clinic: I confess to finding with some surprise that it must combine that of the medical social worker, the family caseworker, and the neighborhood worker. We need to treat conduct problems as symptoms—asking *why*—not as matters for praise or blame. We should not forget that the mental health of the child is absolutely bound up with that of his family. Above all, we must have the long-time look most often acquired by neighborhood workers who know families in good as well as ill times and who know that some things pass but general tendencies endure. We must not, in eagerness for results, forget that 'playing Providence' is not a game for those who wish to see souls grow by wrestling with their own responsibilities. If, as Dr. Richard Cabot says, we can 'unblock and keep clear the channels of understanding,' inspire and learn and patiently let alone when we ought, then only shall we keep close enough to nature's processes of growth so that our experience will add to the sum of knowledge of what *is* the mental hygiene of a young child."

Again, the final paragraph:

"We are not discouraged, because we believe in the genuine love of most parents for their children and that if we can only remove crippling handicaps, nature will, after all, work as surely for mental as for physical health. We reverence the mysteries of personality and natural processes of growth which, taking time, nevertheless go on ceaselessly."

From another paper written a year later, comes the following:[6]

"When we, as a people, care supremely for the upbringing of our children, care enough to provide training for young people in parenthood as carefully as in reading, writing and arithmetic, when we believe in play enough to see that no child misses it because of the accident of living in a city wilderness,[7] when we learn enough about living together to prevent our quarrels from embittering our children's lives or our foolish love from sapping their vitality, then perhaps we shall be fit to be the guides of the children of the future."

I had come a long way since I stood, a timid recruit, on the threshold of social work twelve years before. Twelve years is the time it takes for a child to progress from the First Reader to a high school diploma. What had I learned? What had I to offer to the world? What did I want from life in 1924?

An appraisal of all these questions was precipitated by Professor Everett Kimball, Director of the Smith College School for Social Work, when, on his October visit to the students we were training, he overwhelmed me with this proposition: we want you to come to Smith as Associate Director of the School. This was a decision not for a day or even a week. I felt it was choosing a course for all the rest of my life.

True to my New England nature, I thought of all the objections first. There must be some mistake about my qualifications. I did not have a Master's degree. Though I had studied for years I had taken courses I needed for my work, not the ones to accumulate credit. I had not the background for teaching casework, lacking sociology, economics, and courses in education. Besides, although I enjoyed training students, I wanted to remain in casework and develop skills in it. My direct contact with cases was the breath of my life.

Professor Kimball had answers to all my objections. He told me he could carry the academic dignity of the School, but what it most needed as associate director was a person respected in the profession of social work. My reputation for good relationships with social agencies, as well as my work with students in training, were my recommendations. He was sure that, knowing my subject as well as I did, I could teach by the case method. He outlined a plan by which I would be attached to a child guidance clinic and continue to practice casework in the nine-month field periods between summers at Smith. Supervision of students placed in the field could be concentrated in two month-long trips in the fall and spring. There would be time to carry on research in casework and to write and study as I wished.

Thinking this would settle the whole matter, I told Mr. Kimball that he might not know it but I was really a maverick, an unbranded steer, not orthodox in either social work or psychiatry. I could not stomach philanthropy. I did not care for the way some psychiatric social workers looked down their intellec-

tual noses at all other social workers and lived in a rarefied
atmosphere of the approval of psychiatrists. I would take my
stand for the less mechanical and more human approaches in
casework, and for closer relations between psychiatrically
trained workers and all other social workers without condescension. I wanted to see the closest co-operation with other professions dealing with people. (I thought then that I was rather
alone in these sentiments and only learned later that the best
thought of social work was moving in the same direction.) To
my surprise, Mr. Kimball said that a maverick was just what he
wanted![8]

Of course it was immensely flattering to be wanted that
much; to be given time to think it over but to be urged, "Do say
yes." The salary from the college and the clinic would be
double what I was getting. I had taken a substantial cut when
I had moved from the salary-with-maintenance at Danvers to
live in Boston. I had been glad of my freedom to choose voca-
tionally without financial pressures, since my family did not
ask and would not take financial help. I hoped always to choose
my work for its own sake, but I could not have been unmindful
of the recognition embodied in being paid as much as $3,000.

Mr. Kimball was not a stranger to me, having been my
teacher in American history at Smith when he was a young
instructor and I a freshman student. He was frank to tell me
that he was "the terrible-tempered Mr. Bang," and that he had
had some personality clashes with two previous associate directors in the three years he had been director of the school. He
kept an anchor to windward by offering a full-time appointment
but on a year-by-year basis. He seemed most anxious to know
how I made decisions. Did I "fiddle around" or "think in
circles"? I was able to tell him that I hated fiddling, and, once
the data was in, wanted to decide quickly and definitely. But
this time I took a dreadful length of time to come to a decision.

I could not tell Professor Kimball the real reason I hesitated,
and I doubt if it was more than half conscious on my part. The
decision to be made set off questions about where I belonged,

with whom I identified myself, where I could feel comfortable.
I knew that if I accepted the job at Smith I would travel and
mingle with cultured and capable people of whose world I was
not. Was this class consciousness? I did not know there was
such a thing and in any case had been trained to think that
only what a person was, was important. But I knew when I felt
uncomfortable and felt so now. Also, if I went to Smith, my
social roots would probably have to change, and I was not sure
I wanted them to.

To explain this feeling, we shall have to retrace a good many
steps, to the old farm in Stoughton which had been my home
(at least in vacations) since early childhood. I had gone to
Stoughton for every weekend all through my twelve years in
social work. My roots were there, such as I had, and the New
England culture had shaped me. In our family line, our folks
counted the earliest settlers of both the Plymouth and Massachusetts Bay colonies. We though it undignified to be proud of
ancestry when research would as likely turn up a horse thief
among our forebears as the great American poet of whom we
had knowledge. What we were taught to be proud of was buying
nothing we could not pay for, defrauding no one, living at peace
with neighbors, speaking the truth, serving God and country.

To a surprising extent we lived outside the capitalist system
in which great fortunes were made. We knew almost nothing
of exploitation except as it had been practiced against the
slaves before the Civil War. We had no farm employees except
for the briefest periods. Since selling farm products through
commission merchants in Boston netted less than cost, we
peddled our own in the village (sometimes at less than cost, also,
if they were perishable) and bartered eggs for groceries.

Such an economy, subject to losses from weather and fluctua-
ting prices, can expand very little, even with hard work and
ingenuity. But if we could not earn more, we knew how to do
without and keep our independence. There was no way of com-
bining with others to gain more. We lived in fear of individual
calamities, like sickness, fire, bad seasons, but each family,

alone, had to shoulder the burden. Hardly any were able to help a neighbor much in a time of disaster except, of course, by the personal services that mean most of all. This way of life does not give rise to a consciousness of class, unless perhaps to a fear of being invaded by other people who stick together as a class. We had possibly some fear of labor struggles which might reach into our lives to disturb a peaceful, if precarious, existence.

However, to my surprise and late in life, I discovered that I had been decidedly class conscious when I had lived at Aunt Bessie Capen's school in Northampton. I believe now that I had been made so by the literature I was fed as a child and which has recently turned up in the cleaning of the farmhouse attic. The magazines for children, and for ladies, too, in the nineties, were full of snob appeal, stories of chivalry in England and France, the doings of the millionaires in New York and Newport, the races at Saratoga, the fashions and the balls. Servants, peasants, and industrial workers were mentioned only in their roles as background for display of wealth, aids to the comfort of the well-to-do, grateful recipients of charity. If these magazines seem sickening today (because the form of expression of wealth has changed and appears now as luxury advertising for which every reader is assumed to be a potential customer), their falsely colored pictures of life were authentic information to us.

So it was that I was uncomfortable when I met servants at Capen House, but I soon sensed that the farm women from the hills who worked there were nearer to my way of life than the students with whom I could find little in common. College teachers in Northampton lived better than I had been accustomed to living, knew more about all sorts of things, and had intellectual interests that I did not acquire for some years, if ever. By the time I did catch up in the life of the mind— enough to long for intellectual companionship—education was so definitely associated with an upper class in society that I could not think of myself as belonging in that way of life.

Yes, we were class-conscious in Stoughton, but without so

naming what we felt. It was really class consciousness in the
negative. We knew where we did *not* belong and were glad not
to. We thought our life was better than that of people in car-
riages who rode by and possibly had a low opinion of us. I
said once, I remember, as a child, that I wouldn't live in a certain
large mansion in Brockton for anything, because they surely
wouldn't let me make mud pies on the porch. We belonged nowhere except among farmers whom we could not see and who
never got together. We had our Methodist church group of
people like ourselves, but a group which shut out others, the
worldly and the less enlightened. I pity now the isolation we
cherished. Yet, I am sure a wish to belong somewhere was an
essential part of me.

Sometime before I was faced with the Smith College decision
I had a dream which was so vivid and expressive that I have
never forgotten it. A relative who had held prominent positions
and did not mind a bit of boasting had visited us and said much
about offers she had had at a salary, fabulous to me, of $5,000.
I dreamed I was in the domed rotunda of a bank and wanted
to get to the upper floors of the building where the offices were.
I could take the elevator directly to them or I could climb a
stepladder left in the middle of the floor by workmen, I suppose.
I deliberately chose the ladder, but soon realized that I could
never get to the upper floors that way, only to a point in mid-air
whence I could see the crowds milling below. I still held to my
choice, however. Perhaps I wanted to go higher, but not so
much higher as to lose sight of people busy with their concerns.
I think I wanted to see life even if I was not a part of it.

What did I want of life, now in 1924? Normally, a girl wants
marriage and children. What choices has a woman nearing
forty, confronted with a decision like that which came to me
from Smith? First, she may have put marriage, by this time,
into the "out-of-the-question" file basket. She will probably
check, however, to see if it is still there. Or, she may be seeking
diligently (by now desperately, perhaps) for marriage and
relating every other decision to it. A third choice, which was

mine, would be to consider the marriage question fairly well settled by sublimation, but to look carefully to see if the sublimation would hold under new conditions.

It was clear to me that some of my personal sublimations were threatened. First, of course, was the opportunity to practice casework—my art and my predominant satisfaction in life. Possibly Mr. Kimball's plan would take care of that. I was not afraid of being drawn into speaking in public, for I had done enough of that in habit clinic work to know I could survive the shocks of panic and enjoy sharing something with an audience. My desire to "cast a longer shadow," to carry as much responsibility as I was able, would be amply fulfilled if I could multiply my small contribution through many other lives. My personal enjoyment of living had recently received both a setback and some recovery.

I had not realized how much I would miss the social life and companionship of both sexes, which I had had at Danvers, until I returned to lodginghouse living in Boston. After some rather despairing months of loneliness, a fellow social worker and I found a two-room apartment we could afford. This was much more of an adventure in those days than it is today. Two girls who set up housekeeping were whispered about on no other evidence than that fact. The apartment was in a little old house, said to have been once the home of William Lloyd Garrison. It had stood for years with broken windows, choked by tall tenement houses, until it had been renovated for occupancy by middle-class people as part of a rehabilitation plan for the north side of Beacon Hill. This house on steep Garden Street had two-room apartments on each floor, each room having a fireplace genuinely dating from the days when there was no other heat. Now there was steam heat, but one fireplace was usable—an unheard-of luxury. Out of the back room was carved a bath and kitchenette. The latter was so small that, if one was baking in the tiny gas stove, one would have to open the hall door and project one's rear to the landing in order to see into the oven. It was a sunless place, but we were there only

in the evening. It was the first home of my own, and I loved
fixing it up and having someone with whom to share living
there. We had just become settled and signed a year's lease
when Professor Kimball appeared with his disturbing proposition. If I sublet and went away, come June, could I ever hope
to have another home? I would be at Smith in the summers,
traveling much for the School, and stationed only temporarily
in clinics in the winters. When, indeed, would I have time for
personal life, and of what would it consist?

I did say yes to Smith. All that had shaped me bent at last
in one direction. Much later, I summed up the situation in this
fashion:

"Forty years old and beginning life over again! I was to be
a teacher, which I had sworn never to be, and teach my profession which I had sworn never to leave. I was making impossible, so I believed, having a settled home on which I
counted for personal adjustment, and was to move among
people of prestige for whose company I felt no qualifications.
I did not know how to teach and had no time to learn, except
as I did it. Yet, the decision once made *felt right,* and I headed
forward."

CHAPTER 6

DRAWING OUT AND LEADING FORTH

I proved to be more a maverick in education than I had supposed I was in social work. First of all, what did I find when I returned to the Smith College School after seven years?

The School had grown into a full-time professional curriculum of fourteen months, allowing for one month of vacation. It had dropped the specialties except that a few students still elected training in medical social work. The unifying theme of the entire course was casework from the psychiatric point of view. The disciplines represented on the teaching staff were (besides social casework) psychiatry, general medicine (for medical information), law and government, sociology, social psychology (including measurement of intelligence), and research methodology applied in preparation of a thesis. There were two "extension" courses on the campus: a one-summer course for experienced social workers who wanted the new point of view; and a six-week seminar for school deans, to aid them in student counselling. I had casework classes with two groups, the experienced caseworkers and the seniors back from nine months in training centers from the Atlantic coast to Chicago. Cornelia Hopkins taught the introductory course for students without experience—a course in history of social work and its basic principles.

The School had been strongly impressed by the personality and teaching philosophy of Professor Kimball who had been with it almost from its beginning. He was in his early fifties, a

dynamic person with an immense capacity for work, who added
year-around direction of the School to his professorship at
Smith, where he was Head of Department of government. He
taught government for the School and was a stimulating lecturer and discussion leader. He was proud of the School's record
for hard, mature work, and nothing annoyed him more than to
hear it called a summer school. He often said, "This is not a
country club where you combine a vacation with a little work,"
and he told the students going into their field practice that they
might perhaps find time for a movie by Thanksgiving.

Probably the first showing of my maverick tendencies came
when I counselled adequate sleep and some recreation in my
talks with entering students. Some of the seniors remonstrated
with me: "What is this we hear about your making the new
students soft? We sat up nights working our heads off. Nobody coddled *us*!" My reply was, "And look what it did to
your dispositions!"

From the very plan of its curriculum, the School made a
close tie between theory and practice. The courses which used
lectures the most, such as government, medicine, and psychiatry
drew constantly on experience with cases. The casework courses,
as I conceived them, were advance preparation for field practice
or intensive study of that which work in social agencies had
taught.

Learning to practice an art seemed to me quite different from
the education given in many colleges which was an accumula-
tion of knowledge given by lectures and reading and a
regurgitation of the same at examination time. I heartily agreed
with Professor Kimball that our aim was to give understanding of general principles and teach the students to think for
themselves in applying theories to practice. The field period of
nine months in one agency, while it lacked the variety of experience which other schools obtained by change of assignments,
compensated by a genuine opportunity to identify with an
agency during a prolonged period of almost full-time work,
which was given educational value by much attention to super-

vision and discussion classes. The School was responsible for arranging a weekly seminar for students in each training city, and for guidance of the agencies in supervision, as well as for following the elective reading of the students through written reports.

My casework teaching, that first summer, evolved a method which departed quite radically from routine college courses. I was convinced that we were educating whole persons, not disembodied intellects, and that we had to devise ways to develop the *kind of person* who can do good casework. I thought first of the training of the senses through which experience comes. I believed that most peoples' senses were dulled by the training generally given children: "Don't touch. Don't look at what doesn't concern you. Don't hang around listening." A first exercise, then, would be to recover some of the keenness of observation that children have and equally to improve an adult sense of what it was *relevant* to observe about people. I sent students to public parks, railroad stations and ice cream parlors to observe people. We tested observations by comparison of written reports made by several students of the same scene. I taught them to be keen in separating inference from what was actually observed.

Then we studied interviewing, at first as the way strangers get acquainted in casual conversation, and then how interviewing for a purpose differs from conversation. We noted the primary necessity of establishing a relationship of confidence, the place of questions in an interview, the importance of disciplined thinking when there is a problem to be solved.

We also studied cultural differences and spent much time analyzing prejudices, particularly our own, and how we could become conscious of them as a first step toward bringing them under conscious control. Where personal experience was lacking, we tried to give vicarious experience through a variety of life situations in discussion of cases.

This was new stuff to most of the students, and while they gave evidence enough that it was disturbing to them, I interpreted their questions as indications that the educational system does not prepare people to enjoy thinking for themselves. They asked, especially as mid-summer examinations approached, "What do you expect us to know? We have no notes to study, and how can we review anything?" I had been particularly insistent in class hours upon looking into their faces and not at the top of their heads while they hastened to fill notebooks. I wanted them to listen and to think. So my study was thronged with questioners at all hours, and I did not know until. long afterward how much criticism Professor Kimball had to take on my account.

I did not adequately get across to the students that the course I had in mind was a *laboratory* course to prepare for practice. I did not then understand, myself, that it should have been preceded by a series of talks until a desire to *do* had been generated out of the group experience with a new kind of knowing.

Professor Kimball put it this way in some of our many talks about educational theory: He agreed that education should not be (in my phrase) "stuffing geese for slaughter," and that too often in academic institutions, it was. He was proud that Smith College had a tradition of stimulating thought. He said, however, that if education means drawing out and leading forth there has to be something put in first. Could I not give the students more and *then* draw it out? My query was: Wouldn't it then be only what I had given returned and not their own?

My educational theory went wrong, I now believe, for two reasons. First, and obviously, my own theory of social casework was too undeveloped to lend itself to lecture presentation, and my strong belief in the discussion method of teaching was partly a defense against the poverty of my own equipment.

Another reason is subtler but, I now believe, a concomitant of the kind of person I was. My greatest intellectual asset (and also sometimes a liability) has been that all my life I have been a ruminating animal, spending probably two to four hours out of the twenty-four in weaving a mesh of associations around each day's experiences. It has meant an integration of living, a thorough digestion of experience, a richness of association that has been invaluable in teaching as well as in writing and in sheer enjoyment of hours alone. Perhaps this habit was started by a childhood without adequate social stimulation, with long hours of swinging in a hammock in sight of natural beauty. Whatever its origin, once it was a part of me I took it for granted that everyone desired to think things over as much as I. If I had experienced a good deal of repression, I inferred that others had too, and would seize eagerly an opportunity to bring out their own thoughts in a sympathetic group.

On the contrary, many students had come to Smith from middle- and far-western states which exaggerated the educational prestige of the east. They had heard that Smith was tops and would expect a lot of them. They were prepared to fill notebooks and to sit up nights learning the contents. What did they find? Kid stuff! Exercises in observation, little plays to see how everyday people interviewed each other, illustrations from life, instead of from the big hospitals and from books. I believe they did, in the course of fourteen months of training, learn to value life as the greatest teacher, but they did not come prepared to do so in their first summer.

The seminar of the second summer had its problems too. The big idea, already in operation, was to have a student present one of her cases and have it discussed by the instructors from all the disciplines—psychiatry, medicine, government, and casework. That plan broke down because the student invariably took too long in presentation, and I had not learned how to help her to condense. The psychiatrist also lost himself in asking questions about clinical details. Finally, the discussion of what was to be learned from the case was left with little time, and the psychiatrist generally delivered a monologue. The solution which was worked out after the first summer was to have a mimeographed book of cases which I selected for their teaching value and prepared following my spring visit to the training centers. Discussion time was divided between the psychiatrist and the instructors in government and casework, each using the case as he desired to illustrate principles from his own field. Under this arrangement, the students wanted more psychiatry and willingly spent extra hours to obtain what the visiting psychiatrists were equally willing to give.

During the fourteen summers I was at Smith, the prevailing plan was for one psychiatrist to spend at least one and preferably the full two months at the School (even if only half of each week) and to co-ordinate in that way the lectures of a number of visiting lecturers. Names held in especially grateful remembrance as co-ordinators of psychiatric courses were Dr. Frankwood E. Williams, Dr. Lawson G. Lowrey, and Dr. Lewis Hill. Each year we heard, also, the most famous psychiatrists of the United States. The lectures on medical information under Dr. Faith Gordon were stimulating and practical, those in social psychology under Miss Miriam Gould of Vassar College, an intellectual adventure. Mr. Kimball's course in government made the students aware of the legal structure that underlies all of social work. His distinction between laws and administrative decisions "from which there is no appeal" was especially valuable to the legally naive, which included almost all of us.

Each Monday evening the course in The Field of Social Work brought to Northampton lecturers from a variety of social agencies. Also conducive to breadth of outlook was the presence on the campus of seniors who had come from placements in various communities and many kinds of agencies—their number growing from twenty to seventy as the school grew—and of the group of experienced social workers from every conceivable form of social work. The weekend at the beginning of August was devoted to a conference of as many supervisors from the field agencies as could manage to be there. They saw and felt the School in action, and the students saw and heard what life was like in the training agencies.

The administrative work of the School was the untried feature of the job of Associate Director for which I am most indebted to Mr. Kimball. He not only backed me and covered for my mistakes but taught me principles of organization to get work done which had been unknown to me as a caseworker who ministered to troubled souls under the organization of someone else. His humorous definition of administrative responsibility was: "To decide on insufficient evidence what is the least harmful course to pursue." We began the school year with a spring conference on selection of applicants for training. We promoted harmonious social mingling by assigning rooms in the twin dormitories, Northrop and Gillett, so that probably congenial students would be in adjoining quarters. During the summer we did a weekly reshuffling of seats in the dining room with the same end in view. We had to decide, painfully, what students were not fitted to continue the course, and someone, usually I, had to prepare them to understand that fact. Mr. Kimball used to say, "You can't run a hospital without some deaths." He was most anxious, however, that the School should *not* resemble a hospital, which it might have done if I, a psychiatric social worker, had been left to follow my benevolent instincts. Mr. Kimball taught me to be less absorbed by individuals and more conscious of the whole group. He made me see the purpose for which all of us were together—to give a sound experience in education for a career in a world of real competition—and that this purpose would have to take precedence over the needs of exceptional individuals. He brought home to me that even the development of the individual is best served by a group discipline which relates the one person to the whole.

This was especially clear in relation to the annual senior fever over theses. The students were given time in their winter field experience to gather data which was to be ready for the task of writing on their return to Northampton. They had liberal time allotted to writing in their second summer and had the help of a thesis advisor. All had some pressure at the end from unforeseen delays, but most procrastinated. Some had chosen a subject of interest to them but too involved with their emotional problems to be dealt with objectively. Some had writing disability; some fell into panic at the very idea of completing a study for critical

review; many wanted extension of time. The School found
that only the utmost firmness gathered the scattered powers
of distraught writers caught in a group neurosis and brought
the toilers to Mr. Kimball's door, even at midnight of the last
day, with a completed document in their hands.

The students were as varied in age and experience as had
been those of the famous first class. There were a large number
coming directly from college and coming each year, it seemed,
at an earlier age. Mr. Kimball understood these best, and I
least, for they seemed to me impossibly young and most inclined to follow the collegiate traditions in learning. Then there
were a number, still young, with experience of from one to five
years in some occupation. They knew the discipline of a job, and
something about working with people, and they wanted to know
more. Then there were social workers with whom I could
identify who wanted to add "the psychiatric approach" to the
equipment they already had. Some came for only one summer,
and a few of these decided to stay on and work for a degree.
Some gave up positions of responsibility which they had held
for many years and had corresponding difficulties in placing
themselves again in a student position.

I think it was after the summer of 1926 that I became most
conscious of the presence of the "lost generation" among us.
There was more drinking than was healthy in those years
under prohibition of legal sale of alcoholic beverages. There
was some recklessness and cynicism, though much less, I am
sure, than prevailed in the life of the nation generally in similar
age groups. I asked Mr. Kimball if he didn't think we had
failed the students somehow in giving them so much in technical
proficiency and so little help toward forming their philosophy
of life.[1] He was sceptical whether we could do that without
losing the scientific outlook which was the School's greatest
asset. I agreed that we wanted no return to moralistic social
work and that a personal philosophy could not be taught. It had
to be lived, and I thought our co-operative living together on
campus was as good a way as any to demonstrate what we be-

lieved. I agreed with Mr. Kimball and Dr. Williams in their opposition to introducing anything that would divide the School on lines of religious differences, yet I could not agree that subjects connected with religion (an important part of life to many people) should be banned from intelligent discussion, as syphilis and sex had been a few years earlier. We had learned to take both without gulping. Why not a philosophy of life? Could we not discuss what psychiatry had to contribute to understanding of life and its values? Could we not overcome our reluctance to use the religious resources which clients might choose in their communities for better mental health? Already a movement was on foot, centering at Worcester State Hospital where we had students in training, to give theological students some experience with the problems of mental health for their parish counselling.[2]

My suggestion was for a free-for-all discussion in the living room after supper on Sunday evenings, to which anyone might come and in which anything might be discussed without the School's committing itself to any opinions expressed. Somewhat reluctantly, Mr. Kimball agreed to my trying it. We began, I remember, by discussing fear and how the world's peoples have handled their fear through the ages. We were amused when mid-summer examinations were going on to find that the students could not keep their interest upon any fear but that of being tested, and yet the small number who came in that night insisted that *they* were not anxious. Undoubtedly those who were, stayed in their rooms and studied.

As the summers passed, these gatherings grew more informal and usually filled the living room, even to sitting space on the floor. The subjects brought up ranged more widely, but the last one of the summer came by custom to be devoted to readings of favorite poems. I may be wrong, but I believe this little time spent on our common interests as human beings was a unifying force in a School assembled from such diverse sources and that the Sunday evening gatherings lived on in the memories of many as a source of inspiration and personal growth.

How did I work with individuals in this rapidly-paced group life at Smith? First, Mr. Kimball and I each become acquainted with every student in a personal interview preparatory to assigning field placements. We learned their preferences for winter location, and considered all of them, whether or not they could be met. In the process we learned a lot about each student as a person. Then my study was always open to anyone who had a question or a problem. I planned to be there during recreation hours from four o'clock tea until dinner, getting my own relaxation in the personal touch which rested me. Most of the students and I, also, were in classes all the mornings, but they were sometimes free to drop in, in the afternoon. I sat with them in the sun on campus steps, or under the trees, or we roamed the elm-shaded streets. Education spilled over into life at every point.

This kind of individual teaching could have become involved with personal therapy. Perhaps it did sometimes, but I was learning through it the distinction between helping people to grow just for any purpose they might later choose (as we help clients or patients) and growth which takes place in a specific educational situation where it must contribute to the person's doing a responsible job. The fact that for thirteen years much of my casework was done with students, who were in a situation demanding the meeting of standards of performance, shaped my philosophy of casework to an important degree. I came to see casework itself as helping clients to do a job, *their* job whatever it was, in living, and to distinguish casework from therapy which would help patients to gain health without regard to the use they would choose to make of it.

A continuation of individual teaching followed the students into their field agencies, to which they went immediately after a week's break in September. Mr. Kimball and I nominally took September vacations, but he carried on the work of the School office, and I had occasional mail to answer regarding job references for students and such matters. The whole month of October I spent visiting all the training centers, covering the northern and eastern states as far as Chicago (and for a time to Minneapolis). A second trip, perhaps broken to minimize the length of time away from my own field placement, I took in the spring to register the students' growth and to collect cases for the teaching of the second summer. These tours were at first overwhelming in their round of meetings and appointments from breakfast until late evening, when I perhaps climbed aboard a sleeping car and rolled on to the next city. At first I thought I would have to take one day of rest for every three of visits, and Mr. Kimball agreed, but I soon forgot about the cushioning day and grew to enjoy the many personal contacts with much less strain. Eventually, the trips became a glorious round of seeing old friends and meeting new ones. Between trips I was in constant correspondence with the students, discussing their reading and field reports.

If it were possible to review year by year those visits to Boston, New York, Philadelphia, Rochester, Syracuse, Buffalo, Chicago, and other cities, one could trace the evolution of what we were believing and teaching about social work in those years at Smith. I will review some of these ideas in succeeding chapters. Here I pause just to note how experience often follows a spiral. Here I was returning to the use of skills similar to those I had first developed in visiting children in foster homes. There was a difference in the maturity of the persons concerned, but not in essential problems. For instance, how to be a friend and counselor equally to a student, subject to the authority of an agency, and to the agency whose student is not its first responsibility; how to gauge the objectivity of an agency's reports about a student, and the student's reports about the agency in terms of the experience being offered; how to reconcile personality clashes in a situation where replacement of a student during the winter session was practically impossible. There were students with particular personal problems such as: a phobia about writing comments on reading; inability to make good contacts with certain clients such as husbands or mother-persons or rebellious adolescents; inability to value and use previous experience. Whatever the problems, they had to be handled in the span of a day, or a few days at most, and in such a way that the agency supervisor and the student were left better able to work them out together. This was education in living and very much in the midst of living. It was education that had to draw out what was in people from their own experience as much as it put into them of new concepts and theories.

I cannot close this brief account of a significant experiment in education without recording a disturbing note introduced by Dr. Frankwood Williams as he participated in a senior seminar one July day in the summer of 1926. The problems of an adolescent boy were under discussion, a boy who was a misfit at home and at school, something of a sex delinquent, rebellious against authority, and obviously in need of discipline which "would make a man of him." The social-psychiatric prescription had been to get him into the Navy, and to the Navy he had gone. Everyone except Dr. Williams seemed well satisfied with the plan of treatment, for it relieved the community of a burden and at the same time it looked like doing something for the boy. Dr. Williams objected. With a few deft strokes he pointed out that treating a situation by removal of a troublesome element completely disregarded the known needs of a developing personality. He showed a picture of a bewildered adolescent confronted by the major adjustments of emancipation from his family and the maturing of his own psycho-sexual life. Well-meaning people were doing all that could be done to make impossible this boy's ever becoming a healthy, well-rounded person, capable of a normal marriage and the headship of a happy home. They were taking him out of his home physically but giving him no opportunity to work out his conflicts about authority. "Discipline" designed to make young men unreflecting cogs in a machine was to still his struggle to be an individual. Sex was to be solved for him by depriving him of normal contacts with girls of his own age at the time in his life when such contacts were most essential. Was sex thereby to be eliminated from his life? Dr. Williams showed that it could not be, but under the circumstances could hardly avoid assuming antisocial forms. He then went on to say that until psychiatric social workers could advance beyond guesswork, trying one experiment after another and content that a thing "worked" if there was no vocal complaint about it, there was no possibility of considering social casework a profession mature enough to be responsible for its acts.

There was indignation as the class broke up, and the summer noon was filled with protestations that the resident psychiatrist had no conception of the thought that went into casework decisions nor of the community, as well as personal needs they must satisfy.

How could I know that this incident would be the one I would select ten years later to be my tribute to Dr. Williams at a memorial meeting full of tributes after his death? I was not ready to know, that day in 1926, how right he was in telling us that we could not become a profession by any road other than that of genuine scientific study and actual application of the findings of science to real situations. Dr. Williams was one of the few people most of us have known who could understand being misunderstood and who could go on speaking the truth without blaming those who could not receive it.

CHAPTER 7

CLINICS AND RESEARCH

The All-Philadelphia Child Guidance Clinic, to which I was assigned for the first two winters of my connection with the Smith College School for Social Work, was a project of the National Committee for Mental Hygiene and The Commonwealth Fund. It was a demonstration clinic and was becoming a permanent community institution and training center for clinic personnel. Dr. Frederick H. Allen was Director and Miss Almena Dawley, Chief of Social Service. I was to work with cases during my stay from November 1st to May 31st (with time out for supervision trips in March and April) and conduct the weekly class for the two students from Smith who were placed at the clinic. It was my first experience with the varied problems of children of all ages and in child guidance work beyond the level of habit training.

After a discouraging canvass of Philadelphia for "rooms to let," I found a delightful home for both winters in the family of Miss Amy Smith, General Secretary of Central Branch, YWCA, and her elderly sister, Miss Abigail. Their home was in the Mt. Airy section of Germantown, and my room looked into the woods of Fairmount Park. Here I had congenial companionship and a real sense of belonging.

The contrasts in my new way of living were epitomized in the daily train trip to the clinic. I passed stone houses with gardens, and one could assume, in those suburbs, that everybody who was anybody could afford a stone house or at least half of one. Then, from Broad Street Station, I walked through the Negro slum which flowed southward to the very door of the clinic and spilled over into the playground opposite. I did not sense fully the terrible poverty which must have haunted the little houses whose marble steps were scrubbed so clean or of the flophouses of South and Lombard streets. I liked to see the brown faces I had missed since Atlanta days. But this was clearly not a world in which everybody was comfortable in a stone house or in which serious problems of family life could be solved by a child guidance approach alone.

The clinic was located at 17th and Fitzwater streets, where it had the use of a building, a remodelled dwelling I think, at the corner of the grounds of the Children's Hospital. As I remember, it did not draw its clientele from the neighborhood but largely from other parts of Philadelphia and its suburbs. The staff consisted of the usual clinical team, all engaged in some way in teaching and research as well as in community service. There were internes in psychiatry and psychology as well as students of social work.

Dr. Allen and Miss Dawley gave leadership in thinking through the role of a psychiatric social worker in child guidance. They believed that giving advice on child training was a method to be used with caution. After all, what does behavior which an adult deems undesirable mean to a child who is using it to express his own needs in some way? If it expresses fear or frustration, certain parental responses might be indicated which would be inappropriate if the child was reacting to an urge to be independent of a too-cramping authority. The degree to which socially unacceptable behavior should be controlled or needed to be expressed was another consideration. Dr. Allen came to feel, from his experience in addressing parent-teacher groups, that simple ignorance of child training was relatively rare and that it was the emotional problems of adults which made them distort even the best advice and often apply it destructively. It was noted that some of the most baffling cases in the clinic were those in which the parents had been most active in parent-education groups.

The Philadelphia staff gave much thought to a flexible use of psychiatrist and psychiatric social worker within a children's clinic. Instead of limiting the psychiatrist to treatment of the child and the caseworker to environmental adjustments in the home and transmission of child-training recommendations, it was thought advisable in some cases for the psychiatrist to give the parent some brief psychotherapy. At the same time the social worker might ease the child's problem by communication through play, by some modification of the school situation, or by finding opportunities for group activities.

The clinic began to face the psychological problems connected with payment for clinic service. While the local medical society would allow the clinic to operate only as a free service for families unable to pay, the fact was that the cost of private consultation with a psychiatrist was impossible for many who were accustomed to pay for other less time-consuming medical services and that the treatment by a clinical team, which seemed so essential in child guidance, was unavailable in private practice. The clinic drew its clientele largely from middle-class people who would be hampered in their use of the clinic if they were not allowed to give something for the service. A plan was therefore worked out whereby families could contribute voluntarily on a scale related to cost and to their income.

A quite different economic problem was reflected in clinic work in the case of Mike, an adolescent boy assigned to one of the students from Smith, who took up an immense amount of her time in keeping track of his delinquencies. Mike lived in a neighborhood where the social norm for his age was to go to Reform School, and on return to be hailed as a hero who would have much to tell his fellow citizens. Mike had no warm clothes, ate fried peppers when he had what he called a good meal, and stole when he could meet his needs that way. A clinical approach to stealing as a personal problem seemed a little remote in Mike's case. Our student persisted through one harrowing episode after another, and I have no doubt that her warm interest in Mike did something for him. Perhaps it was from Mike's normal adjustment to a very abnormal environment that I learned what I set down that year:

"There is a minimum of creature comfort essential before any of the so-called adjustments of personality are possible. One cannot, in a clinic, 'cure' a boy of stealing when he is always hungry or keep young people away from questionable resorts when their homes are utterly cheerless. This, however, is a challenge, not to thoughtless use of the resources of palliation we now have, but to more thorough study of the possibilities for community-wide improvement."[1]

Among the rich opportunities for learning in those winters in Philadelphia I remember especially two, outside the clinic. The social workers of the city were then a closely knit group who shared experiences in a committee which met to discuss their most difficult cases. There were, among others, Miss Betsey Libbey of the Family Society, Virginia Robinson from the School of Social Work, Jessie Taft and Irene Liggett of the Pennsylvania Children's Aid, and Almena Dawley of the clinic. I think it was my first opportunity to discuss with a group the meaning of "relationship," as it occurred between caseworker and client, and within families. Miss Robinson's book,[2] which was a milestone in the history of social work, must have had some of its beginnings in those discussions.

The other experience came in the second winter after two Philadelphia school principals had gone to Smith for the summer seminar for school deans. One was Miss Marie Chase, principal of an elementary school in a Negro section of West Philadelphia, an educator in the finest sense of the word, who arranged for her teachers a series of discussions of mental hygiene in school situations in which I participated as group leader. It was a rich experience with this all-Negro group of thoughtful teachers, facing especially difficult problems because of the economic and social discrimination suffered by the families in their school district. They had to be social workers

as well as teachers and build morale in a depressed neighborhood while they met city standards in education. Needless to
say, they taught me much.

The paper quoted in discussion of the case of Mike[3] was
written in the first year at Philadelphia, to be read at the National Conference of Social Work at Cleveland in 1926. The
following excerpts show, I think, a crystalization of ideas about
the place of a professional worker in the life of a troubled
family:

"Why do we include the techniques of understanding as a
part of the processes of treatment? First, because treatment begins in the first interview. . . . I mean that the way in which
a worker obtains information indicates already her skill in
treatment—nay *is* treatment. She may think she is out for information only and that the diagnosis, formally made, is the
temple bell which must ring before the ceremonial of treatment
begins, but the way she questions a client may make the difference between leaving him flat like a collapsed balloon or full
of courage and a determination to win through. One may 'pick
a person's mind' as truly as his pocket, or one may, by showing
him why one asks what one does about himself, make him see his
own difficulties in a better perspective, even in the telling. . . .[4]

"We may think we know an environment well for its liabilities
when we have never even begun to see its assets. Of these, I believe that the strictly so-called social agencies of a community
are the least important.[5] The school, the preventive health
service, the churches, libraries, and recreation opportunities of
a community and above all the personal wealth in men and
women of good will are resources which our clients may use
when helped to find them, without becoming thereby exceptions
in their own group. Caseworkers with individuals should be the
first to see the needs and help to develop community opportunities which shall be for all to use. . . .[6]

". . . a good contact. What is it and how is it achieved? First,
we may be helped by thinking of social relationships as a function as natural to us as walking. We have gotten along with

other people somehow, from our crib days. Our habits, formed when we were toddlers, are the basis of our greater or less success as *persons* now. Bad habits interfere with a function like walking—so they do with our meeting people. That is why I believe that every social worker should take the 'corrective gymnastics' of mental hygiene for her prejudices and faults of character as a part of her training in the same way that a teacher of physical education would be required to correct poor posture. Secondly, I believe that we shall learn most about how good contact is achieved, not through self-consciously scrutinizing our own work, but by observing constantly the successful contacts that are made between people in their natural relationships. We see ourselves as the star performers in a drama, unaware that it has been going on a long time before we came and that our only chance of a vital part is to get our cues from the performers and enter in as a part of the setting. We force ourselves in when the actors are not prepared for us; we hurry things; we magnify ourselves; and we find ourselves alone on the stage, speaking to an empty house, the play moved elsewhere. . . .[7]

"Over and over we social workers adjust everything that can be adjusted in the lives of our clients and wonder why the result leaves no enthusiasm either with them or with us. In other cases, people bear unalterable burdens not only with fortitude but with cheer and are a force in helpfulness to others. I think we should not be satisfied just to banish symptoms. We want vigorous health. We want to make it possible not only that people should live, but that they should have something higher than themselves to live for. We shall not help our clients to achieve in their own experience any goal like this unless we plan for it as earnestly as we do to keep them from being a nuisance to society. Unless we teach them to be of use, to give something, however little, they can hardly hold their own as self-sustaining. We do not want them to remain, unless hopelessly handicapped, as the world's dependent children but to reach up to the limit of their capacities to its adult responsibilities."[8]

By my second year in Philadelphia, the Commonwealth Fund

program had passed the stage of demonstration. Mental Hygiene clinics were being set up in city after city. Where could the trained personnel for them be found? A center for such training was projected for the fall of 1927 in New York City. It would have four units, each a complete child guidance clinic, and each would absorb a group of trainees in psychiatry, psychology, and psychiatric social work. The Smith College School and the New York School of Social Work would each have eighteen places for field work of students. This was an amazing opportunity for the schools despite some drawbacks—one was that at Smith we preferred to have only a few students in one agency so that they would be an integral part of the working staff and not create a "student atmosphere." The clinical work at the new Institute for Child Guidance would be genuine service to the community, although its strong emphasis on teaching and research would determine to some extent its selection of cases. There would be assembled at the New York Institute the best teachers and supervisors to be found in the United States. The students would see and bring back to the schools the best in developing practice in mental hygiene clinics.

I was fortunate that the arrangement with the Smith College School provided for my having winter assignments at the Institute, with the title of research assistant. Dr. Lawson G. Lowrey, whom I had first seen as a dynamic young lecturer at the first session in 1918 at Smith and who had been teaching there in the summers as resident psychiatrist, was Director of the whole Institute project. He was an inspiring teacher, keenly interested in research in this new and growing field. Under his leadership, the Institute entered upon six years of extraordinary accomplishment.

The Institute was located on the upper floors of a business building on 57th Street, near the corner of Lexington Avenue, in New York. Each staff member had the advantage of an outside, private office furnished in mahogany. In the center, on the floor allotted to the supervisors in social work, was an assembly room for lectures and conferences which was seldom empty. A similar room on another floor had desks for the thirty-six social work students. This congregate seating was unfortunate, even though interviewing was not done there, for someone was always talking either on the telephone or in spirited discussion with one or more others. To secure quiet, many students formed the habit of doing their desk work in overtime hours, only to find that too many others had the same idea. The supervisors regretted but could do little about the loss of time in the working day and the formation of irregular habits of work. However, the stimulating opportunities of every day at the Institute balanced any possible disadvantage. There were in the clinic ample facilities for psychiatric interviews, psychological measurement, physical examinations, and laboratory tests, as well as interviewing and dictating rooms and a waiting room and playroom for the young patients.

In living conditions, I was again fortunate. I had dreaded New York City as a home, feeling it would offer only the rockbound canyons of a metropolis or exhausting commuting at the end of each day. I found a housing development called Sunnyside, across the river in Queens, in which two-story houses, built around a central park, had each a bit of lawn and garden in front and the same, hedge rimmed and perhaps with a porch, at the rear. I was directed by the management office to a German music teacher, Miss Johanna Beyer, who owned a new house, rented the upper apartment, and wanted to rent one of her four rooms downstairs. I had just returned from a month of travel for the School and was hungry for contact with the good earth. I never tired of looking out on grass and trees, seeing the sun rise, hearing the rain drip from leaves and seeing it fall into garden soil. I loved that Sunnyside community for all the twenty years it was my home, and my friendship with Miss Beyer lasted as long as she lived.

The Institute developed to perfection the principle of team diagnosis and of treatment based upon the findings thereof. The original study of a case filled many pages of record and sometimes required many clinic and home visits before it was

completed. Parents were eager to be given the report for which
so much information was asked of them, "so that we can help
you." Some dropped out during the process, some were disappointed in that they had known all along what they were told
but lacked the emotional ability to apply it, and some undoubtedly reacted only to a sense of their own failure. The
positive results, however, were impressive, and there was immense value to the whole mental health movement in having a
group of experts working together, ready to explore any and all
ways of helping the most difficult cases. Toward the end of the
Institute experience, Dr. Lowrey was studying well-recorded
first interviews to see if the applicant had not said *then,* perhaps
in disguised form, essentially what came out in the elaborate
study. He was aiming at better *listening* and *observation,* a
keener sense of what was important in the first diagnostic impressions.

The research interests of the staff were varied and generously
shared. I remember especially Dr. David Levy's studies: one
on finger sucking in infancy, one on a "method of integrating
physical and psychiatric examination: with special studies of
body interest, overprotection, response to growth and sex difference," and a group of studies, in which a number of students
of social work shared, on maternal overprotection and rejection.[9]
There were studies on the then new Rorschach test for personality diagnosis. Studies were made of the varying problems
of children who were first, last, or middle in ordinal position
in the family and of children showing stealing as a symptom.
Dr. Lowrey made studies of competition and the conflict over
differences. There were social studies on referrals to a psychiatric clinic.[10]

My first research study centered around what mental hygiene
could offer to Negro families. Some clinic workers thought that
the problems arising from racial discrimination were insurmountable, and nothing effective could be done. I believed that
Negro children, having vastly more difficult adjustments to
make than white children of the same age, should have special

consideration. The initial difficulty, as I saw it, was that mental hygiene clinics were not even reaching Negro adolescents and their families. Why not?

I made an arrangement with the Principal of a Junior High School for Girls in an all-Negro section of Harlem whereby I might receive clinic referrals of pupils needing help, make contact with their families, and try to ease their use of the Institute facilities. One obstacle was the prevailing economic stress which deeply affected home life in the Negro community and made difficult the use of opportunities even when these existed. Another was the belief (widely held by the Negro people and, I must confess, with unfortunate experience behind it) that psychological tests were used to show an inherent inferiority of Negro children and to steer them away from higher education to vocational training for inferior jobs. A third source of difficulty was that delinquency at that school at that time was taking the form of gang life of girls who were asserting their right to be people but in antisocial ways. Their parents and the school were so concerned as to be interested only in repressive measures which they thought would minimize the risk of disaster for the girls.

I do not know how much the clinic helped those who were persuaded to come to it, but the experiment was full of value for workers in mental hygiene. The results were published[11] and indicated a method of examining critically our own part in making difficult good contacts with Negro families. As I reread the study, I am impressed with the changes that have occurred in thirty years. To be sure, the same problems of racial discrimination and economic injustice remain, and some are intensified, but one would not assume so readily today that a social agency or clinic would be staffed by white people. Many more college-trained Negro young people are entering professional fields, and many more would do so were not the barriers so high. The history lived through since the Supreme Court decision of 1954, defining discrimination in public education as a violation of the Constitution, has brought new hope of

an eventual solution fit for a democracy. The stories of
Montgomery, Alabama, Little Rock, Arkansas, Louisville,
Kentucky, and many other places have demonstrated that Negro
young folks do not need white people in clinics to tell them how
to meet life's terrific crises with gallant courage.

A second research study which failed also taught me much.
I devised a questionnaire in three parts, around the queries:
What adjustments does every adolescent have to make? What
additional adjustments confront a Negro adolescent? At what
points would guidance from mental hygiene be helpful either to
Negro adolescents or their parents and teachers? There was a
sheet to accompany the questions, with a rating scale to be
checked for each boy or girl whose history was being considered
by the teacher or social worker using the forms. I thought that,
if fifty or more of these studies of individuals could be collected,
some conclusions might emerge to guide mental hygiene programs for Negro adolescents.

Miss Marie Chase in the Philadelphia school was very
interested in using the questionnaire. In New York I planned a
series of group discussions with Negro and white social workers
and teachers together to see if group thinking would produce
leads. Then nothing happened. The Negro workers who were
the key to the project did not use the questionnaire nor attend
the group meetings. Finally a Negro friend told me why. I had
sobbed out to her the question, "Are relations between us,
Negro and white, so bad even now that we can no longer talk
together of these things as human beings?" "No," she said, "it
is not that." She explained patiently what I should have known,
that the adjustments which Negro children and their elders have
to make to racial discrimination are learned in the earliest
years and often with painful experiences which are partially or
wholly repressed. These adjustments are carried on largely below the level of conscious awareness, much as one learns to
balance on a bicycle, and are better done if the person does not
think too much about the process. Negro people cannot bear to
bring much of this into full consciousness and are literally

unable to talk about these adjustments with white people. So I learned something more significant than my elaborate study had projected.

The Institute for Child Guidance had a brief and glorious career of six years. The economic depression of the thirties terminated the training center which had been set up for five years but which everyone assumed would continue to meet a growing need for expert personnel. It was found that new mental hygiene clinics were not being opened, and well-established ones were closing for lack of funds. The clinic workers already trained were dispersed in social agencies of other types or went into private practice. After a sixth year of tapering off, the staff members were given their office furniture and as many books from the library as they could carry, and the Institute for Child Guidance was only a memory.

As I look back, the experiment seems a last gesture of history in the booming twenties, as if to say there are no problems which enough money and expert knowledge cannot solve, if children are taken early enough and given the right guidance. Even at its peak, however, the Institute program left its staff with a vague uneasiness. One day we confessed to each other that we were not, strangely, even as happy with our work as most of us had been in struggling clinics with never enough to do with. We laughed it off by saying that having plenty of money and time had destroyed all our alibis. Who could stand being left naked in face of problems we were unable to solve? Parents had other problems than child guidance and were often too tense and overwrought to make use of the best of diagnoses and the most cleverly devised remedies. After the depression broke upon us, the shivering man who sold apples on the street corner and whom we passed on the way to a hot lunch, was a haunting symbol of ills that individuals cannot solve and child guidance cannot prevent.

Four other studies engaged my research time during the Institute period. One[12] will be treated with those of a later time. Three, I group together for their relation to the growth of a personal and social philosophy. I take them in chronological order.

The greatest honor of my professional life was an opportunity to present a paper at the First International Congress on Mental Hygiene, held in Washington, May 5-10, 1930. Like most honors, there was as much of chance in it as of recognition for the traditional qualifications of inspiration and perspiration. While the papers contributed in psychiatry and psychology were drawn from fifty-three participating countries, psychiatric social work was hardly in existence outside the United States and was poorly distributed here.[13] Furthermore, Dr. Frankwood E. Williams, Medical Director of the National Committee for Mental Hygiene, was chairman of the Committee on Program. He happened to know my work from association with the Smith College School and to be close to that of the others he asked to participate. It was, in any case, a stimulating challenge to prepare a paper on "The Role of the Psychiatric Social Worker in Therapy."[14]

The paper noted, first of all, a relatively new approach to health and disease: the concept that the human body, including the mental and emotional life, is in active and ceaseless adaptation to the conditions under which it lives. The human organism is not static while diseases and disasters swoop upon it like evil birds, but uses a marvellous mechanism to deal with all except the most extreme threats to its well-being. Some adaptations, like retreat into mental illness, are more or less effective to relieve the individual from psychic pain, but are unsatisfactory for meeting the demands of social living. If, then, adaptation to a *social* environment is the goal of a healthily functioning person, a psychiatric social worker who is a specialist in social environments and the interrelationships of a person with his fellows is an essential member of a team of specialists in mental hygiene. It was brought out that a psychiatric social worker could function in this role only when working with psychiatrists who also thought in a dynamic way about social adaptation.

Here, for the first time as far as I know, I used the threefold classification of treatment measures: those predominantly effecting changes in the environment; those predominantly related to the giving of understanding; and "those concerned with the curative possibilities in the emotional relationship between the clinic staff member and the patient, or the person in his environment who is, for the time, receiving treatment."[15] It was made clear that these measures are never found in pure culture, but each in some admixture with the others. The larger part of the paper was taken up with as vivid illustrations as I could find of the use of these forms of treatment, here called therapy. At the end, I placed the role of the psychiatric social worker in relation to the psychiatrist as follows:

"The psychiatrist, seeing his patients in his office, gives them a security in their relationship to him that may make them able to deal with their own distorted and pain-filled relationships. The psychiatric social worker, among the people who surround the patient, may be doing for one or another, on a more superficial level, something of the same sort of thing. She may try to make them ready to accept the patient in a new way by the time the psychiatrist has got him ready to accept them. She may change unfavorable environmental conditions or, better still, get the people concerned to change them; she may interpret by spoken word or, better, by giving an opportunity for new experience. She may let people try out on her their distorted emotional patterns and use her skill to correct them. Whatever the form of therapy, it is because a maladjusted individual usually means also an environmental situation gone wrong that the trained psychiatric social worker has a role in therapy that no one else can fill."[16]

Another research project sought an answer to the question whether case closing can be planned as a part of treatment.[17] During the winter of 1931, I reviewed all the cases closed by the Institute which had had at least a year of contact, 149 cases in all. The study showed some factors in closing which were not planned, but related to circumstances such as the season of the year when student workers were leaving, family condi-

tions which made it impossible to get to the clinic at the desig-
nated hours, and broken contacts which seemed unlikely to be
resumed. In thirty-five cases withdrawal by the clinic was
considered a constructive move for treatment, stimulating use
of the client's own resources or leaving intact an adjustment
that might not be ideal but was better than anything the clinic
could offer to replace it.

The main questions dealt with in the study were: For what
purpose are we in a case in the first place, and when can we say
that the purpose has been achieved? It was noted that finding a
remedy for an existing acute maladjustment is easier to define
than the results of an educational goal—to leave the client better
able than before to make his adjustments to life in times of difficulty. In this study, I distinguished two philosophies of social
casework. One I called the mechanistic, the other the growth
philosophy. In applying the first, we enter the case situation accepting responsibility to use all possible resources, material or
educational, to see it through to a socially desirable conclusion.
"Advance is along the line of more and better adapted machinery, of more knowledge of what levers to pull and when,
of more controlled techniques."[18] Of the growth philosophy I
said: "We talk less about 'assuming responsibility for the case'
and wonder a bit more just where these forces, working ceaselessly and without haste may find a use for us. We see our clients
accepting or not accepting us into a helpful relationship, rather
than ourselves as doing all the accepting. We think less of pre-
determining the conclusion of our endeavors than of making it
our aim to find out what it is that the surging growth process
itself is striving toward. We become much more like gardeners
than machinists. Knowledge of the forces of life adjustment
shows us where we may improve the conditions for growth as
a gardener gives water, controls insect pests, lifts a stone around
which a little plant is trying to grow, but no more than he do
we create the growth process. We may become wise in prediction
as a gardener, weather-wise, plans his labor in relation to expected sun or rain, but our predictions are based on close study

of how life adjustments proceed so that we may the better co-operate with them. If we accept this philosophy it will mean a development of casework in the direction of minimal interference with life processes which are increasingly better to be understood, but the fullest co-operation with them where the need and the exact nature of that participation is indicated. Once we know as much as that about life forces, we shall both slip in and slip out of case situations more easily, as far as our need to feel our own personal participation is concerned, but with more humility and with more power."[19]

The third paper, "The Church and Individual Security,"[20] was prepared outside the Institute program at the request of Miss Mary S. Brisley of the Church Mission of Help for presentation at the Episcopal Conference of Social Work held in Philadelphia in May, 1932. The question was whether church-sponsored social agencies have something to give because of their religious orientation which distinguishes them from other social agencies. I read records of the Church Mission of Help, an agency dealing with delinquent girls and unmarried mothers, and had a number of conferences with Miss Brisley and Miss Marguerite Marsh of that agency.

My background for dealing with such a question was briefly this: I had been strictly raised in the Protestant faith according to the Methodist tradition of those days, made a gradual and painless transition to modern religious thought in college courses in Bible and evolution, devoted my life to religious work, and now found myself securely planted in a scientific form of social service. My connection with organized religion had been maintained during the twelve years I had practiced social work by weekly visits to Stoughton and participation in the home church. In Philadelphia, and now in New York, I had found no satisfactory church connection. Sermons were either unreal to me or actually irritating in their deductive reasoning while I was daily using thought processes based on induction from experience.

The meaning of one aspect of this transition had been clari-

fied for me by the Registrar at the Institute, a young man who
had graduated in theology and had been diverted to social work
through recreation and youth activities. As he compared his
present outlook with that of his theological school classmates,
now serving pastorates in suburban New York, he found that
they felt an obligation to help everyone who came to them and
counted on a divinely-aided ability to do this. He had learned,
he said, through working with doctors who were scientists,
that we have to face the reality that we cannot help everybody
with our present knowledge and facilities. We can only do the
best we can, without guilt, to increase our skill to the utmost.
I had come to this point of view and could be glad that social
work was outgrowing its own tradition of Jehovah-like responsibility for every need.

The study posed two questions: What did religion have to
offer in mental hygiene, and what sort of co-operation could be
worked out between religious agencies, with their different ways
of thinking, and social agencies, working from a scientific point
of view? I was interested in the study for the same reasons I had
advocated Sunday evening discussions at Smith. Nothing of
value to human beings should be alien to our interest and concern. I focussed the paper upon a statement in the first sentence:
"It is a familiar saying in medicine that science can make it possible for the human body to combat disease and so can prolong
life, but that it cannot furnish reasons why the individual should
want to live. How does anyone find his own reasons for living?
Does religion have an answer?"

I tried to show the stages of normal growth to maturity,
from the baby's rudimentary love of himself and those who
care for him to the capacity for adult love relationships. Growth
can be interrupted at any stage, and the balance between need
for security and the urge for new experience and further
growth is sometimes hard to find. I expressed a belief that religion, defined broadly as a positive attitude toward the universe
as a whole, is a source both of security and of continued growth.
I found that the childish dependence, which sometimes seems

to be fostered by religion, is a symptom of arrested development. Such people "could not *have* a religion on a more mature level than their own emotional growth."

I called religion a sense of *belonging* to the universe, something greater than oneself to tie to, something to evoke effort and responsibility.

I discussed frankly how frequently religion is not a maturing experience even when it could be, and yet that religious and mental hygiene workers do have in common their contacts with people having essentially the same human problems. Can they not give something out of their experience to each other even though they think so differently?

All the studies in those years in Philadelphia and New York were a search for the relationships between the mental hygiene movement and the world in which it was finding itself. There were to be worked out relationships to the mass of people whose problems would be brought to clinics: relationships to an oppressed minority group; relationships of social workers to psychiatrists; and relationships to community leaders, specifically in religious groups. It seemed most important in those days not just to muddle along with clinic work but to get things straight, to know where we were going, and why.

CHAPTER 8

POISED FOR ADVANCE

Within fifteen years after the end of the First World War, new knowledge about human psychology had changed the thinking of vast numbers of people in the United States. During this period, the radio had been added to the press and movie screen as an important means of communication. Mental hygiene concepts had spread from the treatment of war neuroses to the prevention of delinquency and guidance of the growth of normal children. Ideas such as that all behavior is a meaningful expression of personality had permeated theories of education and challenged religious doctrines of sin and prevailing methods of punishment. Everyone dealing with people in school, church, playground, or industry was stirred to ask "why" when confronted by troublesome behavior, and to seek scientific answers. Psychiatric social work was only one development among many, such as associations for child study, parent-counseling magazines, reforms in treatment of prisoners, and use of psychiatry in schools, courts, and general hospitals.

As I remember, the new ideas came in waves to the understanding of the general public. Among the first to be talked about was "the inferiority complex," which explained so well why some people who seemed to be capable always underrated themselves. At first it was believed that others who overrated their abilities had a corresponding "superiority complex," and some teachers believed that children with this tendency needed

to be "cut down to size." Later came the realization that loud
and aggressive behavior is a fairly reliable sign of overcompen-
sation for a mordant sense of inferiority and needs treatment
to build up a healthy self-esteem rather than the reverse.

Rather early, in a culture that made many mothers frustrated
and overprotective of their children, it was possible to hear
people on trains and trolley cars discussing the attachment of
grown sons to their mothers. From being a beautiful quality
described in Victorian novels, mother-attachment came to be
seen behind the unhappiness of many marriages in which the
husbands were otherwise unusually nice young men. Attachment
of girls to their fathers was less easily recognized, probably
because it fitted in with the prevailing mores which demanded
dependence of women to a greater degree than is true today.

Many people began to look to psychology as a means to
better physical health and efficiency—people who perhaps had
not been able to accept the faith-healing cults. It was reasonable to believe that mind influenced body and that everyone had
unused powers of control of physical processes which were occasionally demonstrated in emergencies but which could be used
as a source of strength in everyday life. Sometimes the power
of self-suggestion was used as a magic formula, as during the
craze over Dr. Coué who taught his patients to repeat, "Every
day in every way I'm getting better and better." Sometimes
the use of self-suggestion amounted to a denial of the reality of
the illness rather than an assertion of strength to overcome it.
Looking back over the years, however, I think it is distinctly
less fashionable to complain of illness and that it is now a better social asset to picture one's self as triumphant over physical
disabilities. Concomitant with this trend has been the growth
of preventive medicine so that there is actually less of acute
and devastating illness. Of chronic disease associated with
deterioration, there is another story to be told.

A concept which strongly influenced social work in the early
postwar years was that a "psychological approach" was a new
form of scientific tactfulness. When skillfully used, this newly

popularized science could win friends and influence people even without their knowing it. To be sure, it was not always as resistance-proof as was hoped. I remember the father of a friend of mine who shook his finger at her and said, "Now don't you try to psychologize me." However, social workers rather generally believed that resistance could be overcome if one had sufficient professional skill, and blamed themselves for clumsy practice if they encountered much opposition.

For most of this period, the sense of social responsibility which had been inculcated by the pioneers in social work remained a strong influence in the formation of treatment plans in social agencies and clinics. What was our special knowledge for, if not to produce better solutions for social problems than people could find for themselves? Under the influence of the group in Philadelphia, I had begun to challenge this philosophy of social work,[1] but generally, I believe, social workers welcomed psychological knowledge first for its help in securing the co-operation of the client with their own plans based on social diagnosis.

I marvel to remember that it was not until about 1931 that we made a working tool of the idea that negative and hostile reactions are as normal and necessary as positive, outgoing ones. The strange dream world in which we lived with our benevolent impulses, ignoring or attacking as "resistance" whatever opposed our good intentions, seems incredible today. Why should we have thought that it was not as normal for a person to protect himself against encroachment from others as it was to love and trust them?

The answer must be sought in our culture. The Judeo-Christian tradition has increasingly counselled love and forgiveness toward our fellow men, even to "seventy times seven" offenses, leaving anger and hatred only for evil itself. In our culture, children are taught that fighting for one's own advantage and showing hostility are wrong and that love and sharing are characteristic of good children, or of a desirable process called "growing up." What do children see, however, in the grown-up world into which they are moving? It is a world of ruthless competition for advantage in which they must be aggressive or fail by its standards. They are not at all prepared to understand or deal with the repellent emotions they invariably experience. They can only be guilty about the emotions they have been taught to suppress, or else abandon the "conscience" which they must in turn inculcate in their own children. Perhaps fathers and mothers divide the incompatible roles embodying the ideal and the practical, increasing their difficulties in understanding each other or in making sense to their children's inquiring minds.

Dr. Frankwood Williams was one of the first to voice the new understanding that a scientist is as concerned to know why "good" people (by society's standards) are good as why "bad" people (also by social measurement) are bad. That does not mean that there are no social standards, but that a scientist does not make them. He tries to understand and deal with what is actually present.

When social workers first became conscious that hostility was a normal emotion they saw it in their clients constantly. If they no longer routinely blamed themselves for having created it by their clumsiness, they were nevertheless concerned that they found hostility personally hard to take. A byword (particularly in the Philadelphia group) was, "Can you bear it?" It became a coveted skill to be able to draw out hostile reactions, release them without too destructive effect and, by accepting these feelings without blame, relieve the guilt over them which may have paralyzed or distorted action. For instance, now that it could be faced sympathetically with a mother that she really rejected her child, a plan for her handling of a behavior problem or even for placement of the child elsewhere for a time, did not need to be thwarted by the mother's repeated efforts to prove that she did conform to the traditional concept of a loving mother. Play therapy with children developed great possibilities for release of buried feelings of hostility in aggressive action against dolls and other toys.[2]

Winning acceptance of plans became a very different process from heavy or devious persuasion. It became the release of *all* the client's feelings about his situation. It meant going with him through all his explorations of remedies and his reactions for and against these. It meant his right to refuse as well as to approve, to be a person in his own right, to *use* a service, not to be captured by it.

When Virginia P. Robinson put into her doctoral thesis[3] in 1931 some of the ideas which had been in practice in a variety of agencies in Philadelphia for a number of years, the effect upon social work in general was that of an earthquake. My own reaction was one of "wonder and deep delight"[4] to find expressed so much that I had come to believe. While I could not follow entirely the theoretical background in the works of Otto Rank and the Gestalt psychologists, it seemed to me that the relationships of human beings to each other contained the dynamics of living and that in these could be sought the source of the personal influence which Miss Richmond had found to be the essential core of case treatment. Miss Richmond had conceived personal influence to be transmitted from the fortunate in the community to the unfortunate by means of volunteer service. By 1931 social casework had gone far toward becoming professional, but the secret of helpful work with people was still a person-to-person relationship. That this was not something to be ashamed of—something infected with the hocus-pocus of magic—but a reality to understand scientifically and to use responsibly was a thrilling idea when it first made its appearance in our professional literature.

My review of Miss Robinson's book in *The Family*[5] welcomed a diminished reliance on detailed histories as guide to treatment, and saw in the relationship of client to caseworker the best guarantee that what history was brought by the client would be soundly used, because it would be important to him and relevant to his problems. The client was moved into the central position in the picture which had been occupied by a wise social worker bearing gifts. The challenge was to learn

to understand and use the relationship so that the client would
be strengthened to build up his own resources. While I considered it doubtful if the casework relationship was enough
like that of psychoanalyst and patient to make analogies between them, I nevertheless thought in terms of the client's
"living out" with the caseworker, symbolically, the relationships which have gone wrong in his own life. The caseworker
must develop a maturity, such that she may be "the steady pole
about which the distorted emotions of others may beat until
they straighten out to that steadiness."[6] This demands the utmost in scientific preparation and self-discipline.

My review was published in *The Family* in June, 1931, and
in October, a letter came from Florence Sytz of the School of
Social Work of Tulane University, sounding a needed note
of warning.[7] She could not agree with Miss Robinson's philosophy of social casework. She said, "The time has not yet
come when social workers can confine their interest and activity
to the realm of emotional adjustment, either for themselves
or for their clients."[8] She found attempts to do so as amusing
as when "an application of mental hygiene to our fears is
offered as a solution for the industrial depression." An interest
in social welfare is still necessary, and not to be avoided by
"acceptance of self and acceptance of difference" in the client,
which may turn into acceptance of difference *for* the client
—that is, of unconcern for the client's social situation. Miss
Sytz also questioned Miss Robinson's selection of students on
the basis of attitudes and capacity for the desired growth.
How could tests of attitudes be as objective and reliable as
tests of sound education in the social sciences and tests of
performance in life conditions? Miss Sytz stood for content
in teaching in schools of social work, not just "an atmosphere
in which the student is free to learn, to think, to experiment,
to grow, to change."[9] Content in professional education, Miss
Sytz said, could not ignore inadequate wages, trade unionism,
unemployment, poor relief, probation statutes, criminal law,
old age pensions. It seemed to her that although Miss Robin-

son had left to other writers and later years the needed studies in social welfare, her book had, by implication rather than by design, created a gulf between social welfare and intensified treatment of individuals. Would that this warning had been heeded in the years to follow!

In June 1932, I wrote for *The Family*[10] an appraisal of the effect of Miss Robinson's book upon our whole field, as I saw it after a year's observation over a wide area as well as in my own teaching and practice. I said, "It has created searchings of heart and practice, questioning of old attitudes, tentative or whole-hearted experimentation, confusion, disappointment, hope of a more valid casework philosophy, despair of anything of the kind, a refuge for the passive, joy of power for the active—in short, the positive and negative effects of a most dynamic expression of living experience."[11]

First, I noted, "We have all become more conscious . . . of the *client as a person,* determining the casework process to a degree not before realized or permitted. To 'accept' a client has come to mean more than taking responsibility for his problem, as we may have used the term in the past. We wonder now whether, if we were the client, we should want to be 'accepted' on those terms. We think now of his acceptance of us in any really helpful casework relationship as implying an equal right to reject our help or to use it in any way he can best do so. We 'accept' him when we are able to understand him as he is and to respect his integrity as a fellow human being."[12]

Secondly, I found valuable Miss Robinson's concept that a client's experience with an agency to which he comes for help is a kind of "sample situation" in which he is likely to react as he has done in his relationships with parents. His advances and retreats are indices of what the process of receiving help means to him. Using all the skill we have in observation and in psychological understanding, allowing for sources of error which we ourselves create because we are persons too in the helping situation, we can be much more sure-footed than we have been in helping people to help themselves.

I found two unsolved questions in Miss Robinson's presentation. One was the factor of control which a patient accepts in advance when he enters a treatment relationship with a psychoanalyst but which a client does not understand in a casework relationship. Miss Robinson went so far as to deprecate the use of the term "participation of the client," as implying that the caseworker presents him with a preformed plan. She nevertheless saw the casework relationship as one in which the caseworker is in control of the helping process. The other factor was the training required to become able to do skilled casework by Miss Robinson's definition. She thought a psychoanalysis would usually be a necessity and believed that the handling of the therapeutic relationship in casework would have to be developed (in persons carefully selected) through experience with a similar relationship to the supervisor during training.

I thought at that time that the dangers inherent in a client-worker relationship, which involved a control that was not well understood on either side, and the hazards of a standard of special skill which could hardly be developed in social workers generally, precluded widespread acceptance and use of the new theories, much as they had contributed to our general understanding. I thought we needed a much clearer definition of our field in relation to executive services of agencies, such as administration of relief and employment placement on the one hand, and on the other, of our relation to the psychiatrist and psychoanalyst. I found reason to differ with two points in Miss Robinson's theory.

It seemed to me that the client-worker relationship, as she described it, was essentially a therapy and not social casework. If called by some other name, such as relationship therapy, and prepared for by different training, it would have its own standards and discipline. Social casework, however, while using the relationship of worker and client consciously, would make of it an instrument for co-operation rather than control, and would be allied to a personalized education rather than to psychoanalytic treatment of emotionally sick persons. Similarly, I found it unsound for a supervisor to become involved in the relationship problems of the student of social work. Insofar as these came into the educational situation, they should be dealt with co-operatively as educational problems, and the student should retain responsibility for personal adjustments, receiving therapy elsewhere if it was needed. Exploration of the differences between social casework and therapy was to be a major interest in my research for many years.

No subject was more debated among psychiatric social workers in the 1920's than the question whether a psychoanalysis[13] was necessary for professional success. That it was an advantage was rather generally conceded, and for a period of years New York City, which was almost the only place to obtain an analysis, was overloaded with social workers whose job performance was made unpredictable by the emotional storms they were riding in their personal therapy. Psychiatric workers who resisted the trend had to maintain their prestige either by expressing disbelief in the value of an analysis for successful practice or to let it be known that some authority had assured them that they were already at a point of development only reached by analyzed people at great expense. Those who had had an analysis listed the fact among their job qualifications and hoped that their personal adjustment would show no flaws that would make employing agencies skeptical of the whole analytic procedure. As the emphasis in psychiatric casework was more and more placed upon the dynamic effect of the relationship between worker and client, it became increasingly necessary to consider what our own unconscious conflicts might be doing to the people we were supposed to help.

Probably I was typical of many workers of that time, who saw an analysis as desirable but felt they could not afford it unless personal need for it made it imperative. I had traveled quite successfully for fifteen years with the help of four interviews with Dr. Putnam. The fact that I was hardly ever free from mental pain or from recurrent fatigue and physical discomfort was not of too great concern to me as long as I could fill my days with absorbing work.

The personal crisis became acute, however, in the summer of 1926. In terms of recent events, emotional indigestion was to be expected. I had experienced in one year an amount of radical change of way of life and of attitudes to the mores I had hitherto accepted without question—changes which would have been difficult to assimilate had they been spread over at least five years. Gone was the stimulation of newness which had braced me for the first summer, and the security of a sense of competence had not yet come. If I had known then that in such a situation some maladjustment was inevitable and that it would pass in due time. I would not have been as fearful as I was that my good working adjustment was breaking permanently.[14]

That summer I talked seriously with Professor Kimball about resigning. I could not get a grip on teaching and felt I ought either to leave it or to take time out for adequate preparation leading to a master's degree. I told him that, personally, I was like one hanging by the hands to a precipice, unable either to raise myself or to hold on much longer. Or, to change the figure, I was like a tree with wide-spreading branches, giving out constantly in leaves and fruit but lacking roots for its own nourishment. How could I keep on giving to others, as I knew I did, when I had so little life for myself?

Mr. Kimball advised against academic study for one of my age and experience. He said that a psychoanalysis would help me more, even in my teaching. Nothing, at the time, seemed less possible. The cost was prohibitive, and I was not located in New York City. Within a year, however, I had been assigned to the Institute in New York at an increased salary, and so it was that in November, 1927, I began a six-day-a-week analysis

with Dr. Frankwood Williams, which continued until my
return to Smith the following June. At that time, Dr. Williams
was working under the theories of Dr. Otto Rank, and his
handling of the interruption of treatment was that I was to
return if and when I felt a need. Since I was not able to make
this decision without help and assumed that it would be showing an immature dependence to ask further treatment, five
years passed before I came back to Dr. Williams for another
winter of daily sessions. These ended with the spring trip in
April. During the five year interval, I learned much from
living, but perhaps at greater cost to myself than if I had had
more therapeutic help. In the second period, Dr. Williams
was more Freudian in his methods and I was ready for more
fundamental analytic work and made far greater progress.

The following autumn, I wrote to Dr. Williams to arrange
for continuing treatment in the hope of reaching unresolved
physical symptoms. As I put it to him, "Perhaps my new zest
for living makes me less willing to tolerate physical disability,
or perhaps I do not need the symptoms so much." Dr. Williams
replied that analytic treatment might or might not affect physical symptoms, which, whatever their origin, might in time have
become organic difficulties. He would be glad to continue, but
was at that time, and all during that winter, too ill himself to
do so. I finally saw myself as holding everything in suspension
until his return, shook my shoulders, and decided it was high
time to do all I could for myself. As time went on, other pressures intervened, and I had not resumed treatment with Dr.
Williams when his death in 1936 finally ended the possibility.

What relation has a psychoanalysis to the adjustments constantly made in daily living? In my case, the five-year interval
between treatment periods was something of a laboratory for
experiment. I had gained enough relief from tension to begin to
try out new ways. I moved to a two-room apartment in Sunnyside, Long Island, which I loved on sight and throughout the
seventeen years it was my home. I called it The Little Deck
House because of the sunny porch which looked out on an apple

tree, green grass, and ivied walls. It took a return visit to Dr. Williams, however, to enable me to enjoy living alone, even in this delightful place. I felt guilty because I did not want to be the kind of person who likes to live alone. It was as if it somehow meant being unfit to be wanted by others, or being too self-centered to care. Dr. Williams said, "You put bad names to things," and made me see that for one who works with people all day, living alone is perhaps a needed change.

Not only in that five-year interval but later, the pattern of meeting crises of emotion became familiar. There would be a building up of tension to considerable discomfort, then a discharge into some new insight. I called these episodes "cutting another tooth" and grew to have confidence in the outcome. My belief is that such self-help would not be possible without some previous relationship with a therapist, which, once it is established, carries over to a degree in periods of absence. I am also convinced, from much experience, that psychoanalysis does not solve problems that life has not presented nor solve them without the patient's living them out.

Did psychoanalysis have an appreciable effect on physical well-being, even though it closed without having removed all physical difficulties? Decidedly yes. The release of energy and decrease of tension were phenomenal. After the first demand for a perfect result, the guilt for having any symptoms disappeared, and I could accept myself as I was, symptoms and all.

It was painful to realize, late in analysis, that whatever the outcome, I was forty-seven years old, and the clock could not be turned back. My life situation had not changed, and it was too late for a different kind of living with marriage and children of my own. I was wrong, however, when I thought for a time that I would always be only an observer of the happy relationships of others. When analysis had released my power to see them, I found that love and friendship had been around me all the time, in innumerable people who were perhaps themselves lonely and reaching out. My friends noticed the difference in me. They said, "Sometimes we could get close to you, and then you would retreat behind a wall. Now we can find you anytime."

I began to reach out to wider and wider circles of people with whom I could feel kinship and to whom I could give something. I had already begun to write for people I had never seen, and had found them answering. One day in the bleak winter of 1932, when I felt the confusion of my colleagues everywhere, I had sat down to write as if their questioning, almost despairing faces were before me. *The Things That Cannot Be Shaken* reached into remote places, and nothing else I ever wrote brought so many replies.

What does it feel like to be free of mental pain for the first time and able to begin to live joyously at age forty-seven? I had a curious sense at first of not one but three personalities taking their turns at a belated adolescence. For a while it seemed that I could attend to but one at a time. Later, all three were present in every activity and became inseparable from the person that was I.

One was the familiar social worker, now exploring a challenging field with new insight and confidence. A second was almost unknown, a person I named "The Enjoyer." She had less time than the others in a life already well scheduled, but she capered about and revelled in whatever the working selves were doing. She enjoyed good food, good talk, travel, books, music, nature. Considering previous neglect of this "Enjoyer" person, I made a new rule: When in doubt about doing something that would be fun, by all means do it! A third was a self, hitherto unknown, whom I called "The Citizen of the World." She was quite inexperienced, but somehow had a sense of the meaning of events to which lack of energy had previously made her blind. Magazines like *The Nation* and *The New Republic* which had confused and exhausted her she now read avidly and began to draw her own conclusions. This new self belonged in the world as the total personality had never belonged before.

I was busier than ever in my life. My teaching "took hold" and was more related to the needs of my fellow learners than to whatever technical question happened to be haunting me at the moment. Though I still taught by discussion for the most part, I could give much more to it. Instead of being "Socrates, the gadfly" who too often drew people out with a sort of malicious joy in revealing their deficiencies, I loved to see people grow and did not have to be too critical that they did not grow more and faster. I began to be called on for supplementary teaching in remote places, and there was a demand everywhere I traveled for talks, short institutes, and written papers. Questions to be investigated in the winter months popped out of every corner.

Counselling with students on the summer campus, on winter visits, or by mail, became a rewarding third vocation. A remark of a psychiatrist at the School, relayed by Mr. Kimball, meant much to me. It was to the effect that something happened when students who had problems in learning counselled with me. They became "like different people." It was a sacred trust, whatever gift I had for helping people, and something I could not ignore, nor, in accepting it, fail to give it my best.

One morning, that first summer after my liberation, I thought over the change in my life. It seemed that whatever new paths I might now choose, much of my future was bound up with the Smith College School. A whiff of panic struck me as I asked myself what I would do if I lost Smith. Would all my eggs go with the basket? I found I still had my characteristic sense of mission, but now I somehow felt that I belonged to more than the Smith School. I felt a tie with all social workers in the English-speaking world to whom my writings had gone. If I ever left Smith, I said to myself, it would be to go to other work that needed me more, and I would be content. I felt strong, and as confident as a new college graduate going out into the world.

As I piece together what I learned about psychoanalysis from its use in social work and from my own experience with it personally, as well as in teaching and counselling with students, an analysis falls into place as one among many ways of achieving

or maintaining mental health. Nature's correctives for any im-
balance created by excessive strains in living are marvelous to
behold, and we have as yet hardly begun to understand them.
There is the normal working out in appropriate action of any
disturbing experience. There is conscious thought to find the
best course to take. There is working over in dreams of the "unfinished business" of the day's adjustments. There is the
ability we all have to wall off from consciousness what is too
painful or too complicated to deal with at the time. When these
natural correctives fail, and a person becomes tied by unresolved
and repressed fear, anxiety, or hatred, so that he cannot work
off strain normally in living, he needs help, which has become
possible through the discoveries of Sigmund Freud and those
who have come after him. The analytic method depends not
only upon ways of tapping the mind below the level of consciousness, but upon a relationship to a professionally trained
psychoanalyst, who can create special conditions for the release of deeply buried emotions. This is not magic but a special
development for therapeutic purposes of what occurs to some
degree in all living.

Over and over, people become able to face hard things and
deal with them if they have a relationship to someone in whom
they have confidence who will share their effort. Parents,
teachers, and friends do this for all of us. Social workers are
trained to do it more reliably and skillfully, and psychiatrists
are, of course, able to deal with conditions of greatest difficulty.
People say, "I saw things about myself and my life while I
was talking with you that I never realized before. I thought I
couldn't face that decision, but now I know I can." There is,
then, an emotional readjustment in relation to a person which
can lead to increased understanding, when fear and anxiety
are reduced and energy is released to let conscious intelligence
do its own work. This is a taken-for-granted but deeply significant process in daily living. A psychoanalysis becomes necessary, then, only if a person cannot *live* without it, that is, cannot

participate in the social world, using the natural correctives for strain with reasonable success and happiness.

The mental climate of America showed marked change in the decade after the first World War. There was a debunking of old superstitions and obsolete conventions, a refreshing increase in frankness, and a will to understand and to challenge whatever was inimical to individual development. The revolutionary nature of the changes in social casework can hardly be appreciated by anyone who did not practice both before and after the coming of the new psychological understanding. Psychiatric social work was growing with the amazing vitality of a movement whose time has come in history.

In the meantime, what was happening to social work as a whole? As we surveyed the agencies of Boston before the First World War, we saw a collection of specialized activities for social welfare, each conscious of its difference from others but each aware of its social responsibility. We saw a growing cooperation among agencies to further reforms that might prevent some of the ills that separate agencies were treating. Did psychiatric social work add just another specialty to the list? Did it introduce further division among social workers who were just beginning to find themselves in relation to each other? The answers are yes and no.

Psychiatric social work did introduce a division of which I had begun to be conscious when I joined the staff of the Smith College School—a division which neither the School, nor I considered desirable. However, the very rapidity of the spread of "the psychiatric point of view" among social workers made it possible to say by 1927, as Miss Jarrett did, that even if psychiatric social work was considered a specialty when used in psychiatric clinics and hospitals, it was, nevertheless, in the content of its knowledge the common property of all forms of good social casework.

Agencies which had seemed permanently divided because they dealt with different *situations,* such as loss of income, hospitalization, parental failure toward a child, neighborhood deterioration, now found themselves closer together because they all dealt with *people,* whose troubles could be seen to be common to all walks of life. Schools of social work which had tried to separate out what was basic in social casework for a first year of training found that for a second year of specialization there was less and less that was completely different, even among the specialties. There were differences of setting, method and approach, but not of principles of working with people. A school like that at Smith College, which had pioneered in training for a specialty, found itself describing its work as education for social casework "from the psychiatric point of view," and increasingly its graduates went into every type of agency. It was high time to ask: What is social casework? Can it be identified as something generic underneath all its specific and varied forms?

In October, 1923, a group of seventeen executives and board members from six national organizations in social work met at a resort in Milford, Pennsylvania, for two days of uninterrupted thinking together.[16] They continued to meet each year to try to define social casework so as to distinguish it from other helping professions and to clarify what training in this field should be. Subcommittees were appointed to work between annual gatherings.

After several years of work, the group, now called The Milford Conference, emerged with common agreement on three points:

1. That there was a general concept of "generic social casework" which was acted upon in practice better than it was defined in theory, and which was more substantial in content and more significant than had been supposed.

2. That division of labor among social agencies had separated out various fields of social casework without clear understanding of why, or of the principles which might govern the relations of the special fields to each other.

3. That "while the trained worker was a fact," nobody knew

how he came to be a fact." Professional training had been established for twenty-five years, but nobody knew the requirements of the specific fields of social casework which might guide the formulation of training programs.

The Conference report, presented in 1928, was published by the American Association of Social Workers the next year, under the title *Social Case Work Generic and Specific* and was as definitive a marker in the development of social work as was *Social Diagnosis* in 1917.[17] Certain aspects of this important document are relevant to this discussion, predominantly in its focus not upon the caseworker but upon the client.

First, while not attempting a definition of social casework, the report states that: "Social casework deals with the human being whose capacity to organize his own normal social activities may be impaired by one or more deviations from accepted standards of normal social life," and typical deviations are listed. The client is thought of as a potentially active force in his own adjustment. In crises, "which, to a large extent, must be handled by the intelligence and common sense of the individuals concerned," the use of professional casework service would be indicated by the degree of impairment of the person's capacity for adjustment. Social casework would contribute its knowledge of the environmental setting, of the symptoms of maladjustment which the individual is showing, and of resources for remedy, both in the community and in the person himself. Social casework "has made its highest contribution when its client no longer needs the social caseworker, not because he no longer faces these deviations [from accepted standards of normal social life—B.C.R.], but because his developed capacity for self-maintenance is equal to the task of dealing with them unaided by a social caseworker."

The Milford Conference Report was an appraisal of the progress of social casework as a whole. It found everywhere the practice of an art based upon some scientific knowledge, though it might be unevenly distributed and applied. It found, as Mary Richmond had, that social casework deals with individual case situations one at a time and in reference to all the particular circumstances.[18] It found a philosophy of social responsibility to the client and to the community. It based its social norms upon values generally accepted by the community as essential or at least desirable. All this was not new but was just beginning to be formulated. The need for much more research was clear.

In 1929 there was every reason to believe that our young profession was going to move forward to an honored place in the national life. Professional education was no longer seriously in question, skills for helping people in trouble had been demonstrated, new psychological techniques contributed by another profession had begun to be sought eagerly by hospitals and clinics, courts, and counselling agencies. Social casework would come into its own, not solely to aid society's misfits, but to make sure that children would grow up to be mentally healthy and talented people would be freed to make their contribution to the common life. We were climbing to the top of the world in 1929.

CHAPTER 9

THE SOLID EARTH IS SHAKEN

Crash! Even the word, symbol of a stark reality, reverberated around the world and into every mountain hamlet and prairie town, every city street and slum in America.

At first the break in the stock market, on that October day in 1929, seemed no more serious than the end of a boom and the periodical business blood-letting which would eliminate competitors and insure to employers an enlarged reserve of unemployed labor. Then came shocked surprise and incredulity. The depression did not go away when it should. Factories closed with no likelihood of opening again. Banks failed. Investments were lost. Those who, in losing their paper fortunes, had nothing left to live for, began to throw themselves from high buildings and to litter with their broken bodies the sidewalks of rich cities in which they had been great.

The economic earthquake was felt differently in the various social strata. Some of the luxury hotels in New York City, for instance, found business booming in rentals of residential quarters to families who were economizing by closing their city and country establishments and discharging their household staffs. Other families, deprived of income and losing the comfortable homes which had given them status in their communities, dropped out of sight of their acquaintances, leaving no forwarding address. Many families had relatives staying with them indefinitely. Husbands departed in search of employment opportunities that failed to materialize. Wives who had never

worked before found some ill-paid, pin-money job and turned
the money toward food and utilities. Housewives at home be-
wailed the fact that they were constantly called to the door by
canvassers selling things nobody would want but from whom
they sometimes bought "just to help out."

Moving down the economic scale, the majority of people in
the richest country in the world had hardly ever been free from
the effects of depression. If they were not walking the streets of
industrial towns, finding no one to hire their strength and skill,
they were painfully trying to get on their feet after the last time
they were laid off—paying debts, trying to build up the health
of the children who never quite got over "the time when we had
so little to eat," even paying for the funerals of those who did
not survive. If there was work to be had, they knew well that
any day a discharge slip might fall out of the pay envelope, and
then, in a week's time, they would again be the forgotten men
whom nobody wanted.

Farmers were envied because they were supposed to have, at
worst, a roof over their heads and enough to eat. Now thousands
were losing their farms and joining the long lines of jobless in
the cities. Agriculture had been in crisis all through the prosperity of the 1920's, and farmers were unable to make the cost
of production and pay their debts. The small, family-sized farms
suffered most. Banks and insurance companies increasingly
came to own tracts of thousands of acres on which farming
could be made profitable by use of machinery and by importation
of cheap labor for weeding and harvesting.

Worst off of all were the farmless folk who existed by share-
cropping or as migrant laborers, following the crops in season.
These people had no homes but such shacks, unfit for human
habitation, as landowners who depended on temporary help
would provide. In a share-cropping economy, debt for "furnish"
while the crop was growing held thousands in virtual peonage.
Depression could scarcely make their lot worse, yet it drove
many to the roads in battered old jalopies, searching as families

for a place to lay their heads and a job to do with their hands for a bit of food and gasoline to go farther.

The young had courage, if only that of desperation. When there was not enough food to keep families together, the more adventurous took to the roads and the freight trains by thousands. Sometimes they lost life and limb, sometimes the only chance they would ever have to grow up as stable citizens.[1] Children came out of it with weakened bodies and twisted minds. If they asked why their fathers who mined coal could not get work because there was too much coal, and yet people were without fire, if they asked why farmers burned grain in their stoves to keep warm when others were hungry, if they asked why children could not go to school for lack of clothes and shoes when people who produced these things were forced to be idle, there was no one to give them a satisfactory answer. The leaders of the country did not know.

Those who had seemed to have the answers had believed that the capitalist system was not only destined to last for always but certain before long to abolish poverty. When the system broke down, they were angry and incredulous. Perhaps the ten-year boom in psychological ideas helped to bolster their belief that there could be nothing to fear except fear itself. Optimism would surely bring results in tangible prosperity, if only "calamity howlers" and "agitators" would stop rocking the boat.

Ironically enough, the president whose lot it was to be associated in history with The Great Depression and who had been elected as "the great humanitarian" found that his name had added two new words to the American language. To "Hooverize" meant to chew a little food a long time, as the President recommended, and not only make it last but gain better health thereby. "Hoovervilles" were colonies of the very poor on the outskirts of great cities, where homeless people sheltered themselves in packing boxes and corrugated iron, and raided garbage for food. One more indignity upon the poor goes down in history as the contribution of this man, probably sincerely convinced that prosperity was "just around the corner" and that a "dole" would corrupt the independent spirit of a free people. When thousands who refused to starve quietly converged on Washington to petition their government for the Veterans' bonus which would ease their situation, even if only temporarily, Mr. Hoover had no answer but to call out the army to greet the marchers with tear gas and gunfire and to burn their miserable shelters.[2]

Leaders of the labor movement had no more to offer than did leaders of government. The craft unions affiliated with the American Federation of Labor had never organized more than a tenth of the working people of the nation and did not reach at all the most exploited. When members became unemployed, they dropped out because they could not pay dues, and the unions had no further concern about them. It was even better for the remaining members if there was less competition for the few jobs that existed.

In reliving times like these it seems almost irrelevant to ask what became of social casework. During the winter of 1932-33, the psychiatric social workers of New York City volunteered to help in a study which would show how many applicants at the Home Relief Bureau in a given period were in need of psychiatric services. We talked with those whom the intake workers thought likely to have such needs and who were willing to be interviewed. I do not remember the conclusions of the study, but I shall never forget my own reactions to interviewing an educated woman who had lived for days with no food except bottled milk stolen from hallways. It seemed a bit obscene to ask her what were her personal problems or to think that psychiatric casework could function when subsistence itself was so precarious.

A lecturer at Smith during that period posed the question: What do you do when you have nothing to offer in cases of desperate need? You just listen, hoping the person will get a little relief just by talking out his feelings to a sympathetic ear. Whether or not this was its origin, it is certain that a procedure called "passivity" was in vogue in casework for several years. It was probably compounded of many things, such as revolt against the advice-giving which had cursed our young profession two or three decades earlier, application of the idea of emotional catharsis from the practice of psychoanalysis, growing appreciation of the client as a person and of his right to self-expression, a retreat into doing nothing when there was nothing one could do. Theories justifying leaving the initiative and responsibility to the client were carried to such amazing lengths that in a few years revolt came and "the passive approach" was changed to "dynamic passivity," and that was defined and applied according to the needs of the caseworkers as variously as "passivity" had been. Being dynamic did involve some control of "the helping process" which had been a feature of the teaching of the Pennsylvania School of Social Work.

It was Pennsylvania School which was the first, as far as I know, to encompass in its theory both sides of the contradiction between a conception of social casework which made the client's choice of service and of how he would use it a focal point and a mass program for relief of subsistence need which was applied to meet the threat to the community of starvation, disease, rioting, or social disorganization. The new public assistance services were saying in their procedures almost everywhere that beggars must not be choosers. They must take what the community offers or go without. The Pennsylvania School had led in emphasizing the self-determination of the client, but had also set up controls in "the function of the agency." The client might choose, but only within fixed limits set by the agency and the social order in which it functioned. His willingness to accept these limitations was tested by his co-operation with conditions set by the agency (perhaps in consultation with him) as to use of time, money payments (if any), procedure in treatment sessions, and acceptance of what the agency could offer. It was a logical step from this theory to its application in a public relief agency where what could be offered was determined by law or ordinance. The authority involved was not that of the individual social worker but of the structure of society and the realities of the situation. The Pennsylvania School had something definite to propose in the training of the hastily gathered staffs of the new public assistance agencies. Most other schools, including Smith, waited for the situation to stabilize before including administration of public assistance in educational plans.

One strange phenomenon shook to its foundation the official structure of the practice of social casework. Professional workers in private agencies charged with administering relief had exhausted themselves in home visits so that the privacy of the families might be protected. To their surprise it was found that many preferred to come to the office for their grants, getting out of the isolation of their dreary homes to meet others, even their neighbors, who were having similar experiences. They did not seem to feel the "stigma" which social workers attached to assistance, and some, indeed, came to prefer public aid (even under uncomfortable conditions) to which they felt they were entitled, to private "charity." Some of the workers loaned to public agencies chose to remain there in work that, in a democracy, had the mark of public service, equivalent to that of public education and health care. The aura of prestige around the private social agencies began to quiver at experiences like these.

In the winter of 1932-33, the Milford Conference met again in New York, and this time I was a member and acted as secretary of a committee studying the question of whether social casework could be interpreted as a basic approach to human problems.[3] At that time, as the depression was lengthening into its fourth winter, no one fully faced the permanence of the changes that must come. The concern of the Conference was rather how social casework could survive in a period in which retrenchment was inevitable and in which there was not time for the attention to individual needs which was its basic and valued characteristic. It was a matter of *interpretation* to communities which would possibly support social casework if they could be helped to understand what it was.

Particularly, we asked this question: If a community is suffering economic breakdown so that it has to distribute the necessities of life to a portion of its citizens, have social casework services a place in a mass program of public assistance? We answered that question by saying that attention to individuals under a mass program depends upon their *capacity to adjust* if basic needs are met. Social casework has a role not for those clients who can adjust by themselves, nor for those whose maladjustment is chronic and unrelated to their present situation, but for those whose deprivation of employment has temporarily dislocated their ability to adjust. "Social casework in such an organization would bring in a concern not alone to prevent starvation but to prevent the destruction of responsible personality in the citizens of the nation, and in so doing it would go beyond the cases of individual need to the implications of those needs for community action. . . . Interpretation of social casework in a time of emergency should be related not to saving money in a penny-wise way but to spending money to safeguard interest in human life for the loss of which no money could compensate."[4]

Summing up: "The matter of leadership in social casework in these years of rapid and unpredictable changes involves more than the development of a profession within itself. . . . Social casework has become professionally conscious. It is not conceivable that it can allow itself to be used by communities to cover exploitation or to distribute the gifts of philanthropy while the social order is itself destroying life by its injustices. It grows clearer day by day that the future of social work is bound up with the coming of a sounder social order and that the members of this profession have not only the obligation to work for justice which good citizenship implies but the professional duty to make real the conditions under which their service can be given. Whatever of scientific fact-finding they can contribute, whatever of social vision they have gained in

work with individuals, social caseworkers must be close to the
social engineers in days filled with import for the future of
mankind."[5]

That same winter the American Association of Psychiatric
Social Workers published a symposium, *Gain or Loss on the
Casework Front.*[6] It characterized the period as one of "economic chaos" which would affect our profession profoundly.
Its questionnaire (to which twenty-two representative agencies
had responded) had asked what pressures had been experienced,
what adjustments were being made, what new ventures tried.
The picture which emerged was that psychiatric social workers
were migrating from clinics which could not survive to family
service agencies whence many of the most experienced workers
had gone to administer Temporary Emergency Relief funds.
Great numbers of recruits, new to relief administration, were
coming from other occupations in which they were unemployed.
There was little time to train them, and many and complex
were the hastily improvised policies under which they had to
work. Such trained workers as could be gathered served as
supervisors in the relief bureaus, and of necessity had to direct
their efforts toward conserving inadequate funds rather than
paying attention to people as individuals.

The reports were that both budgets and staffs were being
cut in social agencies of all types. Meanwhile the need for service
increased as insecurity and resourcelessness mounted. Generally,
relief needs took precedence in community planning. Agencies
administering relief could not delay distribution of urgently
needed food by giving much attention to cases, yet were terri-
fied that they would fall into disastrous mass handling of aid.
Taking stock of the function and scope of the agency became
increasingly necessary if it were to preserve its legitimate role
amidst almost limitless needs. There was much thought given
to methods of sifting cases at intake to see which ones needed
casework and which specific problems were within the scope
of the agency's resources. Some tried to keep up the morale
of their staffs by doing intensive casework with a few cases.

More responsibility was left to the clients for assembling information or searching for resources. Altogether, it was recognized that if standards of good practice were to be salvaged, it would be in small pieces and in the midst of mass programs demanding other skills.

My part in the symposium was classified under "Philosophies Emerging." "Social work today is standing at the crossroads. It may go on with its face toward the past, bolstering up the decaying profit system, having to defend what is indefensible for the sake of the money which pays for its services. On the other hand it may envision a future in which professional social service as well as education, medical service, and the like, shall be the unquestioned right of all, conferred not as a benefit but as society's only way of maintaining itself. . . . The new thing the last months have brought us is a better sense of the individual as a social being to whom the social order matters so tremendously that no adjustment is possible except within and through it. . . . If we can form some conception of what a community based on co-operation instead of exploitation would be like, if we can see our casework with individuals as preparing them to live in and carry the responsibilities of such a society, undoubtedly that kind of blueprint of what we are working toward will affect decidedly many of our procedures in casework with individuals. . . . We must not lose our fine touch with individuals, but we see now that we must learn to think mental hygiene in mass terms too. . . . After all, individuals fulfill themselves only in relation to some whole in which they find more than themselves and in which they fill some useful place."[7]

With all the changes in the field of social work, the Smith College School was faced with dilemmas in two directions. First, it had depended more than most schools upon teaching done in the field agencies, because, with its block of nine months of practice, it could place students in a wider than local area and select agencies for their fitness to teach. Now the private social agencies were overworked, if not disorganized, with their best supervisors on loan to public assistance programs. If students came to the School without previous experience in social work, one winter of field training was not enough to develop the quality of graduates for which the School had gained a reputation.

The answer was a bold step which was a risk in those days when Smith College might well feel that a professional school of this type was beyond its means. Professor Kimball proposed and President Neilson agreed to lengthen the course from three sessions to five—two winters and three summers. The school must raise more scholarships, must help the training agencies more, and maintain at all costs the standard of professional education.

My contribution to the new plan was some detailed thinking on the content of field training. The problem was not as simple as in 1904, when a period of "general practice" in a family agency was followed by specialization in some other. By 1918, the Smith College School had defined general practice as "casework from the psychiatric point of view," making understanding of human behavior the basic preparation and giving preference to psychiatric agencies. Now family agencies, in giving up their relief function, were finding more complicated and less defined emotional problems to deal with than those that came to psychiatric agencies. If family service was now suitable field experience only for advanced students, where was the basic training for beginners?

As I saw it, the administrative elements in a casework job were being increasingly differentiated. Besides giving counselling to those who needed and wanted it, agencies were giving material aid, doing employment placement, finding foster care for children, helping travellers to their destination, arranging that medical recommendations be carried out. It seemed to me that beginning students could learn best in settings where the administrative elements were relatively large, the procedures definite, and the discipline of facts compelling. For this I found state hospitals, with their history-taking and after-care visits, excellent. In addition to their own work experience, students would be in touch with psychiatrists and see applied in practice the theories they had learned in school. As fast as public assistance agencies became stabilized I looked forward to using them also as centers for the field practice of the first winter. By the second year, students should be mature enough to face the complicated emotional problems found in psychiatric clinics and family agencies—problems in which skilled counselling was indicated.

The School's second dilemma was involved in the changing definition of social casework in the professional field. Since the psychiatric approach had come to dominate the teaching of casework, not only at Smith but in most schools, there had developed, as the ideal of casework practice, an intensive treatment of emotional problems over fairly long periods of time. It was called counselling and, later, therapy and was increasingly set apart from the administrative services of an agency, such as child placing, relief giving, or facilitating medical care. Professional caseworkers performed those necessary services, but considered that in so doing they were diverted from doing "real casework." Agencies which sent staff members to schools found that either they did not return or came back dissatisfied because they felt they could not practice "real casework" except in a psychiatric agency, freed from administrative duties. The University of Chicago School, and others whom it influenced, resisted this trend to disregard the social work in which, after all, the majority of agencies and workers were actually engaged, and continued its emphasis on public welfare and on the social forces affecting the adjustment of individuals from outside themselves. On the eastern seaboard, however, intensive work with emotional problems was the standard training for all students, even to some degree for those specializing in group work.

I could not accept a definition of social casework which so limited itself to intensive counselling with cases accepted for continuing treatment. After all, hadn't we started out to be *social* caseworkers? Were we to become a cult of elite members, while the majority of workers in public assistance, in hospitals, and in child-placing agencies did not do "casework" and therefore must be outside the really professional fold?

I had come to believe that casework was defined not by a particular setting or procedure but by a *quality* of approach to people that was unique among professions. It was characterized by perceptiveness regarding needs and by imaginative co-ordination of resources directed toward strengthening the client's own capacities to deal with his life situation as a social being. I believed this quality could be found in any agency setting where needs were found and resources could be developed. Particularly, the agencies with services to administer needed from the schools trained workers who could put this quality into any professional contact, however short.

My research study in the winter of 1931-32[8] approached two questions: 1) Could an experienced caseworker apply in single interviews the principles found characteristic of casework in longer contacts, i.e., development of a relationship of confidence (which might have to be limited in favor of a later relationship with another worker), listening with understanding, application of theoretical knowledge to interpretation of what was said, working with the client toward a plan of action? 2) Could this kind of interviewing, which might involve sifting and immediate decisions, be entrusted to students? (It had been done up to the point of decision by clerical workers. Recently, it had come to be thought so important that only the most skilled workers could undertake it.) My conclusions from the study were that short contact interviewing has all the possibilities of good casework (by any definition that I could consider sound) and that students should have experience in it under supervision, with no more risk than in practicing casework in longer contacts. In fact, I found the discipline of not being able to put off to other contacts the resolution of foggy portions of an interview, an excellent stimulus to clean-cut thinking on whatever facts were so far available.

Another aspect of the definition of social casework was

whether it required not only time for a proper relationship to develop between caseworker and client but also freedom from any involvement with authority. As I saw the trends up to the Depression period, we had acquired an outlook almost like that of private practice in psychiatry, even though we were doing our counselling in social agencies. We could only work with a client if he wanted us and found us completely devoted to his individual interests. The paradox was that communities supported the agencies in which we worked. We could be freed from contact with authority only as other agencies and other workers (not quite caseworkers was the implication) took over jobs like probation, public assistance, and the commitment of the mentally ill to hospitals.

My research projects for two winters were concerned with the question whether good casework was compatible with administration of some services involving authority. In 1932-33 I read records in the national office of the Association for Travelers Aid and Transient Service in New York.[9] My conclusions were that the community is always involved in any professional relationship, whether it be that of a paying patient to a physician or of a client receiving free counselling service from a social agency. There are legal and community regulations always to be observed. The relationship can be an honest and self-respecting one on both sides if these limitations are faced, not as personal coercion but as necessities by which both are bound. The opportunity for the client to talk out what he wants with an understanding person, even if the agency cannot meet his desires, is a genuine casework service. In summing up I said:

"The relationship to the client in an agency like the Travelers Aid may (in spite of a rather large amount of community-ordered procedure as compared with some other forms of casework) be of the finest quality obtainable anywhere. It seems to depend on the bigness of the personalities concerned, just as does any relationship. . . . She (the caseworker) may sometimes have to protest on their behalf against community de-

mands that work injustice. She will keep her professional
integrity by being too big to accept a slavish following of either
community or individual. And no one is in a better position
than one who sits at the crossroads of the world to know how
much bigger than local conditions are human needs and as-
pirations."[10]

In the fall of 1933 I had an opportunity to continue the
study of casework in an agency involved with authority. The
Jewish Board of Guardians in New York City, while not itself
an authoritative agency, was in the orbit of service of the
Juvenile Court, which had power to commit delinquent boys and
girls to the schools administered by the agency. Parents and
children could find friendly personal assistance, but only within
the framework of law which controlled the child's situation
without their choice. The J.B.G. wanted to stimulate more
voluntary use of its counseling service for problems the parents
themselves felt to be important. The agency wondered how to
urge the parents to come with their problems without suggesting to them problems that the agency, not they, found important. Could they offer counselling earlier, perhaps as soon
as the child was committed to the school, and in some way prevent a repetition of maladjustment after his return on parole?
I was to be avaliable two days a week at the office through the
winter months, and a letter offering the possibility of counselling was sent routinely to families of the children at the schools.

The study as published[11] was imbedded in a more general discussion of what I called a new philosophy of social casework
freed from paternalism. The ten interviews reported from the
study at the JBG brought out certain conclusions: that whether
or not authority is involved, people do not usually face problems
in advance, as social workers might expect them to do, but only
those that life has already presented to them. Secondly, that
causes of delinquency often lie in social and economic conditions that are beyond the power of a family to master, no
matter how well these have been discussed with a counselor.

My growing philosophy of casework will be referred to frequently as we go on.

This chapter has been a record of change. While the world rocked with disturbance, social work, which resembled a seismograph marking the social cataclysm, was itself shaken out of the grooves in which it had expected to advance. Family service agencies had moved away from their function of administering material relief only to be precipitated into it again and as suddenly out, to seek whatever function they could. Public assistance, which had, where it existed, been a despised stepchild of the kind of social work taught in most of the schools, now came to absorb a large part of the energies of the community. Professional training in social work, which had won some recognition in thirty years, was lost in a mass of untrained workers coping with new problems which had not been included in school curricula. There was a deep chasm between professional and nonprofessional social workers, and fear of each other seemed likely to widen rather than to bridge it. Volunteers had all but disappeared between professionals and public service officials. Where were the standards of yesteryear and the confident workers of the era when psychology and a triumphant capitalism were expected to solve, in time, every human problem? I shall end this chapter with two notes of cheer.

The month of May, 1933, was for me a never-to-be-forgotten spring. I was free, with the closing of my psychoanalysis, to step out into a new and blooming world. I went to Minneapolis to give a month's institute at the University of Minnesota School, headed by Professor F. Stuart Chapin who had been the first director of the Smith College School. In Minneapolis I had the privilege of working with, and knowing personally, Miss Gertrude Vaile, who did as much as anyone to cure my New England and New York City provincialism. Miss Vaile had grown up in the West, in a family devoted to public service. She was a graduate of the University of Chicago School where there was a strong tradition of social responsibility. She had done pioneer work in public welfare in Colorado, taught social work in Iowa and was now, in her position as Associate Director of the University School, a strong influence throughout the rural counties in the state. She had been president of the National Conference of Social Work, and represented new and developing trends in social work of which we in the East had scarcely heard.

Miss Vaile knew what good casework was and believed in it. She believed in it heartily for public assistance agencies where everything depended on stimulating self-help and self-respect. I shall never forget the evening rides with Miss Vaile after work, skirting the beautiful lakes around Minneapolis, seeing lilacs and fruit orchards in bloom, and talking of down-to-earth issues in our profession. It was as if a strong, sweet prairie wind was blowing away the smog of cities and the reek of unnecessary human misery. I shall never be able to measure how great is my debt to Miss Vaile's joyous and practical approach to life in this disturbed time.

The National Conference of Social Work of 1933 was memorable for one evening address, enhanced by the setting in which it was given. Detroit was a stricken city whose economic life had been paralyzed by bank and business failures. Some questioned whether it would dare to undertake being host to the National Conference. The answer was, "Of course." By March, Franklin D. Roosevelt had been inaugurated, all banks had been closed and reopened gradually with some foundation for confidence, and by June the New Deal had begun to function.

The speaker on the evening in question was David Cushman Coyle, whose pamphlet, *The Irrepressible Conflict, Business vs. Finance,*[12] had caused much discussion. He was not an economist, so he explained, but an engineer specializing in wind vibrations in high buildings. He said that, if his qualifications to discuss the economic situation were doubted, his reply would be that, if all the buildings in the world fell down, even a layman might ask if something wasn't the matter.

Mr. Coyle's thesis was that a technological revolution was making obsolete the use of large numbers of workers to produce the material goods needed for human society. Now, under highly mechanized production, surpluses piled up, businesses failed, workers were idle. Mr. Coyle punctured the illusion that, as many times before, the cycle would adjust itself. This time technological unemployment was permanent and growing. What future for our world?

Mr. Coyle's answer was that this surplus of labor power should be employed in productive work for enrichment of human life in nonmaterial ways. Suppose everyone who wanted an education could have it, and millions were trained to teach everything from higher learning and the arts to physical education and sports. Suppose, instead of the enforced idleness and deterioration of unemployment, there was a shortened workday with leisure for everyone to pursue the avocations of his choice. Could not millions more be employed in recreation, the arts, exploration, and travel? Suppose the unsolved problems of man's life on earth were seriously tackled by well-directed research. Could not thousands of scientists be employed to achieve something important in control of insect pests and communicable diseases, in reforestation, in use of the wealth in soils, minerals, and the marine life of the seas?

I do not remember whether Mr. Coyle answered the question which must have been in everyone's mind: Why not? It was so logical, and yet so impossible if we cling to the present economic system with its final condition for every new proposal—will it make a profit? If a people's resources in natural wealth were forever to be tied to the possibility of profit to private entrepreneurs, then there was no answer. Who would finance the education of an army of teachers, recreation workers, scientists? There was wealth enough in this country now for all of this, but the dead hand of profit was laid upon it, the same hand which had destroyed food to keep up prices while people starved.

I do not remember, as I say, whether Mr. Coyle drew the

conclusions which I drew as I mulled over his speech. I do remember his closing sentences:

"You social workers have asked for all these things which enrich human life, and have been called impractical and visionary for it. Now the economic stars in their courses are fighting with you. The so-called luxuries that social workers have advocated have become necessities. If we cannot afford these things, then we will have to afford to support millions on the dole, and in hospitals and prisons, or destroy them in war. Which does America really want?"

CHAPTER 10

VITALITY

I remember hearing social workers say that the saddest thing about the Depression was to see the unemployed so beaten down, so unprotesting, so apathetic. No doubt thousands were as lost as the stockbrokers who jumped from high windows, and for the same reason. They had built their security and their sense of their own worth on what they possessed, and in losing possessions, lost themselves.

The workers of America, however, had always lived with insecurity. Possibly they had known labor organizations in which they had briefly won and often lost in contest with organized Capital. They knew the power of Capital, not only over their jobs but over their ability to live as men, free to organize and bargain collectively. They were familiar with company spies, intimidation, picket lines broken by tear gas and brass-knuckled thugs, enrolled by the companies as cops. The Depression had, however, caught them at a bad time, when the craft unions had been decimated by the company-union movement of the 1920's, when the great industries like coal and steel, textile and maritime, had outgrown the divisive form of craft organization, and when workers had not yet gained protection of their right to organize by whole industries, as they did later under the National Recovery Act.[1] For the first years of the Depression, they could find no voice with which to speak. They knew that they were helpless unless they could meet the organized power of Capital with collective strength. Then,

slowly, necessity drew them together in such organizations as
the Workers' Alliance and the Unemployed Councils, as well as
into labor organization by industries under the Congress of
Industrial Organization (CIO).

I also remember social workers speaking with considerable
apprehension about evictions from homes which were stopped
by determined neighbors who gathered and carried furniture
back into the house as fast as the sheriff's men could deposit it
on the sidewalk (and faster than they could themselves be arrested and carted off). Also I remember hearing of auctions of
farms for foreclosure in the Middle West, when grim-faced
men bid on the property for almost nothing and presented it to
the former owner while no one dared to make it a take-away
sale. A sense of threat was in the air whether the unemployed
asserted themselves or whether they did not.

What leadership, what planned program for dealing with the
crisis came from our profession which was dedicated to human
welfare? The American Association of Social Workers set up
a Committee on Federal Action on Unemployment which
worked for a year and a half to secure the passage of a federal
unemployment relief bill. On April 22, 1933 it called a conference on National Economic Objectives For Social Work. The
conference report[2] stated that partial methods of seeking
emergency remedies might well do more harm than good. The
specific measures recommended were included under seven
heads:

I. Achievement and Maintenance of Labor Standards.

II. Relief Measures, which included federal responsibility,
more adequate organization, work relief, relief for the homeless,
adequacy of relief, the co-operation of government with the self-
help movements.

III. Public Works, so planned as not to interfere with industry.

IV. Unemployment Insurance.

V. Employment Exchanges.

VI. Achievement of Economic Security Through Social Insurance.

VII. Taxation related to ability to pay, and such as not to lower the standard of living.

At a luncheon meeting of the conference, Miss Mary van Kleeck[3] gave a paper analyzing the total situation. She showed that the crisis demanded planning which would go beyond single industries to the whole economy. She said that social work had been predicated upon an economy in which wealth is unevenly distributed. Now the maldistribution is so great that social work can not correct it or even seem to. To secure the economic objective that the resources of the nation shall be used to meet the needs of all of its people requires a totally planned economy such as we see only under socialism. The basic questions of distribution of wealth and of ownership and control of industry must be faced by us all.

It is a sad comment to make that I cannot remember ever hearing of this important conference. It could not be that I was not interested, for I was teaching in a leading school concerned with the whole field of social work, and I had expressed in numerous papers and speeches my own conviction that a fundamental reorganization of the social order was necessary. I do not recall any meetings on this subject at the Detroit National Conference, or in New York during the following winter. Certainly it seems that such an important report of the leading professional body in social work should not have been ignored. Or was it that already social workers had retreated a long way into a shell of protected preoccupation with their own techniques in casework?

I was jarred out of any such preoccupation by contact with a youth group I had not met before. One day in the spring of 1934, while I was giving an institute on casework in a New York agency, I was handed the first number of a new magazine, *Social Work Today*, edited by young workers who called themselves practitioners or just "the rank and file." From it I learned that discussion groups had been meeting for nearly four years in New York, Chicago, Boston, Cleveland, and Philadelphia to try to find answers to problems that were not being faced in the professional organizations. It announced its province to be "all of social welfare" and its aim "to promote an interest in the fundamental reorganization society must undergo to provide security for all" and to support "labor's struggle for a greater measure of control as the basic condition for that reorganization." The magazine would devote itself to the professional and economic status of the rank and file worker and serve as a medium of exchange of experiences for practitioner groups all over the country.

My eyes were caught by the following sentences which had life in them:

"Under the cumulative pressure of four years of continuous contact with the victims of our chaotic social order, some have learned to question the traditional dogmas of the profession and to examine critically the shibboleths of 'awareness,' 'bearing witness,' 'social engineering,' and 'community integration.' They are painfully aware of many things that do not submit to awareness. They wonder who is doing the engineering and whether it is social. They suspect that talk of community integration is a pleasant fiction to hide the ugliness of our class society. They are sick of merely bearing witness.

"There is a growing body which is applying in another spirit the charge to all social workers to know their clients and to help them free themselves. They have heard the voice of labor speak compellingly in its own behalf. They are coming to feel that whatever skill and knowledge they may have, can be put to most effective use supporting by publicity and action the organization of labor and its fight for adequate relief and social insurance.

"They wonder, too, whether their position is very different from that of other workers of hand and brain, for salary reductions and discharges have destroyed illusions concerning their own security."[4]

The first issue of *Social Work Today* covered matters that

were seldom mentioned in professional magazines or the public press. There was a description of two conventions in Washington. One was of the American Association of Social Workers[5] to discuss its relation to the federal government, in which government leaders gave them little except, "You must trust us to work something out." The other was the National Convention Against Unemployment[6] composed of workers, Negro and white, from North, South and West, reporting struggles for relief, hunger marches, action against evictions, and attacks by police. They said, "The real issue is unemployment, not forced labor camps, and abolition of discrimination against Negroes in jobs and relief." They set up the National Unemployed Council of the U.S.A., to work for a Workers' Unemployment and Social Insurance bill.

This first issue of *Social Work Today* contained an estimate by a leading research specialist in social work that the staggering sum of $2,400,000,000 would be needed in federal relief funds to meet the problem of unemployment with any adequacy if the country was left without a social insurance program. There were articles on the NRA (dubbed the Negro Riddance Act because so few had benefited by it) on who benefits by slum clearance, correspondence on the standard of living and on the plight of the social work employee, and an open letter proposing to organize professional workers to promote unemployment compensation, social insurance, and economic security.[7]

A few weeks later another issue was out, covering the National Conference of Social Work, in which I found myself misquoted. I wrote the editor, protesting and yet applauding what the magazine was trying to do. The answer made me smile. The editor said they could not attempt to correct mistakes because they were new at reporting and made so many, but he cordially invited me to become a member of an advisory council of older professional workers who were in sympathy with the rank-and-file movement. I said I would accept and feel honored if the association meant something more than "window dressing." It did—much more. During all the eight years that the magazine survived its penniless origin and became a vital force in social work, it was one of the richest associations of my life.

Nineteen thirty-four! What a year that was for great beginnings!

> *There are years that pass, unnoted,*
> *Shuffled off with sigh of hope*
> *For better days, or else remembered*
> *Like peaceful stream in grassy plain.*
> *There are years that men count time by ever after,*
> *Pregnant with destiny, for hope or fear,*
> *Will watching working living folk*
> *Reach* Annum Domini *this year?*

When I wrote those lines as a greeting for the holidays in 1937, I was looking forward, little realizing that I had already lived through the year of my lifetime most pregnant with destiny.

On April 29th, 1934, at the auditorium of the Engineering Building in New York, I attended the first open meeting of the Interprofessional Association for Social Insurance, to bring together professional workers who were as severely affected by the Depression as industrial workers and were far less accustomed to organize for their own protection. There were engineers, architects, chemists, and actors, with unemployment ranging as high as 80 percent. There were doctors who had so much work that they "could not get to the bank to draw money to pay the office rent." There were salary-cut librarians, teachers, nurses; there were writers without contracts and social workers doing double work for less pay.

The organizer and leading speaker was Miss Mary van Kleeck, who analyzed skillfully the provisions of a proposed Workers' Social Insurance Bill and estimated its cost and also the much greater cost in dollars of an adequate relief program, to say nothing of the cost in lives when millions are cut off from productive work. Miss van Kleeck emphasized that a bill which workers could support would have to be adequate in coverage,

paid for by taxation of those able to pay, and managed democratically with fair representation of workers.

Another speaker was Dr. Frankwood E. Williams, who, as
a psychiatrist, brought out the terrible toll taken by economic
insecurity in the lives of individuals and families and the cost
we pay in insanity, disease, crime, and the constant preparations for war which are the result of fear and anxiety. The cost
of all these is staggering. No matter what it costs, adequate
social insurance is worth it all to prevent social disintegration.

From this small beginning in an enthusiastic meeting which
lasted till midnight, the Interprofessional Association went on
to organize public sentiment for social insurance, eventually
having chapters as far as the Pacific coast. It was instrumental
in forming also protective organizations in the various professions, such as The Federation of Engineers, Architects,
Chemists and Technicians, the Newspaper Guild, the Lawyers
Guild, and union organizations of actors, writers, artists, nurses,
librarians, and others. The Workers Social Insurance Bill was
introduced into Congress by Congressman Lundeen of Minnesota and was campaigned for by labor unions and professional
workers from coast to coast. While it failed of passage, as did
its successor, the Frazier-Lundeen Bill, there is no doubt that
the Social Security Act of 1935 owes its existence to the pressure of public opinion generated by discussion of this far more
adequate even if radical proposal.

The National Conference of Social Work which opened in
Kansas City in June, 1934, promised to be a New Deal Conference. Rexford D. Tugwell and Harry C. Hopkins were there
to praise the accomplishments of government plans which had
been in operation for a year and to discuss those which were
projected. William Hodson, Director of the Emergency Home
Relief Bureau of New York City, was Conference President.
There was a note of optimism in this meeting only one year
after the confusion of the Detroit conference. Many social
workers felt that, with our profession represented in the cabinet
by Harry Hopkins and Frances Perkins, we had arrived and

could give a leadership in welfare matters which had hitherto
been denied to us.

Then, on the morning after the first evening session, Mary
van Kleeck's address on "Our Illusions Regarding Government"
produced more heat, and for many social workers more light,
than any other at the conference.[8] She challenged the AASW
which had, at the recent Conference On Governmental Objectives For Social Work, endorsed a proposal for a permanent
system of welfare services under government auspices, praised
the present administration of welfare services, and even paid
high tribute to Congress and the Federal Administration which
had used "the best traditions and experience of social work,"
adding praise of other New Deal programs not associated directly with relief administration.

Miss van Kleeck noted the recent shift from social services
predominantly privately administered to governmental programs. Then she asked a searching question: Does this shift
commit social workers to the preservation of the status quo,
separate them from their clients, and lead them into defense of
political institutions "against the strain put upon them by the
failure of industry to maintain employment and by the industrial policy which seeks to sustain profits at the expense of
standards of living"? Miss van Kleeck went on to outline two
theories of government: 1) That government is above conflicting interests and can, by majority vote, legislate in a democracy for removal of inequalities in the present distribution of
wealth and "establish a basis below which wages and other
conditions of employment affecting the standards of living of
the working class are not allowed to fall," and 2) That government "is dominated by the strongest economic power and becomes the instrument to serve the purposes of the groups
possessing that power. . . . Government tends to protect property rights rather than human rights."

Miss van Kleeck then showed that proposals that lay burdens
upon property are bound to be resisted at every point. Strikes
demonstrate the basic conflict of interest between labor and

capital. The relief program "is the thermometer representing the political leadership's diagnosis of the effectiveness of the demands of those who need relief." She asked if social workers who happen to have the task of administering relief are to take sides with government "in the three-cornered conflict of interest between those who own and control the economic system, the workers who are claiming their right to a livelihood in an age of plentiful production, and the government which has always most closely identified itself with property rights." She saw an unfortunate result of the capitulation of social workers to government in the inadequacy of the federal relief plan which was announced just eleven days after the conference of social workers had issued its laudatory report. She called for much more clear thinking on objectives and more aggressive action to implement them. Instead of taking positions with government and acting as apologists for it against the mass protests of the workers of the United States, social workers should be organizing to make an effective demand for adequate standards.

The effect was that of a strong wind blowing through the Conference. The audience would not stop applauding, and called on Miss van Kleeck to speak many times during the week to small and large groups. The newspapers considered her ideas front-page news. The New Dealers answered with a prepared statement defending their program against Miss van Kleeck's criticism, and a meeting of nearly a thousand gathered to censure the issuance of the statement. Her paper on "Common Goals Of Labor and Social Work" was another sensation.[9]

What the net results were no one can say, except that the Kansas City Conference of Social Work became a thinking instead of a rubber-stamp conference. The idea had been planted that the young profession of social work did not become a leader for higher standards of public welfare just by receiving recognition and having some of its members appointed to government posts. It could thereby become merely a follower of political programs designed against, rather than for, the interests of clients of social work, and it could be led into positions which would betray those interests it was ethically obligated to protect. Miss van Kleeck counselled that social workers study as never before the facts of economics and world history and that they get into contact in their own communities with the protest movements of working people which were actually grappling with inadequate relief and social injustice. She urged that, even if they should disagree with the leaders of these movements, social workers should learn how they think and why they act.

The story of the practitioners' groups in social work is another tale of upspringing vitality. At the Kansas City Conference they were introduced by four meetings of their own.[10] On Wednesday, they discussed relief practices and working conditions and set up a national co-ordinating committee of practitioner groups. On Friday, at a meeting on professional standards and education, a caseworker from Chicago, read a paper on "New Forms of Social Workers' Organizations," indicating that there were already twenty-one functioning groups of practitioners throughout the country, responding to various local conditions but falling into three general types: 1) Groups in AASW chapters where young workers found themselves without other means of expressing their thinking, under the dominance of agency executives; 2) social workers' discussion groups which soon found a need to take action on issues vitally affecting their work; and 3) protective organizations, recognizing that professional workers need to be concerned with their own economic welfare and working conditions. These groups are distinguished from a professional organization like AASW which concerns itself with professional standards but has never embraced more than ten thousand trained workers while four or five times that number, many of them not eligible for AASW membership, are employed in welfare services. These practitioner groups extend to all employees of social agencies, not just to social workers, and use methods which industrial workers have found necessary in collective bargaining, such as negotiation with boards and commissions, petitions, publicity, and (recently) a two-hour work stoppage which won a partial restoration of salary cuts.

At a luncheon meeting which two hundred attended, the practitioner groups heard a representative from engineers at a city hotel striking against violation of NRA codes, and the meeting passed a resolution of support. It condemned an instance of discrimination in housing against Negro delegates at the Conference and distributed leaflets on these two issues. Miss Mary van Kleeck spoke on the Workers' Social Insurance Bill. On Friday evening, some delegates attended a meeting of an organization of the unemployed and participated in the program.

Moving on from the Kansas City Conference, by February, 1935, in a conference held in Pittsburgh, a national organization of practitioner groups was formed, to which local groups could affiliate. By spring, the number of groups had grown to forty-six, twenty-four of them protective organizations, most of them in public relief agencies, related to one employer, and including clerical as well as social workers. In February, 1936, I attended the National Convention in Cleveland at which the organization drew up a constitution and considered seeking affiliation with the labor movement. I had never seen such a "participating" conference at which delegates sat up all night to complete committee assignments.

By this time, practitioners had, in protecting their own interests as workers, come to experience all the forms of counter-action to which labor was accustomed. They met with intimidation and the dismissal of outstanding workers for joining their organization. They found it impossible to be silent when delegations of clients protesting starvation relief were beaten by the police at relief stations. They had to protest when some supervisors called the police instead of talking out grievances with the clients and doing all they could to remedy injustices. The practitioners considered that the public should know what happened in the public services, and they used leaflets, picket lines, and mass meetings to give this knowledge.

Soon, of course, they had dismissed members to defend as best they could.

By October, 1935, the Social Security Act had been passed, inadequate as it was, especially in its provisions for unemployment insurance (limited in coverage, setting no federal standard, encouraging company plans which decreased labor's motility and discouraged organization, and paid for by taxation which decreased workers' purchasing power). The Federal programs which seemed likely to exhaust all the letters of the alphabet were constantly being revoked, sometimes with others substituted, sometimes not. So it was with projects under the WPA, the Youth Administration, cultural projects, the Service to Transients. While each withdrawal was publicized to be an indication that the service was no longer necessary or was succeeded by something better, the unemployed and those close to the suffering of relief clients could see little but readjustment downward. More and more, however, labor groups and the unemployed, and social workers with them, were learning how to act as normal citizens in their own behalf.

These movements in social work now had a voice. *Social Work Today* had become a well-edited journal of fact and opinion, contributed to not only by the young workers who had initiated it with their vigorous thinking, but by leaders in the profession and by others who had something to say about what was happening to people in this critical time—economists, congressmen, labor leaders, doctors, lawyers, artists.

Going back to the summer of 1934, immediately after the National Conference of Social Work, I was invited, among other representatives of schools of social work, to attend a conference at the University of Missouri on the training of relief workers for the rural counties. I found there another fresh wind blowing. Young, eager college graduates from the Middle West were gathered to learn as much as they could before tackling the overwhelming problems of country districts which had never before had a standardized program of relief. The educators conferred on "how to" while the young workers studied under the direction of Miss Lucille Cairns from St. Louis. Outside the formal sessions of the conference, I learned much from talks with Miss Cairns and from the student group to whom I spoke during the Sunday lunch hour. If I had lingering prejudices against newcomers to social work via public assistance services, they were dispelled. These were not beneficiaries of a political spoils system, outsiders destined to destroy all good standards of work. They were clean-cut young Americans ready to pioneer in a new situation for which no experienced body and no established school had the answers.

My monograph, *Between Client and Community* (including the study made at the Jewish Board of Guardians), was published in September, 1934.[11] It expressed a philosophy of social work which discarded paternalistic condescension in favor of a relationship with clients which could open doors and windows for them so that they could use new understandings in their own way and for their own purposes. I had come to see that worker and client alike were enmeshed in a social order that does not favor growth of human personality, yet I believed that this spirit and philosophy could be applied even in settings where administrative duties carry authority and demand action in brief contacts. Writing my credo in social work was a growth experience for me, and it created much controversy in professional groups.

One day in the fall of 1934, I received a letter from one of the field supervisors of the Smith College School who was Program Chairman of the New Jersey Chapter of the AASW, asking if I would take part in a symposium at a Chapter meeting on November 8th. The subject was to be the new rank-and-file groups, their aims and philosophy. Other speakers were to be the President of the New York Home Relief Bureau Workers Association and an architect representing the Interprofessional Association. I was asked to give the point of view of a member of the AASW, who could "carry the thread along to the relationship of the Association to the movements which are already in our reality and about which most of us are sticking our heads in the sand. . . . you are the only person I would want to do this for us, and after reading your book and seeing you at IPA meetings, I know you are sympathetic and have the experience and range to help us think out our relationship to these challenging, dynamic movements."

I accepted the challenge and on November 8th said what I thought about the economic system which had failed so miserably to make possible even the minimal essentials of a decent life for vast numbers of people. Some of the young were delighted and took me to their hearts. Some of the old were frightfully disturbed. I remember a prominent board member almost stamping in her agitation as she said such radical changes as I proposed were unthinkable. She wanted, on her return to Wellesley College, to find the same huckleberry bushes on the campus which had borne fruit in her day. She did not say whether the hungry could subsist on huckleberries.

To some of the rank-and-file leaders who talked with me later, I said that I stood by every word that I had spoken. This did not mean, necessarily, that I could go as far as they would. I had to move ahead at my own pace, backed by solid conviction, but I saw no reason why I could not work with them for a better life for the clients whom, after all, we were obligated to serve. From that day I came to have a place in the new movements which were sweeping through social work.

This chapter would not be complete without a record of the impact upon us of the upsurge of vitality in a land across the sea. It came to us through Dr. Frankwood E. Williams who published a book in the summer of 1934 which brought together articles in the *Survey Graphic* and speeches he had made in the past three years. His book, *Russia, Youth and the Present Day World*,[12] came at a time when the United States had just recognized the seventeen-year-old federation of Socialist Republics and when interest in knowing the truth about Russia was very keen.

Dr. Williams had gone to Moscow and Leningrad in 1931,

as part of a vacation tour of Europe and because a Russian
psychiatrist at the First International Congress on Mental
Hygiene, in 1930, had aroused his curiosity about what they
were doing there. Dr. Williams wrote:

"I received such a shock on this first visit that there was
nothing to do but to go back the next year to prove to myself,
at least, that what I thought I had seen on my first brief visit
was actually true. This led to a journey of over ten thousand
miles from one end of European Russia to the other, through
cities, towns and villages, factories, hospitals, schools, prisons,
wherever I could poke my nose—and I found I could poke it
anywhere I wanted to. If I came away from my first visit
shocked and stirred, I came away from my second visit deeply
thoughtful."[13]

What did Dr. Williams find in the first socialist society on
earth that survived wars of intervention, famine and pestilence
and economic prostration, and had become in a few years a
world power? First, he was looking in clinics and hospitals for
what he called "mental hygiene" and found little of interest.
After a while he began to see that mental hygiene was not
in these remedial institutions, but was "all over the place"—in
kindergartens and schools, in factories and public kitchens, in
health education and vocational training, in marriage and divorce bureaus, in measures to deal with alcoholism and prosti-
tution (which the Russians claimed had been virtually wiped
out), in treatment of prisoners and their rehabilitation.

Dr. Williams could not believe his eyes when he finally identified the outstanding characteristic of Russian life to be *regard
for the individual!* Yet their regard for the individual was
even different from that in other countries where individual
interests were often set into competition with those of others.
Here the individual was always part of the group—the whole
group, not separate groups with competing interests.

The first Russian contribution to Dr. Williams' new idea
of mental hygiene was, then, that *the whole of life* can be so
organized in a socialist society as to reduce the causes of anxiety

which are so common elsewhere. Remedial hospitals and clinics
are provided, but have less and less to do, even in a population
undergoing very rapid change, as, for instance, from rural to
urban life and from farm labor of the crudest sort to mechanized
industry. Always, he found national planning concerned with
making their common life fit for individuals and individuals
healthy and fit to do their part in building it.

Dr. Williams had led our thinking in psychiatric social work
to a consideration of the role of the hostile emotions in mental
life and their use in constructive ways—in work, in overcoming
obstacles, in conquest of natural forces. Now, for the first time,
he made us see a whole society, organized on the simple principle that *there shall be no exploitation,* in which the devastating
effects of personal and corporate hostility are strikingly absent.
Dr. Williams spent much time in Russia with youth groups,
workers and students, hearing their comments on life and their
questions. He found free expression of anger at exploitation
and at the bad conditions under which people throughout the
world are forced to live, but was amazed to find so little hatred
of people. He heard them say, "Our enemies in other countries
are misled by their exploiters. When they understand they'll
be all right." Or, "Enemies of the state here must be kept
from destroying what we are trying to build, but maybe it is
our fault that they have not understood before this."

Dr. Williams died at sea two years after the publication of
his book, and the notes he had taken on a third summer trip to
Russia were never found. He did make a bridge for us in psychiatric social work between our immersion in study of individual conflicts and the place of individuals in a society that, for
the first time in history, claims to have found the source of conflict within and among nations—exploitation of man by man.

The first five years of the Depression in America, through
1934, were bitterly devastating. Yet they gave rise to amazing
instances of courage and resourcefulness. Most important, they
were not individual and scattered instances, but the drawing
together of groups, first to think together and then to express

their thought in action. Those years saw the unemployed lifting their heads again as men, thinking not only of their needs but of their obligation to do something about them for the sake of everyone.

Many people learned only as much as to rely on their government, though, as a Negro porter in Washington put it, "Santa Claus ain't going to keep on coming." Some learned that their government was not theirs unless they made it so, for it was easier for it to act for the money-seeking aggregations of power that pressed upon it. Some learned that great numbers of people of like interests have to act together to have any effect. To reach their fellow-citizens they had to use the only language of appeal that was available to them, even if it were the unpopular speech of demonstrations, picket lines, and even strikes. Professional workers began to learn this, too, the hard way, the persecuted way. Fortunately, they had leaders like Miss van Kleeck, who were not fooled by easy, specious solutions, who had the facts of economics and history, and who knew there *was* an intelligent way of dealing even with a depression, if one had courage and vitality.

CHAPTER II

RETHINKING

After an earthquake it is well to look to the foundations, not only of man-made buildings but also the mountain slopes and deep ravines of the earth's crust. What has moved permanently, what has weakened and is about to move, and what irreversible changes are to be understood and made part of the heritage of human experience?

The timing of my personal liberation through psychoanalysis was fortunate. Its release of energies and broadening of sympathy and understanding coincided with a similar release and broadening in a large and growing sector of the young people in social work. They went beyond use of the frame of reference of the 1920's in which new problems were to be solved by the old methods.[1] They knew that it was not possible to muddle through a great depression without applying to human society the scientific thinking which was demanded by a complex modern world. They used group thinking, welded by discussion into a firm belief as to the purpose of social work and how that purpose could be carried out under today's conditions. They believed they had a science of society and were learning how to apply it.

If there was a science of society, how did we social workers come by it? The decade of psychiatric teaching had prepared us to extend the area appropriate to scientific study from the physical and biological world to that of human behavior. In psychiatry we had stopped with the behavior of individuals, assuming that once they were "adjusted" to a norm of mental health which we had set up, they would themselves be in tune with a society which was believed to be stable and for the modification of which we were not in any case responsible. Now it was evident that society itself was sick. Individuals were powerless either to adjust to its feverish tossing or to change it in the direction of healthy functioning. Was there no science of the behavior of human beings in societies?

A century earlier, Karl Marx and Frederick Engels, out of their study of German philosophy and French political economy and out of their experience with the combined efforts of workingmen of several countries to better their condition, had discovered the laws of motion of all human societies, whether their economy was that of primitive communism, slavery, feudalism, or capitalism. Lenin had brought study of these laws of motion into the age of imperialism which Marx and Engels had not lived to see. A multinational federation of republics had begun in 1917 to shape its entire life on this new scientific outlook and by 1934 had survived wars of intervention, famine, pestilence, and economic ruin to become the fastest-growing economy of the world. The United States had just recognized the existence of this country of nearly 200 million people and had begun to trade with it.

The world of capitalist economy did not welcome this new embodiment of a scientific world outlook. It furnished forces for military intervention which failed and an economic blockade which only increased (under tremendous odds) the industrial development of the new Soviet state. News about the U.S.S.R. was systematically distorted to prove, first, its weakness and inevitable end; then, its menacing strength and intention to conquer the world and its deceitfulness in that it used the welfare of people as an appeal for the world's acceptance of its system. The welfare of people was our business, but most of us knew as little as anyone else who read the papers how a scientific outlook might modify our theories and practice. In 1934 many people supposed Marxism to be a dogma (not a science to be tested by experience), and to be the property of socialist debating societies (which dabbled in politics and always failed), or of strange and dangerous people called communists.

I think it was early in 1936 that I saw the first communist I could identify as such. I was attending a conference on unemployment insurance, and one of the participants representing the Unemployed Councils, threw into his brief talk a surprising sentence, "Now we communists believe. . . ." I looked at him startled, as much by my own reaction as by his simple declaration. Did I expect to see horns above his thoughtful face? I only noted about him a quiet manner and a grasp of facts and logical thinking that was unusual even in a professional group. I had heard about communists—that they were wily and cruel and always plotting violence. But as I came to see them in the New York labor movement and in the struggles of the unemployed, I found quite the contrary. They could be depended upon for more devotion to the interests of working people than anyone else, for clearer thinking on better facts, and for more determined action—which could not be selfish since they got nothing for it but abuse. I could not believe that they were paid by Moscow gold, since nobody had less. It did not seem any more reasonable that the Soviet Union was plotting to take over America through a party smaller than most religious sects than that the existence of an Episcopal church in the United States was evidence that the Church of England was conspiring to control American religion.

I did not find the key to a science of society until later in 1936. At the end of the summer, as I was packing to leave Smith, a student came in with two or three books and remarked (probably more casually than she felt), "Here are some books for your reading list. I shall expect a reading report on them." I laughed with her, making some quip about "sauce for the goose is sauce for the gander," and put the books into my trunk. During vacation I read them—classics of the science of political economy worked out by Karl Marx and Frederick Engels in the western Europe of a hundred years ago and by their followers in later periods. It was my first contact with the books themselves rather than with versions sifted through the prejudices of others. I had to stop often and wait for emotional assimilation of what they were saying, but they made sense of current and past history as had nothing else I had ever read. By the time I could write the "reading report" (which I took seriously) some three months later, I had the beginnings of a world view that made a consistent whole out of nature and history.[2]

It is impossible here to summarize this world outlook which immeasurably enriched the thinking and practice of many social workers in the 1930's. It is enough to say that it followed the principles of scientific thinking everywhere: the collection of data with increasing accuracy and better methods of testing; the sharing of tested experience; the placing of isolated facts in relation to other facts and to the framework of discovered laws of motion which govern development and change; the learning how to co-operate with the forces of nature in human history instead of acting blindly in ignorance or in defiance of them.

During the seven years from 1934 to the outbreak of war at the end of 1941, I was growing slowly, but fortunately as I said, in company with a vital young generation of social workers. The simple principles that the so-called rank-and-file workers of the Depression years were putting into practice were not new to social work. It was only a new thing to take them seriously. They were, first of all, that social work exists to serve people in need. If it serves other classes who have other purposes it becomes too dishonest to be capable of either theoretical or practical development. Secondly, social work exists to help people to help themselves, and, therefore, one should not be alarmed when they do so by organized means, such as in client or tenant or labor groups. Thirdly, social work operates by communication, listening, and sharing experiences. Those social work administrators in the Home Relief Bureau in New York who worked out ways of dealing with grievances by

receiving client delegations as equals, instead of treating those
who came to protest like wild beasts to be controlled by police
clubs, achieved a genuine professional practice of their best
theories even under the inadequate and repressive laws and
ordinances which controlled relief administration.

Fourthly, social work has to find its place among other movements for human betterment, to be concerned with civil rights,
equality of opportunity, decent housing, public health, and community sharing of common hazards like unemployment, sickness
and old age through social insurance—all needful things
which cannot be secured without the whole community taking
some responsibility for their being available to everyone. If
social work is a remedial service only, it can not be remedial
for the ills beyond its scope, like mass unemployment, but
neither can it ignore the existence of such ills as make impossible a sane administration even of "tinkering" services.
Social work must look to the setting as well as to the minutiae
of its professional practice.

Finally, social workers as citizens cannot consider themselves
superior to their clients as if they do not have the same problems. Social workers, too, are beset as others are by human
problems, not the least of which is how to earn a living. If they
are glad that their profession offers more than just a pay check,
so much the more does it require that they give something to
the common life of the community. Social workers have to take
adult responsibility to see that conditions prevail which make
sound professional functioning possible. They learned during
the Depression that they had to organize and exert pressure
as groups to protect their service to clients, and themselves as
citizens. They could not regard themselves as especially privileged and noble characters who could talk their way into a
community's sympathetic understanding of their best intentions.

It all added up to a maturing process in our profession. I
analyzed it in *Between Client and Community*[3] in 1934 as a
four-fold growth which I was myself experiencing: to be more
sensitive to people and their needs; to ask *why* (instead of

taking for granted that as things were so they would always be) ; to find a place for the self among other selves (not having constantly to climb on the backs of others to enhance personal prestige) ; to be able not only to live but to give life, to think but to help others to think, to act but to act with others.

In 1935, I was expressing this potential for maturity in another way. "Life is for growth,"[4] meant that social work must be dedicated to fostering growth and to opposing whatever made growth of human beings impossible. I saw social work as if it were in its adolescence, looking back with admiration to the early pioneers but distrusting some of their formulations, made for the quite different world prior to 1918. Today, the future must be built on principles found valid in today's stress of change.

In 1936, I compared the maturing of social work[5] to the growth of personality from the stage in which infants can form relationships to others, only on the basis of using them for their own needs and desires. Gradually, a person comes to relate to others as persons in their own right, to be responded to and to co-operate with, rather than always to use for one's self. So social work had progressed from getting clients to do what someone else wanted them to do to seeing them as individuals whose co-operation must be on the basis of mutual respect. This lesson had to be learned in relation to fellow workers also. In school guidance work, for instance, psychiatric social workers had to learn to work with teachers and school administrators, not to get them to contribute to *our* work with the child but to form with them a partnership geared to better service to the education of youth. In the same way we had to grow to a new understanding of our relationship to all other professions and social forces.

Throughout this whole period the magazine, *Social Work Today,* was the speaking voice of the new movement in the profession and a powerful educational force. By 1937, its volunteer editorial board could no longer carry the load, and Frank Bancroft became managing editor and one of the most beloved and influential personalities in the whole field of social work. I first met Frank at a meeting in Cincinnati which goes down in my history book as the most uncomfortable I ever attended. I did not know at the time that the Association of Public Welfare Employees, which had asked me to speak, had been forced into the mold of a "company union" or that an officer of the administration had invited herself to chair the meeting. I did know that the air seemed somehow charged with resentment, which I supposed was directed against what I had to say. As a detail, the labor hall in which we met was hot and bare, and the ventilating fan in the ceiling (which could not be turned off) made a noise like a lawnmower. Frank, who represented the welfare employees on the sponsoring committee, was soon to be fired from the Welfare Department for his activity in the union. That evening, when it seemed to me that I had failed the group who invited me by doing so poor a speaking job, and when, by the discussion period, I felt hopelessly bogged down, Frank earned my enduring gratitude by pulling together the answer to what may have been a heckling question. His good humor and keen intelligence never failed the group around *Social Work Today* in all the stressful years that followed.

Later, I learned more about Frank's colorful life. He had come from an old New England family on his father's side, had been educated at Princeton and ordained as an Episcopal clergyman, and had spent three years in India, knowing intimately the great poet Tagore. He had landed on his feet in Cincinnati in the Depression years as a public welfare employee, After his "release" from this employment, he became a reporter until *Social Work Today* claimed him for a long career in journalism.

Frank Bancroft could inspire any group to phenomenal group thinking and action. Though the magazine was never free from financial difficulties, it began to have organized backing from Social Work Today Co-operators, a body of friends who stretched from ocean to ocean and from the Great Lakes to the

Gulf. They pledged funds and organized forums in the larger cities which were the source of important thinking in the profession. At each year's National Conference of Social Work, the *Social Work Today* luncheon meetings were overflow affairs, commanding outstanding speakers and living in memory long after the event. One year, at Atlantic City, vocal with boardwalk attractions, there was some fear that the large hall which had been engaged would not be filled. It was packed—and in spite of a cloudburst which was rending the heavens at the time. Frank met the occasion with his usual gaiety. "We prayed for rain, just a *little* rain to keep people off the beach, and after us comes the deluge."

Social Work Today published four kinds of material obtainable nowhere else: 1) reportage on world events affecting social work and on political changes and the growth of workers' movements everywhere; 2) relief and welfare measures and first-hand case illustrations of the way these were working throughout the country; 3) growth of organization of social workers for their protection and the affiliation of such professional unions with the labor movement; 4) professional content of theory and practice. This was partly in a special department known as "Casework Notebook," and partly in full-length professional papers.

These articles drew upon the fresh experience of practitioners as well as upon the writers who were accustomed to be heard at National Conference and in the professional journals. Whatever these young workers knew about casework they dared to set down and to submit to the criticism of other practitioners and students of theory. In the winter of 1937-38, a group which had been working on a re-evaluation of social work in the light of recent history asked me if I would write some of the conclusions which I, too, had reached. All winter I labored over and threw away many versions of this evaluation, for I had to grow with what I was trying to think through. The group helped immensely with ideas and criticism. The paper was finally published as a serial in *Social Work Today*[6] under

the title *Re-Thinking Social Case Work*. Later, it went through
many reprintings as a pamphlet, expressing the best understanding I could reach at that time of the relations of social casework
to the world of the Depression period and to its historical development.

I defined social casework as an individualized form of social
work and found it evolving with the years and becoming
focussed at the time of publication of *Social Diagnosis* in 1917,
when it was centered in the family and oriented to economic
need. By that time, "Society had a need to place outside of
itself those who were not economically successful, and employed
social caseworkers to see that it was not troubled by these
individuals and their families."[7] Social caseworkers were in a
position of conflict between this purpose and the needs of their
clients. Trained social caseworkers were for some time in the
stage next beyond that of volunteers, with many of the same
traditions, such as that they wanted to do good and were a little
ashamed of being paid for it. They felt a need to justify their
service by results in cure or prevention and hoped to segregate
the unhelpable so that they could seek out and deal with the
really worthwhile cases.

The First World War brought a movement toward democracy in social work. The Home Service of the Red Cross was
"*we* giving to *ours,* not one group handing down something
to another which was outside its self-defined community."[8]
Everyone, even the poorest, had some part in giving during the
war, "if only to sew, knit, or farm."[9] Out of the neuropsychi-
atric services in the army came a body of psychiatric knowledge
which was to be applied to personal problems in civilian life.
Psychiatric social work became within a decade "a new approach
to human beings and to every kind of problem which concerns
them."[10]

The postwar period was one of fear that people who had
begun to move and think in masses would not be silent about
very real wrongs. In addition to persecution of the foreign-
born, suppression of labor organizations, and the breaking of

strikes, the 1920's were famous for the cultivation of individual psychology. Was it a safer way to expend philanthropic funds to trace the sources of social unrest to psychopathic individuals rather than to allow attention to be turned to low wages, industrial accidents, poor housing, and inadequate health care?

If, nevertheless, psychiatric social work moved toward democracy in those years it was mainly for four reasons. First, it was serving a new middle-class clientele which could not be treated with condescension; second, it was dealing with emotional problems common to all classes in society; third, the *kind* of problem demanded emotional rapprochement between client and caseworker; and fourth, the new approach to behavior was scientific rather than moralistic. Coercion and superior attitudes became not so much wrong as simply silly.

While psychiatric workers were at first more or less isolated from those who dealt with economic problems, and awareness of the conflict inherent in their position came to them late, they were forced by the Depression to see that all caseworkers had the same difficulties, just as all types of agencies claimed their services. When public assistance became a battleground between forces upbuilding the morale of masses of unemployed people and forces organized against democracy, social workers had to ask themselves whom they were really serving. They had to be aware that the base of support for social work had widened to include the whole community, that government responsibility for mass need for subsistence was coming to be recognized, that taxation and the relation of taxes to ability to pay had an important bearing on welfare services, and that insurance was a sounder way of dealing with hazards affecting the whole population than was relief which could never be adequate to the need and was essentially demoralizing.

Social workers were learning slowly that community resistance to any kind of welfare measure was not due to ignorance which could be "interpreted" away, but was organized opposition based on centuries-old fear of the poor and of working people generally. Even psychiatric caseworkers could begin to see that their temporarily protected position did not guarantee them an opportunity to practice their profession ethically. While the separation between psychiatric (or intensive) caseworkers and the large numbers employed in public assistance and health programs seemed to be growing greater, nevertheless the struggle for democracy in social work practice, carried on by employee groups organized eventually into unions, benefited even the social workers who did not consider it "professional" to take part in such organized efforts.

To quote from the closing paragraphs of *Re-Thinking Social Case Work:*

"In reality the threat of the forces opposing democracy hangs over the field of private social work—a threat of control if not of financial obliteration. The Community Fund movement has by and large been under the leadership of the oligarchy of wealth. Increasingly, the professional group finds its standards challenged by organized business interests. The following are only a few instances: The objection to giving relief to strikers is a common issue. There is sometimes a demand for dismissal of a caseworker who has been too active in investigating cases of industrial disease. Manufacturing plants ask for names of clients who are their employees in order that they may check up on what "welfare work" they are getting done in return for their contribution to the Fund. Sometimes there is approval only for those subjects for research studies which do not concern themselves too much with wage rates and working conditions. These are interferences with practice which the ethics of no established profession would tolerate. Social caseworkers are increasingly being forced to choose between practicing their profession ethically (that is, refusing to use their clients for the interests of any other group) or becoming slavishly obedient to powerful forces which must in the end destroy every vestige of professional integrity.

"If private agency workers take the attitude that nothing can be done about these conditions, it is because they have not realized the power of organization which the forces opposing democracy know only too well. To resist alone is professional suicide. To resist in a strong protective organization inclusive of all who are employed in a given social service and allied with thousands of others in organized labor and professional workers' unions, is to have real effectiveness in the fight for democracy in the whole community. It is to belong to the whole community in a new and real sense. . . .

"What of the future? Social caseworkers have learned to respect the nature of man, to learn from it, and to follow it. They know that they may supplement—but never replace—the interplay of other forces within and without the person. They are looking up from their preoccupation with individuals to see what is happening to them, and to all of us, in society. They are beginning to see that we must build a good society on the same principles as those of good casework—mutual respect and co-operation. In such a society will there need to be any social casework? The question is immaterial if we remember that the citizens of that future society will decide. If they want it—a skilled professional service to supplement what friends can do for each other—they will undoubtedly provide for it."[11]

The rethinking of our professional theory and practice may seem, from this brief account of it, to have had two roots: its own professional development in a time of depression which forced new formulations under new conditions; and the Marxist science of society which guided the thinking of some of the leaders of the "rank-and-file" movement. In reality, these were not disparate influences but one. Our profession could not develop otherwise than in conformity with the laws of motion of human society in general. Either it would live out those laws in ignorance of them, and even in antagonism to them, or it would proceed with such understanding and conscious co-operation as serious study could make possible. Fortunately for social work in this critical period, it had come practitioners with Marxist vision and scientific understanding. That they were for the most part a young group, not "well fixed" professionally, did not destroy the vitality which they brought to the whole profession. The AASW took on new life under the stimulus of the union movement in social work. That I was one of the few older leaders who saw what the practitioner movement stood for and heartily supported it, meant to me a great privilege and an inescapable obligation. To the movement it meant added and most welcome reinforcement in the difficult pioneer work they were carrying forward. On my trips to visit students I found in each city groups eager to discuss professional standards in social work, as they related to the changing forces in world history, and the necessity for union organization to carry out our responsibility to protect standards of ethical practice.

While one cannot summarize in the compass of one volume what Marxist thinking brought to social work in this period, I can be specific about some ways in which its world outlook increased clarity of thought and personal and professional morale.

The Marxist outlook welcomed, instead of fearing, change. It found the world not a static interlocking of forces not to be disturbed, but an ongoing struggle of opposing forces being constantly resolved in syntheses which themselves gave rise to new opposing forces. We were familiar with this process in nature, positive and negative charges of electricity, opposing muscles playing against each other in our bodies, the upbuilding and dying of bodily cells which make up the balance we call life. We were familiar with the ambivalence of impulses in psychology, with the resulting choices partaking of both sets of desires. We had not dared to apply this principle to changes in economic systems, change being condemned by the public opinion of our day as unthinkable. Marxist science saw economic changes also as the inevitable result of constant movement and struggle of opposing forces, not to be deplored and impossible to prevent.

The thinking of our age (dominated by those most successful in a profit economy, those who could command the mass media of communication which form public opinion) was permeated by fear that change might be sudden and violent, brought on by "agitators," crackpot individuals who must be caught and disposed of in time if surface peace was to be maintained over the boiling caldron of exploitation and human misery. Marxist thinking was that the new grows in the womb of the old, accumulating by slow, gradual changes potentials of energy for change which burst out, when the time is ripe, in something new in quality—an irreversibly different phenomenon. We were familiar with that process in the change from chrysalis to butterfly and in the suddenness of the birth process after gestation. We knew that suddenness is not in itself destructive, except of the discarded integument of the old which is no longer of any use. In human society, change comes with violence only when elements of the old society create violence to hold back change and to preserve their privileged position. The goal of a Marxist scientist is to work for necessary change before hate and violence so accumulate between classes that destruction is inevitable.[12]

Marxist thinking heightened morale in this period in a threefold way. First, it increased a rational social responsibility while decreasing guilt. Our profession had a tradition strongly rooted in our religious heritage that we could be responsible for helping every needy case, and in some way, perhaps with divine assistance, righting in time every wrong.[13] Part of the destructive effect of a major depression was the crushing sense of need beyond any responsibility we could take. A scientific outlook measured need and resources by the yardstick of facts. Realistically, what needed to be done, and what did we have the forces to do? We could then be really responsible for what we could find the means to do.

Then, a Marxist outlook finally relieved us of the "Jehovah complex" which had always plagued our profession. It was not we, a handful of social workers, against a sea of human misery. It was humanity itself building dikes, and we were helping in our own peculiarly useful way. So we saw fellow workers in our clients, in labor unions, in organizations of all kinds for mutual betterment of conditions of living. We were not separate from but a part of the life of our time.

Morale received a great lift in times of discouragement from another Marxist principle—that measure of progress is not by what we see at a particular time, as if everything were static, but by the *direction of movement*. It is important to pay attention not to what is passing away, no matter how menacing and destructive it is, but to what is developing and coming to birth, no matter how weak it now appears. To understand the movement of social forces and their direction is precisely the reason why scientific study of history, past and current, is imperative.

The seething life of the 1930's was essentially a struggle for human welfare. If welfare was our business, here we were in the midst of it. In this period, there was shaping a polarization toward extremes with the democracies of the world being pulled both ways. The capitalist system could maintain itself and its trend toward monopoly only by extending itself to new sources of raw materials, new controls over cheap and docile labor, and new markets. The great powers were rivals for penetration of the undeveloped territories still remaining. Fascism was one extreme of the polarization, a drive to power through crushing all opposition and through war.

At the other pole was socialism, tried out first in one country which had shown in two decades that it was physically and economically viable, despite all that the rest of the world had tried to do to destroy it. It has been customary in our day to say that fascism and socialism are both dictatorships opposed to democracy and amount to the same thing.[13] Actually, the critical issue with regard to a dictatorship is *by whom* and *for whom*. Granted that in a time of sudden change some power has to assert itself to organize against chaos, shall it be a small group for its own interest or a majority of the people for the interest of the majority? A small private group fears the majority and uses all its power to suppress contrary action and even speech and thought. The first socialist country, with all the mistakes and crimes which accumulate in any country undergoing rapid change, followed a pattern which every country moving toward socialism since 1917 has also followed —a consistent pattern never seen in other dictatorships: universal education (schools set up before the battlefields were even cleared), universal health and welfare services (hospitals, public health measures, fair distribution of available food, and housing), universal arming of the population for militia service for defense (what other dictatorship ever dared!), equality of status for women and minority groups, no matter how backward (in the U.S.S.R. extension of full citizenship to tribes that had never had a written language!).

During the period under review, what we call the Western World tried to remain in ignorance of this new thing in dictatorship and the polarization between it and fascism. It was constantly defending and capitulating to fascism, spreading hatred against the Soviet Union and in our own country decrying any welfare measures that could be labelled "creeping socialism." The Roosevelt era was a brave attempt to make capitalist democracy workable by some welfare reforms called the New Deal. We saw them vanish one by one, even while President Roosevelt was alive. The hatred of the monied interests for this regime was in no way appeased by its moderation. In Germany, social work saw its gains of years destroyed under fascism, as the machinery of its welfare agencies was used to enforce Nazi decrees and to provide jobs for Nazi party supporters. The immediate issue in America was to understand our day and time, in our own country and all over the world, and learn how to serve the interests of our own people. Never had there been such need to know what we believed.

At the end of 1940 and early in 1941, *Social Work Today* began to publish a series of Credos in which persons in a variety of situations related to social work tried to express their most vital beliefs. A quotation from mine follows:

I BELIEVE

That is it possible to understand scientifically the movement of social and economic forces and to apply our strength in intelgent co-operation with them.

I BELIEVE

That the needs and desires, the feelings and the will to act, the strength to endure, and the power to change the conditions of their life are in people not only utterly real but indestructible.

I BELIEVE

That common experiences, common needs and aims make certain that in the long run men will work together instead of in competition to achieve their goals—theirs, not the goals of others for them.

I BELIEVE

That the fulfillment of individual life is in belonging with others who share the same purposes. In this relatedness an individual finds use for what is unique in him, responsibility which develops him, and a sharing which gives both glory and meaning to life.

These four articles of belief do not enter upon the field of religion in which there might be honest divisions among us and for which formulations of belief have come down through the ages. These are, however, a working equipment essential for living, I believe, in these difficult days. If liberals whom we once trusted say, in effect, that the world is utterly irrational and hell-bent for destruction, we need not believe them, for we see history while it works. If they wail that social planning is inevitable, but it means fascism, we see no necessity for a people's handing over the planning to its exploiters when it has the power to own and plan its resources for itself. To the cry that we are facing the end of "civilization as we know it," we reply that we have not yet seen what we call civilization here, but we hope to make it. If the fainthearted weep that war is inevitable and brings fascism and the blackout of all our liberties, we solemnly swear that we will prevent both if we can, but if the seeds of oppression which have been sown must be reaped in bitter sheaves, the workers of all countries will in the end make impossible ever again such sowing and reaping. We need not run and hide ourselves under stones to save our individual skins. If we do there are loathsome creatures under stones to receive us. We have the strength of millions. Oppression produces the resistance which will in the end overthrow it. Fear creates panic only at first. Then it disappears in the release of unimagined reserves of power. We have seen it in Spain and China, and we shall see more. We shall learn how to struggle when we care most what happens to all of us, and we know that all of us can never be defeated.[14]

CHAPTER 12

NEW DIRECTION

Early in November, 1934, I was in Washington attending a conference on parent education at which I was to discuss a paper. As I was more than usually nervous about my talk, I remember, I had gone to the Washington zoo to relieve my jitters by contemplation of the larger animals.[1] Then I had a talk with the executive of a family agency which disturbed me very much. He begged me to do something about an appalling situation—specifically, to help establish a training program for supervisors in social agencies. He pointed out what I already knew, that the weakest link in education for social work was not in theory (which the schools presented very well) but in application of theory to practice. Advance in the practice of social work was held back because caseworkers were pushed into supervision because of seniority or need of increase in salary, without training for the new responsibilities of teaching.

Mr. Kimball and I had been aware of this, and in the summer of 1932 I had been released from casework classes for two weeks to conduct a seminar on supervision. It was not long enough to prepare supervisors, and it broke the continuity of my courses undesirably. Clearly, I could not be spared, and neither I nor anyone else had made a thorough study of what was involved in preparing good caseworkers to become good teachers of practice. It was also clear that, if nothing was done, excellent theoretical teaching in professional schools would be

189

cancelled out by practice which could not rise much above the level of apprenticeship.

As I rode on the train to Baltimore that afternoon to visit an agency, I was mulling over this problem and, also, a dilemma which had faced us at Smith for some time. The School was growing. My way of teaching depended upon close attention to the development of each individual student, which meant much conference time outside of classes and a heavy load of visits and correspondence in winter sessions. Mr. Kimball and I had talked of dividing the work with an assistant,[2] but we both recognized an embarrassing fact. In a few years, without my wish or will, I had gained a "whale of a reputation." Mr. Kimball foresaw endless difficulties if the student body were divided between two of us unless the assistant had an approximately equal reputation. However, such a person should not be hampered by a coequal status with one whose ways of working might be different but should be free to develop the work in a leading position. Neither of us thought it practical to divide supervision of the students' growth on a time basis, leaving each to co-ordinate for a given class during part of the course. The dilemma had proved impossible to solve. I knew I could never change to a less individual way of teaching, yet every year the load for one person became more onerous.

Somehere on that journey to Baltimore the solution flashed into my mind. I was so excited that, when coming back to Washton, I let the train go off without me, arrived too late for dinner at the hotel, and dined on an avocado which I shall evermore associate with enthusiastic planning that lasted far into the night.

I am afraid I gave Professor Kimball the shock of his life when I wrote him next day resigning as Associate Director of the School so that he would be free to accept or reject the new proposal I had to make. For the School's present dilemma I suggested that a new Associate Director, bringing her own assistant, would be in a better position to divide the work and to develop the School, perhaps along lines different from those that had been appropriate in the decade that Mr. Kimball and I had worked together.

I then outlined a plan to which I wanted to give myself in my remaining years of service—the training of supervisors and teachers of social casework. I hoped that Smith would be interested in establishing such a course, but if not, I would try to find a sponsor somewhere. I pictured using the present Smith plan, living quarters for two summers on the campus, the summer teaching force with additions, and a winter field practice which could be carried on by the experienced people taking the course in their paid jobs, provided their agencies would allow them to supervise students or staff workers and to lead discussion groups. In this way costs for the School and for the students could be kept to a minimum. I outlined a course in supervision of casework practice which would include content of theory to be taught, and thought of one in group process, especially in relation to teaching by discussion. A course in psychiatry was desirable as a "refresher" and a guide to practice. Because public assistance was so much "the growing edge" of social work at that time, I wanted to add a course in economic principles as applied in social work. I hoped the students would "chase a problem through every one of the disciplines and find their answers in group thinking."

Mr. Kimball and Smith College accepted the plan and offered me the title of Associate Director in Charge of Advanced Courses. The course was to have the title of Plan D, following the other courses labelled A, B, and C. Mr. Kimball backed the plan liberally, rejecting some economies I had proposed, saying that it deserved the financial resources to do the best possible job. He had some misgivings about training students to teach too exclusively by the discussion method, for fear that groups would just get together "to share their ignorance." I thought that teaching by the lecture method could be learned as one learned how to handle subject matter in any familiar discipline and that the content of what was to be taught would also be included in the courses on how to teach it. In teaching by discussion, however, one had to come to grips with understanding the people to be taught and their difficulties in learning, so as to shape the subject to their needs.

It was November, and we had very little time if a radical addition to the Smith training program was to be incorporated in the catalogues which went to press in December for the following summer. We met and conferred intensively over questions ranging from the choice of an associate director to the assembling of the new faculty. The source of a leader for the course on group teaching was a real problem. The choice lay between educators, many of whom used a subject-centered rather than group-centered education and experts in group process who might not be conversant with educational principles. We wanted both, and finally drew from the parent-education field Dr. Muriel Brown of Rochester, New York. Her knowledge of group process could be applied both to teaching and to conducting of staff and board meetings and client groups in social agencies. For economics, we found Miss Elsie Gluck, Ph.D. from the University of Wisconsin, who had had some experience with labor education in economic problems. I would teach casework supervision and co-ordinate the other disciplines around their application to it. For psychiatry, we secured Dr. Evelyn Alpern of the Institute of the Pennsylvania Hospital, Philadelphia. Since there would be no senior seminar the first summer, I would take Dr. Brown's course in group process to prepare to supervise the students' winter practice in leading discussion groups. We hoped to assemble a class of about twenty-five trained and experienced caseworkers for this new kind of education. Something had been worked out to give training in supervision at the Pennsylvania School but nowhere else as far as we knew.

One of the major questions was what we had to teach. My research, that winter of 1934-35, was concerned with the perennial question: What is social casework? In the past few years identification of social casework as a modified form of psychotherapy had been gaining ground in the schools and in the larger cities of the East where psychiatrists were available and where the intellectual centers of the profession of social work were located. Year by year, as more psychiatrists found placement throughout the country (especially after the Nazi regime drove out many of the best psychoanalysts in the world), the movement in social work toward psychotherapy spread to the Middle- and far-Western states.

At Smith we had already made a choice of a sort. We would not limit the definition of casework to what could be done solely in consultation resembling therapy, in agencies which offered supervision by psychiatrists. We expected to educate students for the whole field called social work and were already taking public assistance agencies into our area of responsibility. We could not teach solely a casework that was alien to the situation of the majority of social agencies or that was limited to long-term, intensive treatment when only short contacts were possible in many places. I was convinced (as the studies of previous winters had shown) that social casework was a *quality* of service to people, not dependent on quantity of time expended. Psychotherapy was also a quality, even though it was usually undertaken only when more time was available than was frequently offered in a casework agency. How could the two be distinguished from each other? I suspected not only a different preparation for a caseworker or a therapist but a different *relationship* to the person to be helped. This was not a matter to be settled theoretically. It had to be lived through in practice. How could I experience the *feel* of the difference between a casework relationship and that of a psychotherapist to a patient?

An unusual opportunity presented itself in dual form. Dr. David Levy had developed, even before the Institute for Child Guidance had closed, a procedure called Attitude Therapy, in which he believed psychiatric social workers could be trained. It selected certain problems concerned with the patient's social relationships, selected certain patients ascertained to be free from psychotic or serious neurotic illness, and certain workers

who were qualified by psychiatric training and experience to be
prepared for this special therapeutic work. His seminar in Attitude Therapy included supervision of the cases they were working with, through discussion of detailed records of interviews.
I could be admitted to this seminar if I could arrange an experience with attitude therapy. One requirement was that the patient
share in the decision to undertake this and understand that it
was *not* a psychoanalysis and what limitations were involved.

At the same time, through the social service department of
the New York Psychiatric Institute, I found a patient in a
peculiarly open situation. A young woman in her middle thirties,
single, intelligent, and eager for help, had been under psychiatric
therapy for three years with a psychiatrist who was now leaving the staff. There was no psychiatrist available to take on
this patient, and there was some doubt whether it was indicated
to continue the same plan of treatment. Problems of social adjustment adequate to return to full-time employment as a secretary and problems of personal relationships were still evident.
The hospital had nothing further to offer and was willing to
refer the patient for attitude therapy under Dr. Levy's direction
if he approved and she desired it.

In our getting-acquainted interview, I talked over fully with
the patient what we could offer within limits of time, since I
must leave New York in four months. I think we planned for an
hour's interview twice a week. I tried to make as clear as possible what social casework help with her employment and personal problems would be like, or the alternative of a special
form of psychotherapy which would be different from the "talking-out" which she had experienced with the psychiatrist who,
she felt, had understood her, although her symptoms had not
changed very much. She preferred attitude therapy to social
casework, saying she knew something about the latter, having
worked as a secretary in a social agency. She thought she could
do for herself whatever casework could do for her. She felt
her troubles involved her feelings more deeply. The nature
of the supervision given to my work in attitude therapy was

explained to her. She thought she might gain substantial help in the time available.

The results of the four months of work with this patient were not conclusive, nor could they be expected to be. I found it a useful experience *not* to do what I would have considered essential in a casework relationship, i.e., to focus upon stimulating the patient's awareness and active participation in fulfilling her role in her life situation, or, if necessary, changing that role. I had the conscious experience of focussing upon the patient's psychic life, her desires and attitudes, and how she might enter into better relationships with people in her work and family environment. Whether this approached a psychotherapeutic relationship, even under the guidance of Dr. Levy's seminar, I cannot be sure. It seemed to me that both the patient and I were so conditioned by our past experience that we could not approach this one with the freshness which would be desirable. She had found satisfying the opportunity to talk of her feelings in the previous therapy and showed some resentment at my tendency to press toward some resolution of her conflicts. In this mood she took action in joining a discussion group where she felt she would get help. I, on the other hand, could see in myself the caseworker's ineradicable perception of action possibilities. I welcomed the patient's joining a study group as a more *social* solution than endless individual talking-out, yet I also saw it as another escape into talking rather than facing her problems with the mind-set of doing something about them. I do not think I grasped adequately the therapeutic problems in the case, and it is possible that this patient could not be reached by the kind of therapy that could be offered. I do not know what the net result was for her. For me, the experience was useful if mainly in broadening and deepening my conception of casework, which I was trying in this instance *not* to use.

During this winter, I looked forward with keen anticipation to the first summer's work with Plan D. For ten years I had been learning how to teach what I firmly believed was an art, based upon somewhat undeveloped sciences. Now there would be a group learning together and sharing experiences. We would have the advantage of years of study of psychiatry as it had been applied to casework. Its possibilities in application to teaching casework had scarcely begun to be tapped, and I believed they were impressive. Learning could be studied as it takes place in whole persons, not in disembodied intellects. Guidance of learning could use the skills we had developed in helping clients to master their life situations, but with fascinating differences as we prepared people to help others to grow. It was an uncharted course over which we proposed to sail, but we had some valued instruments in psychiatric studies and casework experience to guide us.

CHAPTER 13

LEADERS AND TEACHERS

The Smith College School for Social Work opened its summer session in 1935 with memorable changes. The new Associate Director was Miss Annette Garrett, a graduate of the School with rich experience in the field of school counselling and at the Judge Baker Foundation Clinic in Boston. For the summer, for casework teaching in collaboration with Miss Garrett and Cornelia Hopkins Allen, the School was fortunate in securing Miss Florence Day, Field Secretary of the Family Service Association of America, who was destined to follow Mr. Kimball, some years later, as Director. The Plan D course for supervisors and teachers of social work was launched with a faculty of four, teaching casework supervision, group process, psychiatry, and economics.

For the first time since its inception, the School could not be housed in the twin dormitories, Northrop and Gillett, which were due for renovation. Two of the campus houses were used for the main school, and Plan D students and those coming for the two-week seminars were located in Chapin House, perched on a little hill overlooking the College Garden and Paradise Pond. Our association with the seminar students added stimulus to the meal hours and moments of relaxation at the house.

The twenty-five students who composed the first class of Plan D were as conscious of their pioneer role as were the sixty who made up the School in 1918. They were given much less in the way of lectures containing new information, and

more responsibility in shaping the new course as their experience
in casework made them aware of their needs. Perhaps half their
number had had some experience in supervision. The others
were making the transition from doing casework to the new
approach necessary for teaching it. Several of the group were
graduates of the Smith School whom I had known as students
before.

One of the things which intrigued me that first summer was
the difference of my relationship to the student group from
what I had known as a teacher of casework. They were still
individuals to me, but also fellow workers united as a group
in a more conscious common purpose to prepare for leadership.
They had different educational problems. Some resisted preparing to become leaders when they preferred to be followers
or to have an exciting educational experience for themselves
without thought of how to pass it on. They did very little
consulting individually since they had an instrument which
they were learning to use for resolution of difficulties—that of
group discussion. I was one of the group, yet more challenged
to see that the group had a worthwhile experience in exploring
a new field.

Probably many of the difficulties the faculty faced that first
summer could be traced to our lack of clarity about our role,
as between active givers and passive guides of the eager
curiosity of this unique group of learners. We were conscious
that we were dealing with experienced adults who should be
able to help us formulate the best curriculum for their needs.
Undoubtedly we overestimated their capacity for this, just as
I had overestimated in my early teaching the students' capacity
for independent thought. This was most evident in economics,
the newest subject to all of us, and the one whose applications
to casework as we knew it were least clear. Miss Gluck did not
know casework and depended on the class for questions about
economics which they were unable to ask. At that time, the
students and faculty alike were absorbed in study of "the democratic process" in Miss Brown's course and put it to the test

in their other courses. The faculty were prepared to receive a lot of suggestions as to how a course should be conducted, but learned, as the students learned, that some subjects are more appropriate than others to be thrown open to discussion by the whole group and that there are administrative decisions that are best made as such, smoothing the way for discussion and resolution of those problems in which the whole group is concerned in some significant way.

There were periods of mounting tension over the "passivity" of the faculty, which were often resolved in laughter and in trying a new approach. Dr. Alpern's class, for instance, went into a hilarious outburst of new understanding when a student suddenly exclaimed, "I see now what you are trying to do. You want us to have a natural birth, and we're all yelling for a Caesarean." In economics class it was finally agreed that what we all needed was a series of background lectures out of which could come our questions about taxation, living standards, relief budgets, and the like.

We did indeed "chase a problem through every discipline." We faculty members who took each others' courses had to learn, also, how to behave. Having experienced the dismay felt by a teacher who is working a class slowly toward seeing a point for themselves and who finds the bright faculty auditor leaping ahead to that very point, each of us pledged that we, as auditors, would not participate except as we could contribute a pertinent illustration here and there. We also found it more profitable to audit courses from the angle of studying teaching method rather than expressing our own knowledge of the subject matter.

The whole theory of the course was that casework is an art, based upon whatever science has been developed in our field. We were far ahead of the first schools at the turn of the century, but admittedly we had made too little use of sociology, economics, and anthropology, in our intense concentration upon psychology and psychiatry. Whatever science we had, we must know thoroughly and must try to apply more adequately. In our study of the process of teaching and learning, we found a wealth

of resources in the psychological principles we were familiar
with in casework. We were often chagrined to find how little
we had applied what we knew about people (and could use
when they were in the client relationship) to staff and administrative relationships and interagency contacts. Still less
had we learned to apply such principles in teaching through
supervision. We had many problems to discuss about relationships to authority, for instance, the authority of position and
that of expert knowledge and experience. We had to learn the
right balance of listening and talking, of taking in and giving
out, in relation to what was happening in the lives of the people
with whom we were working.

Even under the pressures of that first summer, I began a
collection of experiences of teachers of other arts for comparison with the art of casework. We discussed painting, music,
novel-writing, dramatics, and how these were taught.[1] I was
eventually to find, for instance, at the Rhode Island School of
Design, a method of teaching that releases the rigidities and
suppressed fears of pupils, so that first of all, they can let
themselves go and express creative ideas without fear. Contact
with art teaching in progressive schools also taught me that
relaxation is only the beginning. It must be followed by disciplined study of the rules of good work or the child loses
interest and has no urge to develop beyond what he can do
naively. At Smith we were feeling out the arts as an important
part of the art of living a well-rounded life and helping others
to achieve it in their own circumstances and with their own
goals.

Two instances illustrate how study of the arts was interwoven with our educational experience. One student had not
come by choice but because she was led to believe that her job
depended upon her qualifying as a supervisor. She volunteered
to take shorthand notes of the class discussion which, it soon
became evident, she was using as an escape from dealing actively
with the subject matter. Then one day we discussed self-expression in the arts, and this member of the class blossomed into

full participation, because she had an artist friend who had taught her much. Another student who had great difficulty in expressing herself took to drawing as a means of release when she was preparing to write a paper and carried this further in an art class in the winter session. When it was asked of us, in mid-session, at the time of the Supervisors' Conference of the School, that we prepare a statement of what we were doing in Plan D, the group produced, co-operatively, a little drama called, "The Fireless Cooker," in which they showed the changes in their thinking in those few weeks.

What was the fireless cooker—an instrument now as obsolete as the horseless carriage? It was an insulated chest in which containers of food were placed on discs of hot soapstone, after being partly cooked over a flame, to continue a process of long, slow cooking. The pressure cooker, of course, rendered this procedure obsolete. Our use of the term, "the fireless cooker," as a symbol of a learning process and teaching method, went back to a psychological principle which was called in my college days "unconscious cerebration." It referred to the continued functioning of the brain in periods of rest and even sleep after hard thinking has been applied to a problem. Solutions do not come of themselves; the hard work has to take place; but then one need not stop and perhaps abandon a problem in frustration. Nature will work with us if we allow time for the readjustments in mind and emotions which are necessary before a workable solution can be achieved. So we learned to wait and to say when baffled, "Let's put it in the fireless cooker now that we have gone as far as we can, and perhaps new light will come in another connection some other day." This meant that we were not limited to attacking problems that were already so well solved that the faculty could deliver them neatly packaged in lecture form. We tackled everything, including many unsolved relationships between social work and the world around it and, if we were baffled, were able to turn to other work and trust time to do something for us. Surprisingly, it often did and sooner than we expected.

Many of us got the subject of "relationship" in the learn-ing-teaching process into our bone and sinew through the experience of swimming together at Pine Lake at recreation time. Those who had not learned to swim because of fear of the water were being taught by the others. Several got the thrill of swimming alone for the first time. "I knew my teacher was right there and she would not let me drown." It was a "rela-tionship" giving courage to try something new.

Many in the course gained new confidence in themselves through finding that, as a group working together, we could always be sure that something good would come out of this number of minds. "You can always trust a group" replaced the fear of frozen silence or of group domination with which most of us had come to the experience. To some of us, a group working together had meant fear of a struggle for personal prestige, which we could now forget about as we took part in group thinking under good leadership.

In all our studies of casework process and of group process there was involved an element of timing. How could we get rapport with a client quickly, bearing in mind that a short con-tact might be all that we would have? How could we gain in work with groups that prompt welding of divergent interests and perhaps conflicting feelings, which would ensure a profit-able working together of group and leader? We developed for both situations a conscious use of what we called "the type situa-tion."[2] In studies of short contact interviewing we had found the process of getting acquainted much shortened by using as background all we knew, all we could presently observe or infer about the *situation* of the person before us.[3] How would *any-body* react to being sixteen and in conflict with parents? To being unemployed after eighteen years in one job? To offer ing a home to a foster child and perhaps being turned down?

In gaining rapport with a new group, what did we know about them already as to age, sex, occupation, the kind of com-munity they lived in, and special points of sensitivity in relation to subject matter or leader? If all we knew was that a certain

group was middle-aged then what could they have done with
their time?

This search for and correlation of knowledge of background
is to be sharply distinguished from making snap judgments on
the basis of stereotyped ideas as to what people of a certain
age, sex, occupation, or nationality are like. No one knows
better than a caseworker how differently individuals react to
what seem like similar situations (or is it that their inner
differences make the situations different?). What we gain by
awareness of the type-situation is a flexible understanding of
background and how most people would react to it, open to
correction as one is told and observes more. With this understanding, the interviewer or group leader is freed to explore
further the individual differences of the people concerned from
the expected reactions. It is not only that time is saved when
rapport with person or group is gained quickly. The whole relationship is enriched to a more imaginative dealing with
constructive possibilities in the situation.

We spent some time in collecting what the Plan D group could
contribute of type-situations such as: What does it mean to
grow up in an Orthodox Jewish home? To be the only girl in
a family of six to eight boys? To be the wife of a nightworker
on changing shifts? To live in a wheel chair? We learned not
only to sense situations but to distinguish in them what is inescapably sure to be there and what is put into them by individual reactions which may be subject to change.

The study of education in groups reflected back a new illumination upon our casework thinking. We began to see that it
is only by an artificial abstraction that we ever think we are
dealing with individuals alone. Even when social casework
contributes most fruitfully to a person's better adjustment,
probably nine-tenths of his problem solving is done in groups
in the process of living, and it is to group relationships that
he must take his released or enriched self. Family casework is
group work, really. We isolate an individual for treatment
only temporarily and with great risk that what we thought

was excellent work will be undone in the complex of family relationships. In medical social work we find our patient perhaps literally isolated in a hospital, but our major task is to keep him connected with his normal life in groups and return him to it. In child-placing we are constantly beset by the problems a child faces in being part of two family groups, either or both of which may be damaging to him. So it was that experience in Plan D touched off studies not only of teaching by group discussion but of the interrelations of social casework and social group work.

During the winter of 1935-36 I was able to work as volunteer assistant to an experienced leader of a girls' group in the New York City YWCA. Here was a different kind of group process from teaching by discussion. It was leadership to insure that a social group was actively social and achieved what its members desired in recreation and fellowship.

The next winter brought a unique opportunity. A new graduate school of social group work was being formed at Temple University, in Philadelphia, and I was asked to teach a course relating group work to social casework, as this involved referrals between agencies of the two types and as group workers might need to understand and counsel with individuals, while maintaining their role as leaders of groups. The course was to be offered the second semester, and I was attracted to it first of all by finding in the planning for it the same principles of dealing with people and of open-minded exploration which we felt to be characteristic of Smith. I said I would accept provided that, as preparation for it, I could meet with representatives of the group agencies of the city who were backing the school and learn from them how they envisioned the course and what problems they found in their staff and volunteer workers, to which training might be directed.

The seminar so organized ran from November to February, when the course with students at the School was to begin. It was an extraordinarily useful sharing of experience, starting with a frank facing of the misunderstandings common between the two fields. I began with two questions. First, did they like the term "casework" with which the projected course was to be concerned, or did they prefer some other, such as "counselling"? This brought out negative feelings such as that casework is associated with callousness, remoteness, "charity," disregard of personal privacy, and association with dependency. Second, are these qualities inherent in casework, or do they seem so, due to bad practice? The group began to find evidence of similar characteristics in different forms in group work and finally concluded that they were not inherent in either setting, but remediable.

In succeeding sessions they charted problems to be covered by the course, keeping in mind that group work was still using volunteers largely for leadership of groups and that the students taking the course would be quickly placed in supervisory positions. An amusing incident occurred on the day the seminar group took me to visit several agencies. When I asked one staff worker what problems his group leaders brought to him, for which a course might be helpful, he replied, "They wouldn't think of bringing any. Either they get rapport with their groups, or they don't and we get rid of them." When the course at Temple University finally started, it had the backing of the leaders of the group agencies of the city, and its prospectus was closely related to real, day-to-day problems.

The winter sessions in Plan D were as exciting as the summer ones. The first year the students were found to be working in eighteen different cities, some familiar to me because of Smith placements there and others quite new. Communications with students were kept wide open between the fall and spring visits. First, they reported monthly on their course of background reading—"Economics, Government, Medicine, Psychiatry, Sociology and Social Casework," to quote the curriculum of Course 72 which carried six hours of credit. Reports also came from the students on their work in supervision and their leadership of a group. I replied with individual letters of comment and by a series of monthly mimeographed Notes, distilling from the reports and my own reading and experiences whatever might be stimulatingly interesting to the whole group. Even now, after twenty years, I find those Notes live reading.

A third course, Bulletin number 70, was hard to describe. It was not a research study in any formal sense, though it did involve investigating something new and writing a report about it. Its subject was to be selected for its relatedness to social work and yet its difference from it. Perhaps I had best quote from a discussion of it in the monthly Notes for January, 1938:

"There is no one word that describes Course 70. The phrases 'an exercise in perspective' and 'a cure for myopia' are only fairly good. They do imply that there is more all around us than we ordinarily see, and that we do not always get what we see into relation to the whole of which it is a part. . . .

"Why do we register only the tiniest fraction of the stimulation that comes to us through our senses? The answer, 'We would be exhausted if we did (see more),' is so obvious that we take for granted that it is a mark of maturity to shut out all but what is relevant for the purposes of the individual. The very young give themselves up to seeing, hearing, touching, tasting and smelling everything that comes their way. Only they and those who have no purposes or have not the mental equipment to be selective are interested, so we say, in collecting sense impressions indiscriminately.

"One of the major changes which occurs when a young person emerging from adolescence enters a school for professional training in social work is the taking on of new areas of purpose and interest. The 'professional self' must become sensitive to observe things which had no relevance for a child or college student. Those of us who try to enlarge a student's powers of observation realize that even at age twenty-two the process of organizing the self around a limited range of interests has gone a long way. Now the student of social work is called upon to see things as the mother of a large family sees them, as a longshoreman sees them, as a tubercular patient sees them. In the course of every day's practice there are new areas of life opened up in which attentive observation is not only relevant but demanded. No wonder that students sometimes feel as if they would burst, lose their identity, become a hundred selves and no self. You are guiding your students through that period. How have you come through it yourselves?

"Limitation to what is relevant to us is quite normal and necessary. The penalty is what every person pays as he grows older—becoming less able to see new things, to be alive in new ways. Do we have to economize energy, however, to anything like the degree to which habit and laziness impel us when we take the easiest, because the most familiar road? The tragedy in our profession is that, if we let ourselves get rigid, we cramp instead of stimulating the people with whom we work. . . . Our art demands, then, that we take 'corrective exercises' for the particular blindnesses which our very devotion to our work may produce.

"Course 70 cannot be an elaborate activity since it has to be an interest carried along by a busy person so as not to interfere with the mainstream of occupation. It is best that it be something simple enough to be a sample of what anyone may do continuously to keep fresh streams of interest flowing into a life that is apt to become clogged with detail. It may have some relation to social work (as what has not?) but it is better that it should not be just another way of being a social worker all the time. One of the D's has been wondering where the goods come from that she buys every day, and how to trace them to their source and the people who produce them. Another is studying what horse racing means to her community. Another looks for migration streams from the rural South into her city. Won't you all let me know by the February reports what you have found to look at with your Course 70 field glasses?"

There was notable progression through the nine months of the winter session. Supervisors could see their students or staff workers growing in ability to use supervision to develop their own art of social casework. Since most of the groups which they led held together only for six to eight weeks, the Plan D students formed a second group in the late winter and spring, in which they experienced the joy of being much more comfortable and finding their group more responsive and productive than the first.

The second summer brought one unforeseen problem. The students who had not met for nine months, but had had individual counselling, came back, apparently, with the unconscious expectation that the discussions of the summer would be directed to their personal concerns. They resisted participation in forming an agenda for the course and for a few weeks were obviously not inclined to "become a group." Then, to their own amusement one day when there were visitors, they suddenly drew together in resistance to those outsiders and worked together as a team thereafter.

Certain changes in curriculum from session to session showed progression. A teacher of casework was added to the staff to give the "refresher" course that all the students felt they needed to be surer of what they had to teach. After two winters of study, I taught the course in group-process-for-teaching, as well as the one in supervision for both juniors and seniors, so as to relate it closely to our needs. Visiting lecturers from the fields of progressive education and social group work made up a two-hour course. Economics was changed to a course in economics and government, and a course was added on administrative problems of social agencies, taught by a hospital superintendent and the teacher of casework.

Late in August, 1937, Mr. Kimball announced to me the closing of Plan D as soon as the class which entered that summer should graduate, that is, in a year. He had come to the decision painfully, giving as reason that the course had not attracted a sufficient number of qualified students to justify its expense. I knew that the real reason was deeper, in differences between us not only on methods of work but on basic principles, and I had already decided, as painfully, that I could not continue. Mr. Kimball believed that the School should return to being a leader in teaching a conception of casework which he defined in a more isolated sense than I found possible. For me, it would have been a step backward to keep casework out of relation to social living in groups or unconnected with the social movements of people, solving their own problems in a time of rapid change. Even if I had wished to do so, it was impossible for me to wipe out an integration of life and practice which was my most real self and, I believed, my only contribution to the world of my time.

These were honest differences which I was most anxious that the alumnae of the School should understand, to prevent the possibility that my leaving might touch off the formation of factions around unsubstantiated rumors of rivalries and personality clashes. Mr. Kimball and I agreed thoroughly that the School was more important than either of us and that the loyalty of the alumnae to the School should be strengthened and not be dependent on ties to either of us personally. I wrote this to President Neilson and to the Alumnae Association, urging that the School needed closer bonds with the College, with the whole field of social work, and its own graduates. Actually the discussions of this period did result in a reorganization of the Alumnae Association, so that it became a much more vital force in the life of the School.

For the remaining time, Mr. Kimball and I continued to co-operate as always. I remember that, in answering letters from alumnae asking why I was leaving, we had different answers to give, but we dictated both in the same office and mailed them in the same envelope. After the closing was settled, Plan D was carried through a third year which I found in many ways the best of all. For the last summer, we took in a one-session group in supervision which was an inspiring gathering of experienced people.

Plan D was an experiment which went to other places in modified form, shedding some of its mistakes on the way. It was the most vital educational experience of my own life, and to this day its members write to me and say to others that it meant more to them than any other. I shall always be grateful for those three years of rare opportunity.

CHAPTER 14

TEACHER ON WHEELS

One early morning in August, 1937, I lay in bed asking myself, "What next?" I knew I was committed to developing leaders in social work, but had no illusions that I could do so without the sponsorship of some educational institution, or that, with my lack of a graduate degree, I could knock on the doors of any. I was burdened by a sense that social workers everywhere needed help as they faced almost insurmountable difficulties, problems of theoretical clarity as well as of practice. Most of them could not leave their jobs. Perhaps experience was destined to be their teacher, if only they could have the lift, the illumination here and there that would help them to think about their jobs for themselves. If I could only go to them! I had done a great deal of institute teaching while I was at Smith. Could I ever make a living doing just that? I believed I might so organize professional counselling for social agencies that I could. I rolled over in bed and said three decisive words: "Well, I will!"

Some time in the fall I met at a conference Miss Leah Feder of the George Warren Brown Department of Social Work, Washington University, St. Louis, who inquired about my leaving the Smith College School. By February it was settled by conferences with Dr. Frank J. Bruno, Director of that school, that I was to go there as visiting lecturer for one academic year, to give a course for supervisors before launching my plan for self-employed counselling.

The situation in St. Louis was interestingly different from that of the Smith College School which drew students from a nation-wide area and could direct their work in a variety of cities. St. Louis had a relatively small group of social workers in a one-city setting. Mr. Bruno and I realized that the course must be shaped for the needs of that city, and, if workers were to be given time to take it, must offer the agencies something tangible in return. So the school made the following offer:

Classes in theory of supervision would be given at the University three times a week, open only to qualified students who enrolled for the whole program.

Supervised practice in supervision would involve weekly reports in writing to Miss Reynolds, and return comments in writing would be received from her. Once a month a two-hour individual conference with Miss Reynolds would be scheduled.

For each student of supervision sent by an agency, two hours of Miss Reynolds' time per month could be used as the agency desired, either in a seminar with the staff or in case-reading and individual consultations. Several agencies sent two students, one, four and one, six, so that they had time for a substantial amount of educational service.

There were precautions to be observed in a social work community so small that everything was talked over and apprehension could spread like morning mist. Social agencies might well fear that a counselor at the school would be telling their workers what to do on cases. Students and staff workers might worry lest their mistakes in casework become teaching examples in class and their fellow workers recognize who was who. So we began, with the earliest publicity about the course, to stress the difference between educational and clinical or administrative use of case examples. Discussions in classes, based on other than local cases, would be related to what we could learn rather than what should be done. Those who were to be supervised by members of the course were assured that while supervision notes were kept, no one would see them except supervisor and instructor. The meetings with agency groups did much to

create a general feeling of community participation in the
project.

That year in St. Louis was a very happy one for me personally. I had excellent health after surgery had relieved long-
standing physical handicaps. I lived in a pleasant one-room
apartment overlooking a row of poplar trees and the morning
sky. I had a most friendly and stimulating group to work with
and a challenging experience with varied types of casework
agency, from a large teaching hospital to the newly-merged
childrens' and family agency. The year was at the same time a
tragic one, being the year of Hitler's advance helped on by
the appeasement offered by the European nations and the betrayal of democracy at Munich which many people actually
believed would produce "peace in our time."

St. Louis was an interesting city to meet, after living in the
New England tradition and in the sparkling formlessness of
New York City. Walking about St. Louis streets and meeting
its people, one could sense its ties with the South and those
of the pioneer West, its relatedness to the great river, to the
conservative rural state behind it, to the mountain folk in the
Ozarks who were constantly drifting into the city slums to
work at low wages and drifting back to the mountains again,
perhaps to die of tuberculosis while others took their places.
Wages were always low, because St. Louis drew its labor from
Negro and mountain workers who had had much less or were
banned from earning more. Industries moved here (like shoe
manufacturing from my New England state) to take advantage of cheap, unorganized labor. The standards of public assistance were appalling (in refusal of aid to able-bodied men,
for instance, whether or not there was work to be had), yet
Missouri, dominated by rural counties, could never see St.
Louis as benefactor to unemployed people whom the farms
could use in season as underpaid labor and forget for the rest
of the year.

That was the period of agricultural readjustment when
government payments to farmers for reduction of planted

acreage were not extended to tenant farmers, in many cases, but tenants-on-shares were suddenly declared wage laborers, employed for a pittance, and then ordered to leave the farms after the crops were in. In Missouri a group of Negro and white dispossessed families had camped in the bitter cold of winter on the side of the Federal highway, challenging their government to put them off. I attended a mass meeting on Sunday afternoon, January 22, 1939, to consider what could be done for these homeless people. I believe the Farm Resettlement Authority finally placed them on government land. The episode, not an isolated one, emphasized the need of organization of white and Negro workers, but any form of organization was bitterly fought by planters throughout the South. The Southern Tenant Farmers' Union had its baptism of fire in beatings, evictions, and lynchings during that period.

Two experiences with areas of need and of effort not reached by professional social work stand out in my memories of that fruitful year. One was an Easter weekend visit to Delta Farm, a co-operative in Hillhouse, Mississipi, south of Memphis. Some twenty-four Negro and white families who had been forced to camp on the highway because of participation in the Southern Tenant Farmers' Union had been settled in 1936 on two thousand acres purchased for a co-operative by a group of Southern men. They were led by Sam Franklin, a former missionary to Japan. This producers' and consumers' co-operative was founded on four principles: economic efficiency (using government experts in agronomy, lumbering, etc.), building a socialized economy of abundance, interracial justice (Negro and white families in equal numbers and sharing equally), and "realistic religion as a social dynamic." I visited the Farm as guest of a St. Louis friend who had worked there as Director of Religious Education.

As we rode through the rich agricultural lands of the Mississipi delta, I saw the homes of the white farmers, no better than a workman's bungalow in the North yet so infinitely better than the windswept board shacks of Negro laborers that I could not but wonder, "How much *fear* does it take to maintain this disparity without visible outbreaks of violence?" I can still see against the pale sky at dawn the forms of Negro laborers riding or driving mules, going to work in the cotton fields.

At Delta Farm, life was primitive but full of hope. Homes of some thirty families were lined up, Negro and white on opposite sides of a ravine. The Negro homes were noticeably poorer, not by design, I am sure, but probably because Negro workers were less often equipped with skilled trades that netted more in the co-operative's system of payments. People of both races had come illiterate and were studying at night school. The Farm had a supplementary school for Negro children, who were denied equal opportunities by the State, and was beginning to supply medical service which was not available in the area.

Social life was kept separate as Mississippi law required. At church services, Negro and white people sat on separate sides of the room. Easter parties for the children were segregated. However, at a business meeting of the governing Council which I attended after church, Negro and white members seemed to participate equally.

The Farm attributed its survival for three years to its having dealt fairly with its neighbors and paid cash for everything it bought. I doubted if compromise on social equality could save it in that region if it challenged the economic exploitation of Negro and white laborers on which the social system rested. Eventually, it seemed that the race issue would be used to destroy it, despite all efforts to conform with regional mores and despite its origin in Southern philanthropy. It was still a heartening demonstration of what self-help, rooted in hope, can do to release energies and develop talents in depressed peoples. I do not know to this day what became of this little island of hope and courage.

The other experience was a five-hundred-mile bus trip over the Memorial Day weekend from St. Louis into the Ozark mountains at Mena, Arkansas. This time, I went alone but with previous knowledge of Commonwealth College, a labor school, of which the Director was Rev. Claude Williams[1] who had visited St. Louis that winter and invited me to come. Mena was in an all-white county of Arkansas where signs had been posted on the roads warning, "N——r, don't let the sun go down and find you in this county." Interestingly enough, the history of these "white" counties was of people driven from the rich bottomlands by the plantation slave economy, who protected their mountain farms from contact with slavery by banning Negro migration into their territory. Commonwealth was the successor of a socialist colony formerly in Louisiana, now devoted to the rising movement for organization of the most exploited laborers of both races in the South. While it had to be all-white in student body, its principles were those of interracial equality and uncompromising struggle for social justice. I was there long enough to attend some classes and feel the spirit of the school in its group singing. There I met Miss Winifred Chappell, who had gone to visit the place for a brief rest and had stayed four years. She had been a staff worker and writer for the Methodist Federation for Social Service in New York. At Commonwealth, she taught political economy and current events and was the friend and counselor of everyone on the place. She became one of my own dearest friends.

Commonwealth was a second illustration[2] of contact with grass-roots movements that were reaching out to the causes of the human misery that social work attempts to relieve. Its message was one of *organization* of workers for their own protection, not excluding the most exploited. The movement for organization in those years was clear that *all* workers must be organized. Racial divisions could only work to the advantage of exploitation.

Back in St. Louis, many of the problems with which social workers struggled had their roots in just the conditions I glimpsed so briefly. The private agencies were turning families in need toward public assistance, which was so inadequate in coverage that private social service could not do the job it had theoretically chosen—to give counselling service to people able to choose and to use it. The mental hygiene approach was growing vigorously, and private agencies had begun to use psychiatrists as consultants, in the absence of a sufficient number of clinical facilities in the city. There was much groping to find the real function of private family service.

The agencies were greatly concerned for the children in the city slums which were deteriorating, as families who could afford it moved to the suburbs in St. Louis County and took their taxes with them. One discussion, I remember, had reached an enthusiastic proposal for a block-by-block organization of parent-counselling on children's behavior problems in a Negro district. It stopped cold when a Negro family caseworker from the district brought out a few facts: that many mothers had to leave home at five in the morning to cook breakfast in suburban homes; that children of all ages were left to get themselves to school, or to stay with other children, or with women too feeble to go out to work; that often mothers did not return from work until long after the children's normal bedtime; that children had no hot meals, no guidance. Could counselling of mothers who had to exist in that fashion and who loved their children do anything but increase guilt and resentful despair?

After this, I saw differently the pleasant homes in the University district and the richly gardened suburbs of the city. It was good that women there had time to be with their children and to be active in civic organizations in which they could be very useful. The cost was paid by Negro women, robbed of their motherhood, and children, losing their heritage of health and guidance and even of a sense that anybody loved them. Surely a civilization does not have to exact such a price for its "gracious living"!

Another contrasting impression came from a discussion on volunteers in one of my groups. One member present had been trying to develop a program of training volunteers from among the church women of the city. She was almost in despair. On the one hand, there were plenty of unmet needs in which volunteer service could supplement professional help. But the personal touch needed just wasn't there. On the other hand, women of good will and intelligence were bored by insufficient use of their time in home duties and longed to be of service. How could they be used? Again, the right personal touch was lacking. Their lives were too different from those they would serve. The barriers of a different standard of living, if not of condescension, would seep into the best conceived projects. The volunteers of Mary Richmond's day either did not exist now or were not welcome any more, either to clients or to professionally trained workers who measured their service in technical skills. We had no answer.

So this rich year of experience drew to a close. I had thought that a course in supervision in one city would saturate the local demand in a year or two, and knew that I must move on, although Mr. Bruno asked me many times to consider staying. Interestingly enough, and perhaps by coincidence, the students of that year moved on also, probably to better their situation professionally. I met them in New York, Pittsburgh, and elsewhere, and I believe that at least half were scattered within two or three years. After all, nothing is local. Nothing alive can be confined.

The summer of 1939 was the first in twenty-seven years that I had spent with my family in Stoughton. It brought long peaceful hours in a deck chair in sun and shade, with much reading and thinking. However, anxiety and tension were there, too. The New Deal was turning up the same old cards. The clause in the NRA code which had seemed to guarantee Labor's right to bargain collectively through unions of its own choosing proved to do nothing of the sort. Every step forward had to be fought for as heretofore. The only advantage was that the new industrial form of organization, the CIO, had the vital force to speak for the workers it represented.

Europe was like a bird, fluttering but unable to move while a snake poised to strike. Britain and France dragged their feet at every proposal for collective resistance to the Nazi advance which would include the USSR. They preferred to gamble on a turn of the Nazis to seize territory to the east and on a hoped-for war in which their two enemies would destroy each other. Meanwhile, the crematories smoked and the "civilized" western nations prayed for an uneasy peace for themselves.

In the midst of such tension, and just about the time war burst upon the world, my small adventure in education was launched. In late August I sent out an attractive leaflet of four pages, carrying first an announcement that I was prepared to be a "consultant in staff development for social agencies" in five areas of study: social casework, supervision, group relationships in social casework and supervision, the relation of social casework and supervision to administration, and the relation of these to the life of the community.

Two more pages outlined my professional qualifications and terms.[3] One page was devoted to a statement which I quote in full:

"A consultation service is an experiment in education for social work. In a new profession, finding its function in the midst of extraordinary difficulties, education of staff is of crucial importance yet the need and demand for it tends to outrun all existing facilities. There are gaps to be filled in stimulating workers who have not yet had professional school preparation to want and to find ways of obtaining it; in helping supervisors to learn how to produce real growth in their staff workers; in aiding trained and experienced people to carry on the continuous education which is essential to a progressive professional leadership. Public social work has brought into use a new combination of skills which are not as yet adequately absorbed into the teaching of formal courses. There is need of research in the field to bring theory into closer touch with practice and to enlarge and enrich the theory we have.

"A consultation service can enter flexibly into the field of practice at the points where workers are most baffled—for example, in problems of relationship occasioned by the uneven development of social work itself; problems of fitting skillful casework in with the activities of other professions and community groups; problems of becoming more professionally reliable in the dynamics of counselling with clients. This consultant has no packaged wisdom to offer. Her own learning has been gained in helping a large number of students, of little or much experience, to learn. She can come to staffs of social agencies only with aid in discovering themselves, in using more effectively what they have, in learning with more understanding in the laboratory of their own daily experience. The aims of an education of this sort go back to the simplest principles we know—respect for learners, not as receptacles but as human beings, stimulation to growth, cultivation of sound and fine relationships between individuals and within and among groups, understanding of the dynamic interplay between what we are and do and the social forces of our day."

I included in the plan keeping my home in Sunnyside and spending weekends there to enjoy some personal life. From that center in one of the boroughs of New York an arc of six hundred miles would include most of the concentrations of population of social workers in the East. In a night's run by train I could be in Buffalo or Toronto, Boston, Pittsburgh, Cleveland, or North Carolina, stay a day or two meeting various groups, and be back in New York for weekly seminars or individual consultations. In the summers, trips of several weeks could be arranged, with pro-rata sharing of expenses among the sponsoring groups.

The demand was waiting for me. In November, the first full month of the project, I was meeting weekly three groups on supervision sponsored by the American Association of Medical Social Workers (on Saturday mornings and Monday afternoon and evening), two casework groups of probation officers (on Thursday and Friday evenings) and also the staff of the Department of Public Welfare of Passaic, New Jersey, for a seminar on casework on Friday afternoons. On alternate Tuesdays I went to Providence for two sessions, sponsored by the

AASW chapter, on the relation of social casework to the life
of the community. One Tuesday and Wednesday I spent in
Richmond, Virginia, beginning a series of institutes with the
State Welfare Department staff on supervision, as it related
both to administration and to the growth of individual workers.

At the end of six months, I reported to myself that I had
worked with thirty groups, and all accounts were paid. Appointments were booked well ahead. My salary had been paid,
and funds had accumulated to insure its being paid the first of
every month. I had no office expenses except a mail-receiving
service, and took care of correspondence myself.

The variety of the work was fascinating. In a two-year
period,[4] some of the highlights were these:

A series of lectures and seminars took me to Buffalo for
three days at a time, once in two months, and involved a large
part of the social work community in discussion of casework
and supervision in both public and private agencies. An evening
lecture each time was open to the public. The arranger of this
program said he, himself, got out of it a free course in community organization!

The City of New York, through the Bureau of Training of
the Civil Service Commission, employed me to give two con-
current courses in casework for probation officers of the Domestic Relations Court. Also, the city's Juvenile Aid Bureau,
under the Police Department, had two courses in casework as
it could be used in an authoritative setting.

The social service staffs of Presbyterian and Neurological
Hospitals arranged for a combination of seminars and individual consultations on cases originating in their work.

One group of psychiatric social workers held a clinic on
leading study groups, and several people used individual consultations for help in teaching courses or institutes.

The National Board of the YWCA had a series of thirty-
nine discussions to study education for workers in their field
in relation to what had been learned about education for social
casework.

Two summer programs gave breadth and added personal enjoyment to the working year. In 1940, after the National Conference of Social Work at Grand Rapids, I turned west and from June 3rd to 14th met the medical social workers of Chicago in five institutes located in various hospitals. Then I had a psychiatric group in St. Paul for two days and went on to ten days in Salt Lake City, covering seminars with the Utah Department of Public Welfare state staff, the AASW, and the Family Service Society. On that visit, two weekend trips were memorable. One was to Mirror Lake in the mountains northeast of Salt Lake and one to Zion and Bryce canyons. The social workers who took me on these tours were wonderful people to know.

I prize greatly this brief contact with the Mormon culture, rich in pioneer tradition. I wished I could have studied further two features of special interest to my profession. One was the farming on irrigated land worked in co-operation while the people lived in villages clustered around a church. One worker told me of the strong tradition for co-operation brought to Utah by Scandinavian pioneers. The other feature was noted in my seminar groups—unusually good discussion, expressive and to the point. I was told that young people in the Church of the Latter Day Saints are trained to think on their feet and to say clearly what they think.

In July of 1940 and again in 1941, I went to East Lansing, Michigan, for a five-day institute for supervisors under the Michigan Institute for Social Welfare, a gathering of supervisors of county departments.

In 1941, I went to Erie, Pennsylvania, in late June for two courses in the Department of Public Welfare and from there to New Orleans, which I remember as extremely hot over that Fourth of July, the city filled with soldiers on leave. After seminars with the medical social workers and supervisors in the Public Assistance Agency, I moved to Baton Rouge for an institute on supervision at the State University School of Public Welfare Administration. My comments in letters to my mother are applicable to this whole period: "The folks are making a spoiled brat out of me, taking me around outside of sessions," and "This place is full of friends."

Preparation for all this work involved a good deal of time, including some reading of cases sent in advance for discussion. Thereby hung a problem, for my method of teaching was so closely geared to study of the learning needs of the people in the seminars that it was impossible for me to go armed with detailed outlines before I had seen them. I did go equipped with the rich experience of Plan D, ways of stimulating groups to eager discussion, and examples of the many type-situations which confronted social workers everywhere. The local color, the particular adaptations to a group, I had to pick up quickly on the spot.

For a while I felt guilty over so much reliance upon what looked like spontaneity. The peak of it was probably on the day I was to give an institute at a State Conference of Social Work and helped a fellow institute leader out of a cab. She came loaded to her chin with books, some of which were tumbling about her feet. I laughed with her as we scrambled them together, but the wave of self-reproach that swept over me, I shall never forget. I think I had brought one book. Here was my teaching self, naked as the day it was born, and did I think I had any business appearing before the public?

Actually I worked out a solution that satisfied both my sense of scholarly propriety and my convictions about teaching an art. Preparation had to be incessant to maintain growth in the teaching person. It might be in books or in learning from life and from the cross-fertilization of minds in discussion. It was not laziness which determined my aversion to outlined courses, but refusal to inhibit either teacher or learners by setting in advance molds of thought to which our interchange of thought must conform. We could and would plan together courses which would fit needs flexibly.[5]

One of the fascinating aspects of the work was the process

of getting rapport with groups with ever-changing characteristics. Most groups were prepared to be friendly, and were eager to learn—perhaps too eager, if they conceived learning to be having something poured over them with which they could fill their little pitchers. I came with a scrap of a case situation (we called them miniatures in Plan D), and usually got immediate participation either in unraveling it or in matching it with another of their own. They usually had a good time in those first sessions but then, perhaps, at the second or third, wanted to stop exercising their minds and be fed. I had slowly learned to do just this and then to stimulate them to further exercise.

To some groups, I was a distinct threat. A psychiatric social worker was supposed to be "high hat," if not actually an enemy of the "common sense" approach to a job which represented security to untrained workers. Medical social workers who had been trained as nurses and who sometimes resented the new theories about how to treat patients were apt to be doubtful if a course arranged for them would be more than a disturbing nuisance. I wrote my mother about one such group that: "The second time they acted less like scared kittens who come up and sniff something to eat and then draw off and spit."

I remember one group of nurses with whom I wanted to discuss how we might understand behavior, in patients or their relatives, of which we do not approve. The best point of contact I could find was a preliminary discussion of a child who eats chalk. They knew about strange physical hungers and could tell me things about cases they knew. Then we could move on to the "careless" mother who has never satisfied her hunger for adolescent fun or the over-solicitous mother who is so hungry for approval that she spoils everything she does.

Another time I looked over a group of untrained relief workers in a rural state and racked my brains to find one point of contact with a city-trained social worker. At least, however, they were middle-aged, and most of them must have or know adolescent children. So we began on the problems of adolescents with money—allowances, earnings, how much they keep for themselves, and how many things they want. Everyone took part and I think hardly noticed when we shifted to adolescents in relief families whose problems are so much greater because there is no money.

What the groups taught me was beyond price. To sit, hour after hour, with the Public Assistance staff of a rural state, for instance, and to learn the skill with which they must work with local relief directors and Poor Boards is to bring casework and group work and community organization so close together that the urban distinctions between them seem irrelevant. To hear the heartbreaking stories of child exploitation in backward states, of lack of remedial resources for crippled children or the blind, and of the havoc wrought by ignorance and superstition is to have the greatest respect and admiration for these workers who are often almost alone against great odds. What little I could bring them seemed so inadequate to match their courage and endless labors!

One of the contributions I could make to *Social Work Today,* in this period when I was writing for it frequently, was to keep the magazine in touch with the grass roots of America. Frank Bancroft used to say that if BCR ever got lost she could be located by noting the place from which new subscribers were coming. However, it was not so much stimulation of interest in the magazine that was needed, but to be sure it did not become exclusively New York City-minded. It must speak to rural as well as city workers, and those remote from organization, as well as those actively involved.

A small but important part of my counselling was with groups of administrators, most often those connected with social service departments in large hospitals where they had to relate their staff to other professions and to a huge organization. I said to such groups that I could not come with special knowledge of administration but could help with the human problems involved in it, or, if I did nothing else, could lead them in group discussion to sort out what they knew from their own experience.

I did have a process of maturing in my background that I had retraced as I struggled through with Plan D students the administrative problems of their own jobs. Probably all of us have, at some time, thought of administrators as authoritative parents in the social agency who set limits on what we caseworkers could do or expected of us more than we could produce. If we did not look forward to being administrators ourselves, we at least hoped to rise above some of their hampering restrictions. Moreover, it was always convenient to have an administrator to blame.

Later in our practice we came to realize that administration not only furnishes the machinery which allows casework to be done, but that it is itself an inextricable part of good casework. The office location, appointments, and personnel either say "welcome" or "keep out of my way." A raise in the board rate for placed-out children may do more for morale and good home care than any amount of child guidance service to overcome friction and behavior difficulties. Where time and money are saved and where they are lavishly expended reveal where the agency places its accent of importance in its work.

So I found study of administration inseparable from study of good social work. An administrator becomes, in my thinking, a leader of a working group, using all possible skills with individuals as a group worker uses them and focussing upon the *interaction* of persons with each other as they work together for a common purpose. An administrator has the delegated role of decision-maker, not to hamper the group but to facilitate its working.

Furthermore, study of supervision convinced me that administration is not a necessary evil which sometimes stands in the way of a supervisor dedicated to fostering professional growth in the staff. There may seem to be a conflict between pressure to get work done and educational goals. Some supervisors I have known, especially those highly trained in psychology, have wanted to wait until their students were "ready" to be reliable about office routines and had overcome "resistance" to being reminded to keep dictation up to date. These supervisors learned, from the endless friction generated in an office when time-saving rulings were not observed, that it was better, even from an educational point of view, that their students learn quickly to fit themselves into a structure intended for the convenience of everyone. Pressure of work, also, was not a hindrance to be deplored but an inseparable feature of the reality which students were being educated to meet.

The discussions with administrators in my counselling practice did not often involve the question of union organization of social workers, perhaps because few, if any, hospitals were organized at that time. Undoubtedly, the total picture of my relationship to administration could not exclude the fact that I was known to be in favor of unions for professional workers, that I never refused an opportunity to speak before union groups, or to write for *Social Work Today* papers on civil rights and other problems for which there was no solution except organization. How could I work at the same time with two camps so opposed to each other as most people supposed administrators and unions to be? The answer is that I did not see two camps but one unified purpose of social work to serve human need. What I saw was two ways of making sure that human need was served, both necessary and each supplementing the other.

Good administration of an agency's job is essential but is often defeated in this period of history. Why? Because the community itself is divided. Part of it, undoubtedly much the larger part, wants good, honestly administered social services, both publicly and privately supported. A small but influential part does not want a thoroughly good job done for needy people. It wants social services as a sort of community public relations gesture, but more deeply, it wants a reserve supply of unemployed labor to keep wages low. It wants relief grants always less than such a low standard. It wants no interference with discrimination which keeps certain minority groups in low-paid status, no troublesome claims in industrial accident cases, no labor legislation that hampers industrial management from doing what it will with what it calls its own.

Both sets of wishes in the community are represented on Boards of social agencies, and at various times one or the other may predominate. In a social agency, the staff can only rely for support of professional standards of good work upon that part of the community that wants good service and that part of the Board that represents it. Otherwise, the best administration is often cancelled out by conflicting purposes which destroy the human values which the agency is set up to serve.

The administrators of social agencies are in a position to feel the full impact of the conflict of interests in the community and especially as this is reflected in the Board or in legislative committees. The point of view which has generally prevailed in professional circles is that the administrator of an agency or a federated group of agencies must be in a position to maneuver among opposing interests and to count on unquestioning support from the employed staff. Such a conception does not face the reality of a basic class conflict in society. It considers opposition to good social work to be due to ignorance and believes the problem to be how to "interpret" our work to the public skillfully enough to secure generous support. Community Fund organizations have increasingly taken on this function for social agencies. To this way of thinking, unions in social work are utterly out of place, disruptive of good staff relationships and of community acceptance which has been built up over the years.

The young people who formed the "rank-and-file" movement in the Depression years faced an abnormal situation. Events forced them to ask how social agencies fitted into the total community picture which was badly disorganized. They had to carry frightening responsibilities beyond their experience, in which they should have had backing and counsel from older workers. Instead, in many cases, the young workers who could not help seeing what was happening to clients and who had to speak out were dismissed as unfit to continue to belong to a

professional group. So they organized—for self-protection
partly, but also from a deep conviction that they could not
tolerate abdication of their ethical responsibility as workers.

I could not subscribe to a concept which placed administration
in a parental role while the staff was to adopt that of unquestioning children. For one thing, my maturing belief in the
dignity of an administrator's job demanded preparation for it
through all the grades of staff responsibility, from the bottom
to the top. Many I knew were pushed into administration without preparation for it, and many a good administrator was frustrated by not having a staff in which each worker was trained
to accept responsibility in subordinate positions. Also, as maturing casework demanded a more responsible relationship to
clients, workers were needed who would use their intelligence
in the field and would use a supervisor to help them think, not
to make decisions for them.

Many people were sorely hurt in those days when unions
were new. Executives who had done personal kindnesses for
staff members for years could not understand what seemed
like a rejection when the staff sent a delegation to talk over
grievances or even to suggest that some of the agency's ways
of treating clients would bear reconsideration! A Board which
had voted to pay the salary of a staff member through a long
illness could not but condemn what seemed like "biting the
hand that feeds you" when that worker joined the union. Of
course many women members of the Board had husbands to
tell them that, in *their* world of business, unions would not be
tolerated, and undoubtedly "outside agitators" were at the bottom of it all.

Many new union members felt hurt and guilty. Their mind-
set was that of their childhood—to leave responsibility to those
above them. It was the easier road, and many workers took it.
Those who did not were predominantly in the less-protected
public agencies, where no voice from the rank and file could
reach the upper echelons unless it was backed by organization
in impressive numbers. Or, perhaps, they were in the agencies

supported by voluntary giving but organized into financially controlled federations, where again, no single voice could be heard, and the illusion of a family where things could be talked over was long since dead.

Neither union members nor agencies worked out their relationships all at once or evenly. I remember one executive who told me this: "I fought with the Board for years to get salary increases for my workers. Now they have a union, but they come to me for help just the same. I tell them to grow up and do their own fighting. It isn't my role. Now I can devote myself to the program as I should, and I welcome the union which takes a load off my mind." I think it was the experience of most agencies that entered into contracts with the Social Service Employees Union that staff relationships were stabilized; and common problems were better resolved than when grievances festered and personal benevolence or misunderstanding decided questions which were too important for the agency's service to clients to be relegated to personal decree.[6]

In the history of unionization in social work, it is impossible to separate the two motives of protecting one's own condition as a worker and safeguarding the right to treat clients ethically, as against allowing them to be used for the benefit of other community groups. There was desperate need in both areas. Defense of themselves and their working conditions marked a transition from the early concept that social workers were "agents" of the Board, hired only to do its bidding. Trained workers had to become thinking workers. Could they stop short of thinking about the conditions needful to do their best work? Should a worker be dismissed for this and all her skills lost to the profession as well as the agency? Should professional workers be exhausted and underpaid and insecure until it was impossible to give much to clients? The answer was not in single protests which marked individuals for separation from the staff, but organized protest, based on a collective conviction that in the long run social agencies stand or fall by the quality of their working personnel.

I could sum up my job in those days like this: to develop personnel in the profession of social work, wherever found, at all levels of responsibility; at no level to deny responsibility and adopt a child's view of being "supervised"; to keep clear the purpose of social work to serve people in some kind of need; to study social work as a living part of the whole community, buffeted though it must be by conflicting community standards and purposes; to rely on those forces in the community that are in sympathy with the purpose of social work and reach them with understanding. With such a set of specifications for my job, all of my work was of one piece, one whole, in the midst of a thrilling diversity.

CHAPTER 15

PAUSE IN TRANSIT

Somewhere a door blew shut. I came back to New York in the fall of 1941, expecting to be as busy as ever, and there was no work except for a few appointments planned for in the spring. I was puzzled, but there was nothing to do but wait to see if this was more than a temporary lag. To fill the days, I began to write what would be my first full-length book, setting down all I could of what I had learned about casework and how to teach it.

The project recalled a worry my mother had expressed when I began "teaching on wheels." It was that my stock of ideas would run out or that someone would "steal my thunder." My reply had been, "If I started to worry about that, I would have cat fits all the time, for all I do is tell everything I know." Actually, I was dealing not with packaged knowledge but with principles applied in situations that were never twice the same. The task now was to get those principles into organized form and the wealth of detailed applications into examples which workers, who were endlessly running to keep up with their jobs, could read. I blocked out four main sections: what it is we have to teach; who they are who will learn; teaching in groups; teaching through individual guidance of practice.

The problem of how to live, meanwhile, was happily solved for me in the second semester of the school year by an offer of a temporary position as teacher of casework classes for a professor on leave from the Institute of Public and Social Administration of the University of Michigan, then located in Detroit.

So I closed my Little Deck House in February and transferred my home to Webster Hall, a residence hotel in Detroit, later to be a dormitory of Wayne University.

Being part of a staff and a community again had interesting differences from the St. Louis experience. The personality of a city is a fascinating thing to try to assess in the light of its history. Where St. Louis was German and pioneer, Southern and Western, conservative and out-reaching, Detroit seemed an adolescent, outgrowing its clothes, unrepressed, full of rebellion and of hope, welcoming change. The great "sit-down" strikes which had climaxed years of labor struggle and finally won union recognition were only five years back in history. In wartime when production must be kept at peak, Labor was putting forth tremendous effort, and the strength of Labor could be *felt* in the city. At the hotel where I lived, union conferences were often held, and an occasional representative of Labor met men from management on Boards of social agencies. Money from the auto industry spoke in every program for civic betterment.

The social work community was less organized than in St. Louis. The University of Michigan School, which was then located in Detroit, was in some competition with the Wayne University School to which many social workers employed in the city looked for courses. My two casework classes were soon increased (on demand from the workers in the Department of Public Welfare) by a course in supervision similar to that in St. Louis, including individual conferences and written reports but not an allocation of time to the agency. It was a full teaching schedule. However, since by choice of the participants, all my classes were set for afternoons, I could allot three hours every morning to writing on the book. I did not work in the evenings, because I found any time so gained was sure to be subtracted later in the slowdown of fatigue. It was probably the most efficiently organized period of my whole working life.

One question which was agitating the social work community was the function of the Consultation Bureau, the private family agency. The Department of Public Welfare had developed many forms of casework service to families that, in other cities, had been pre-empted by private agencies. The Consultation Bureau had been tending to become a clinic for psychiatric diagnosis, and even treatment, through its part-time psychiatrist, since other psychiatric facilities in the city were limited. I was asked to read cases there and to see what indications there were for further developing its psychiatric emphasis. Out of these cases, I gleaned an appreciation of what a flexible private agency can do to explore the frontiers for a progressive public agency and to develop a psychiatrically oriented casework which is nevertheless distinct from the services given by psychiatric clinics. I thought there were groups of cases coming to a family agency for problems of economic, marital, or vocational adjustment—groups which needed psychiatric help but would never go to a clinic. I thought there were ways of treating persons who were even quite sick emotionally (perhaps on parole from a mental hospital which did not have social service) so as to secure for them the best possible social adjustment. If the agency in succeeding years moved toward psychotherapy instead of toward this experimental casework, I had at least said what I believed—that there was a field for casework permeated with psychiatric understanding which would be neglected if everyone were diverted to practicing psychotherapy, for which I believed social workers were not properly equipped.

In Detroit, I met Rev. Claude Williams again and he opened windows to the South and the grass roots of America. He had been convinced that if fascism came to the United States it would have its base in the rural South where poverty was desperate, where ideas of race discrimination were deeply ingrained, and where Bible-belt religion fed antagonisms with doctrinal differences. "Rev. Claude," as he was affectionately called, had left Commonwealth College to found The Peoples Institute of Applied Religion, a traveling service to the preachers, Negro and white, who worked as laborers, preached to rural congregations in circuit on Sundays, and were the real leaders of the poorer masses of people in the South. Rev. Claude had taken the social message of Jesus and the Hebrew prophets, distilled it into visual-aid charts that even illiterate people could understand, preached it at camp-meeting-like gatherings, and organized conferences of Negro and white preachers together to open their eyes to the *social* message of the Gospel. These became missionaries of "the religion of three square meals a day" all through the South. The practical outcome was organization to better the desperate lot of Negro and white working people—together, or they could only wilt before the fierce persecution which was certain to overtake them.

Rev. Claude had a group of such devoted southern preachers working over a wide territory when Pearl Harbor shook everything into new grooves. Soon, there was gasoline rationing, and Claude and his battered car could not travel. Even earlier, thousands of Negro and white laborers had migrated to Detroit, being recruited by the automobile companies in the hope that they would break impending strikes. They had not done so, but they, and their preachers with them, were living precariously in that industrial city, easy prey for the fascist-like movements which centered there. If Claude wanted to reach them, he had to go where thousands of them were. In 1942, he was employed for a few months making a survey of the migration from the South for the Dodge Christian Community Center. Later, when the Presbytery of Detroit called him as labor chaplain, he brought his family and spent three years there.

I learned as much from Rev. Claude about the life of the working people of Detroit as from all the social agencies. He walked the streets studded with "store-front" churches, the sponsorship of which no one could tell him. He found the preachers only by inquiring, in his southern drawl, in candy stores and poolrooms, for so-and-so "from my home town." "Well, maybe the preacher would know." So he sometimes found a preacher. But would a Negro preacher trust a white man? Would anyone believe a man, in the life-and-death scramble for survival that was Detroit, who said, "Say brotherhood and mean it"? Some of the strangers in the city were

learning, in spite of instances of betrayal, that union solidarity
meant brotherhood. Many were held back by narrow religious
creeds until Rev. Claude (who never interfered with whatever
else a man believed) made a bridge from faith in the teachings
of Jesus and the Hebrew prophets to a trust in each other,
sufficient to join a union and struggle for human rights. So
it was that many Bible-belt people whom Claude and his preachers influenced began their union meetings with prayer and hymn
singing set to union words and then stood firm in face of beatings and death itself.

While I was working on the book, which I christened *Learning and Teaching in the Practice of Social Work,* I was putting
into theory form a concept of stages of learning a new activity
which I had found illuminating and useful to those who were
guiding the learning of others.[1] It was a biologically based
and psychologically oriented theory that conscious intelligence
is employed first for survival, and then for functioning in the
most economical way possible while well-learned processes are
relegated to the automatic parts of the nervous system. Something new evokes curiosity and, perhaps, fear of danger. Once
it is settled that flight or battle are not indicated, the first
stage of learning about the new thing is to get fear of it under
control. The traditional stage fright is conquered by resort to
older habitual patterns of activity, such as walking or saying
something. This fear period usually passes quickly. Then the
second stage, which may be long, is one of responding to the
new situation without understanding it well. Third, comes
beginning to understand but with uneven application of what
one knows. Performance in this stage is perhaps even worse
than when the responses were more or less automatic. The
fourth stage is one of mastery of the new activity when understanding and unconscious responses move together in harmonious adjustment. A fifth stage is the relearning necessary to teach
the activity to others.

Each of these stages, on the plateaus during which little
progress is visible, accumulates energy for advance to a higher

stage. The lesson for us, as supervisors, was to be willing to wait for this natural evolution, not to try to force it. Strong *don'ts* to observe seemed to me to be these: Do not focus on the self when, in the first two stages, the indications are to look outward and see the situation as it is; don't focus at first on what the learning caseworker is doing, but on the client; don't be discouraged in the second and third stages that learners do not leap to mastery; and above all, don't discourage the learners who must of necessity learn in nature's way.

I ended the book with a section which I called "Social Work Goes Back to the People." It was parallel to the first section which had enunciated a belief that social work had its taproot in what people did for themselves and for each other. Only temporarily, in the long view I was taking, had social work been captured by alien forces, to control the poor of whom the well-to-do were afraid. It seemed in wartime that the crust of giving to the disadvantaged from above had been broken through in visible places, showing the initiative of plain people who knew what needed to be done and could work helpfully with skilled social workers if given a chance. Sometimes they even put us to shame. In the matter of day nursery care for children of mothers urgently needed in war production, for instance, the CIO unions waited for weeks in some cities while social workers offered their services to help mothers to decide if they *should* work. Finally, the unions demanded of the cities, and got, the establishment of a few more nursery facilities.

The question of use of volunteers looked entirely different in wartime from the picture which had distressed us in St. Louis only three years earlier. Now, not just a leisure class but everybody volunteered to do something. In Detroit, I led a study group of volunteers being trained to assist in the public agency and the Red Cross and found them eager to learn and not far removed from the same problems the clients were facing. When I returned to New York in June, I had an opportunity to study interviewing in an agency placing teen-age boys and girls in farm families in Vermont for war service in food production.

The volunteer interviewers of the agency were seeing large numbers of applicants and trying to assess which ones were likely to succeed. They welcomed consultation with a professional, and I, in turn, gained insight into another form of use of volunteers. So it was that "Social Work Goes Back to the People" was a new appraisal of volunteer service in wartime.

When the last class of my teaching in Detroit was over, the book was also nearly done. Rinehart and Company had contracted for it through the fortunate circumstance that they were publishing Helen Witmer's sociological study, *Social Work,* and two books would justify opening a series on social work in the college textbook department.

I remember the summer of 1942 as one of almost intolerable tension. I was practically in confinement in my apartment in Sunnyside, revising the manuscript, reading proofs, and indexing, while I awaited the worst of news from overseas. The second front in the west, long promised by the Allies, did not materialize, and as the fascist armies swept eastward, we could not but wonder what would ever stop them short of their amalgamation with the forces of Japan.

The last day I spent on the book was dramatic in a grotesquely minor way. I had promised the final section, including the index, for the Friday before Labor Day. Aside from an inherent respect for deadlines, I was aware that, if I had to stay in New York over the holiday, Mother's vacation on Cape Cod would be badly disrupted. I fell to counting minutes as I typed—three pages to the hour—and estimating possible delays on the subway to Manhattan. I delivered the pages with ten minutes to spare before five o'clock on that Friday afternoon, mopped my brow, and felt as I used to on the farm when I helped load hay ahead of an already rumbling thunder storm.

In the fall of 1942, there was no doubt that I was unemployed. At first, I had thought it was the effect of war, the tensions of which had begun to be felt by social workers as early as the Atlantic City National Conference in May, 1941, and had made it seem that social agencies must devote more energy to the war effort than to professional development of their staff workers. After Pearl Harbor, of course, community organization for war activities became feverish and all-pervasive. When, however, a letter I sent to the Red Cross, which was begging for qualified supervisors, brought no reply, I realized that there might be, in the background, a boycott of my ideas. At schools of social work, I knew there would be the difficulty that I did not have a Master's degree.

In back of the problems which only affected me personally was a situation which had been often debated in our profession. Social work was not organized to promote the skills in social casework which it called its greatest asset.[2] Only relative beginners did casework or those who could not advance because of lack of professional training. When trained workers had passed through the time it takes to develop mature skills, they could advance professionally only by one of three paths: administration, supervision and teaching, or research, all of which tended to take them away from continuous contact with cases. Some Plan D students who had struggled with this trend found their agencies blocked from giving salary increases to excellent caseworkers because Board members who were businessmen thought in terms of higher salaries to foremen and executives (in social work, supervisors and administrators), but not to rank-and-file workers. Those agencies had even devised some research titles to keep in casework some senior worker who wanted to develop her skills in that art.

This trend in social work decidedly affected my chances of employment. I had not the personality for administration, even if a Board would consider me, lacking as I was in administrative experience. I was also not fitted for nor interested in research of an academic sort. If I could not find a way to teach large numbers, which I loved, I wanted to do casework or to supervise caseworkers in an agency. However, the prestige structure in social work stood in the way. No one wanted a case supervisor who knew too much and had traveled too far, and

nobody believed, as I did, that I would be happy as a caseworker.

A temporary solution came when Mrs. Ida Segal, of the
Jewish Social Service Bureau of Newark, New Jersey, at whose
agency I had given an institute previously, offered part-time
work as Agency Consultant. She was regretful that her budget
allowed only a caseworker's salary, for which she could compensate only by reduction of hours, but since I spent four hours
a day commuting from Long Island City, a ten o'clock to four
o'clock day suited me admirably.

The agency had been a recent casualty of a surveying team,
which had left it depressed. It had a history, common to many
sectarian agencies, of developing out of small benevolent
societies which had an interest in seeing, for one thing, that no
Jewish family lacked the means to celebrate the high holidays
with dignity. It had fostered family life in an immigrant group
with many problems of poverty, ill health, and lack of opportunities. It had become, after two or three generations, a
modern casework agency in a thriving Jewish community, related to all other welfare services of a growing city. The survey
had been made from the point of view of a school of thought
which turned the spotlight of attention on a "helping process,"
closely defined and developed within the agency. By this measurement the agency had serious lacks. What other measurement
was there? The agency wanted to know what mine would be.

I spent the time at the agency, for some four months, reading cases and talking with three groups: the whole staff in discussion of cases; the supervisors of students with their problems
of teaching; and the small number of workers who lacked
school training in individual consultations. Mrs. Segal herself
took me with her to community meetings, and we spent profitable hours in discussing the relationship of the agency to the
whole community.

My feeling about the older, untrained workers (whom the
agency was criticized for continuing to employ) was that here
were women of judgment and warm human sympathy, whose

way of working might be impossible to tabulate under modern professional techniques but whose principles were essentially true and sound. I read cases going back over so many years that one could see more than one generation growing up in almost impossible conditions and becoming successful (if sometimes baffled) parents under new stresses. I felt that here was a sustaining service that a city could not afford to lose, any more than the agency could afford to lose the services of the remaining members of the early staff who had brought it about.[3] There was merit in the modern idea that social workers should consider their function more carefully, should watch for "movement" in their clients toward change, and should drop those cases in which change did not occur within a reasonable time. However, a review of some fifty years in the life of poor families in Newark could not fail to leave one with profound respect for a service, unscientific though it might be, which was always there when sickness and poverty brought emergencies which human strength could not overcome. Over the years, conditions had changed for the better for this group of people. Now an agency might concentrate more on psychological change in people as a test of the effectiveness of its service, but could not some room be left for service that would sustain trapped human beings until something better in prevention could be worked out in the whole community? I felt that the Jewish Social Service Bureau had filled, and would fill, an important place in relation to community needs.

In the early winter of that year came the death of *Social Work Today* about which I felt as if it were the loss of a member of my family. It was actually self-supporting when it had to close, strangled by the debts it had incurred in its early years without capital. When it was gone a light went out of social work which has never been rekindled.[4] It was especially missed, because it was so needed in wartime to keep morale high and the issues clear for a whole sector of the front —workers in a new and bewildering profession. After all, it was *our* issues that were the crucial issues of the struggle: profits and destruction or people and the good life.

It was wartime, that winter of 1942-43, and we could not forget it. As I closed the study in Newark, another temporary job was offered in the Essex County Hospital in nearby Cedar Grove, New Jersey. The staff was short-handed and might be called on to assist the draft boards in getting personal histories of draftees who were dubious risks for military service. If I was working in that region, I might be available for some war work. I moved, then, to a mental hospital, for the second time in my life.

The living conditions were a little odd. The hospital could offer a room in the administration building but not meals (under the war-rationing system). We were a good mile from stores or the nearest diner, although there was a commissary at the hospital where some food items could be bought. I had no car, but it was expected that I would be working in some city at noontime or could catch a ride or walk to a hot meal once a day. Breakfast and supper, I could well provide with the aid of a dresser drawer for supplies and a hot plate and refrigerator in a staff kitchenette. A complication, I remember, was that the large room assigned to me proved impossible to sleep in, because the water pipes in the bathroom next door let out a scraping roar at frequent and irregular intervals, so that one spent the night waiting for the next one. It was said that nothing but total renovation would silence them, and, anyway, the former occupant of the room had been deaf. So I was allowed to go to an upper floor to sleep.

At Essex County Hospital, I had the Rip Van Winkle experience of returning to mental hospital work after twenty years to find it transformed. Shock therapy had shortened greatly the hospital stay of many patients and presented new problems in aftercare. The antibiotics and the tranquilizing drugs that were to revolutionize further the care of mental illness were not yet discovered. There was little psychotherapy, especially in that period when the psychiatric staffs of civilian hospitals were cut to the bone. However, it was a vastly stimulating experience, especially the rare privilege of being supervised, after so many years of teaching and theorizing about the

process. I shall always be gratefully happy in my memories of
Mrs. Elizabeth Bech's supervision during my three months
there. She combined the warmth and keen intellectual grasp of
situations which together make an ideal consultant and teacher.

I had a varied program of aftercare visits, combined with
some case discussions with the staff and the weekly student
class for the three students from the Smith College School.
Mrs. Bech delegated to me a piece of community work which
she would otherwise have done, as Director of the hospital
community clinics—that is, a seminar with the nurses of the
Health Department of Montclair, New Jersey. I found it very
stimulating to work thus with another profession on the human
problems which were encountered in their daily rounds.

I noted with amusement that I was illustrating, in my own
person, my theory of the stages of learning. I was facing much
that was new in aftercare visiting under strange conditions
and stopped myself short one afternoon with the comment:
"Why, I'm not using my brains at all! I'm just responding!"
It was the second stage, when energy is tied up in response to
newness, and conscious mastery has not yet come. I made many
mistakes and am not sure that I ever got out of the second
stage in the three months I was at the hospital, but it was
something to *feel* the experience through which I had helped
so many students.

One evening in March, while I was in Sunnyside for the
weekend, I received a telegram from Constance Kyle, a former
student. It said, "Would you be interested in social work closer
to people directly concerned?" I telephoned her and learned
that a recently formed agency called United Seamen's Service
was seeking personnel for expansion of its service. Its purpose
was to aid merchant seamen involved in transportation of troops
and supplies overseas. I was wanted particularly for a new
unit to be set up in the hall of the National Maritime Union.
Nothing in years had excited me so much. I talked it over with
Mrs. Bech, who had no immediate war work at the hospital,
and arranged to go to the new job on May 1, 1943.

CHAPTER 16

KEEP 'EM SAILING

It was exhilarating to be where history was being made and the fate of millions decided by whether or not supplies reached the battlefields, and on time. Submarines had taken a frightful toll of the Merchant Marine since before Pearl Harbor. New ships must be built and manned with incredible speed. Something must be done in the port cities to stop the waste of skilled manpower due to illness and injury and the drift to other occupations—even other war agencies—because of intolerable conditions in the carrying service.

Seamen were not eligible for the ameliorative efforts of the USO[1] nor for the protections given to enlisted men and their families. Seamen had for generations been considered wards of the government in foreign ports and treated like second-class citizens in their own land. They had suffered a higher rate of casualties in 1942 than had the armed services, yet they had no dignity as defenders of their country. United Seamen's Service[2] was set up in the fall of that year to be a USO for seamen. It organized centers in ports all over the world where shipping was concentrated and war problems acute. Its hotels in crowded coast cities where seamen could find no decent lodging offered clean, pleasant surroundings for a man's few days ashore. Its recreation centers made relief from tension possible. For men with shattered nerves, rescued from torpedoed ships, it provided rest homes with psychiatric help. Its Personal Service for emergencies that made men sick with worry enabled seamen to

face with heightened morale the hazards of submarine attacks
at sea.

Most of the USS units for recreation and personal service
were located in port cities where they could serve members of all
the maritime unions. Where numbers of seamen were concentrated at one union shipping hall, as at the NMU, and could
not leave it for long without risk of missing a shipping assign-
ment, the USS placed its unit in the union hall itself. At the
NMU there was already organized a personal service department with which USS entered into co-operation.[3] In my role
as USS representative in the Personal Service Department of
the NMU I was responsible for the use of a loan fund provided
by USS for seamen's emergencies and for supervision of the
four or five caseworkers paid by USS who worked under the
administrative direction of the NMU department.

This kind of double-headed organization might be expected
to produce conflict and such there was, but not within the department itself. It was natural for me to identify and refer to
Miss Kyle any questions involving union policy or department
procedure which came up either in my work with the seamen
or with the staff. As supervisor, I was educator, not administrator, in the staff organization.

The conflicts which did grow out of the peculiar organization were actually based on the different interests of two social
classes which divided the community, and which affected the
work of social agencies. The division was masked in wartime
by a common purpose to win the war, but it was never absent.

The USS was organized to be neutral in regard to class conflict, but the group comprising its Board had differing ideas
as to the sacrifices necessary to win the war. The shipping
interests held out for government subsidies which would guarantee profits without risk. The seamen who risked their lives on
the ships pledged themselves not to strike for the duration of the
war and saw directly and daily the sacrifices that must be made.
Their labor power was so essential to keeping the ships sailing
that concessions had to be made to them—of which the ex-

istence of USS was an example. The USS Board, however, did not interpret this to mean that seamen should be given ideas, which might be embarrassing after the war, about their worth to the industry and their right to bargain about wages and working conditions. Philanthropy was one thing, business another.[4] The union representation on the Board was in a small minority.

The NMU was frankly partisan in the interests of its members. It had fought its way into being (under the CIO in 1936-37) from racket-ridden craft unions which had offered small protection to men who earned as little as twenty-five dollars a month plus their living while at sea. The NMU offered a variety of services to its members in addition to the basic ones of negotiating contracts, controlling shipping assignments so that they would be made fairly among those qualified, and processing grievances known in the industry as "beefs." It assigned a man, full-time, to visit disabled men in marine hospitals and pay them the Union's sick-benefit for small comforts. It had special departments for legal aid to sick and injured seamen in prosecuting their claims and for the interests of foreign seamen, often entangled in legal difficulties, and for men sailing under foreign flags.[5] It had an educational department and operated a bookstore. The NMU was glad to cooperate with any community agency which offered genuine service to seamen, but was definite about one principle—any service operating in the Union hall must be responsible to the members through their elected representatives and to no body outside. The General Secretary, Ferdinand C. Smith, was the official responsible for USS service and ably supported sound professional principles in its operation.

The inevitable organizational conflict arose from the differences in these two points of view. The USS expected its Personal Service, which it established at the NMU hall for the convenience of the Union's members, to be under its administrative direction through its representative. So I was periodically ordered to "take charge" of the NMU program, and it was often made plain that I could not work except within the framework of the Union's department. If I wonder now why the USS did not fire me, it is also clear that no one else could operate at NMU on any other principle, and the NMU, which shipped some 80,000 seamen a year, was too important in the industry in wartime to be ignored.

How did an old professional worker like me happen to be sought for this job? Both the USS and NMU wanted professional competence and mellowed experience. To USS, in an untried new area of social work, its standing among community agencies depended on professional expertness. The NMU, too, had a high respect for trained competence, not only in its own field but wherever it needed professional service.[6] Less easy to find than professional skill was trade union membership in a social worker. I was a member of the Social Service Employees' Union of the UOPWA[7] and had for years written and spoken in favor of union organization for professional workers. I knew I was sought for this particular job precisely because of this facet of my life experience which had often been considered a liability. It meant a great deal to me in 1943 to find an opportunity thus to express my whole self in my chosen field.

Why was it desirable to have a person with trade union consciousness doing professional social work in the setting of a union hall? Aside from the confidence it might give seamen to find a fellow union member to whom to tell their troubles, was the work any different from that in any social agency? Yes, there were real differences in approach and in thinking when a social worker moved to serve an employed group in an essential industry. The principle of relating social work to its community was unchanged, but it was a community quite different from most of those ashore.

First, this was a man's world of intense competition in which a wandering maternal instinct could well get lost. It was not competition of individual against individual but of organized groups of immense size. The seamen were formed into unions to protect their interests against the pressures of well-organized shipping companies and of government bodies whose regulations were most often set up to give incentives for profit. Within the union group, the individual was not lost, but constantly related, through union meetings in the ports and on ships, to the interests of all. Only by such organization could the strength of all be united to protect each one. In situations where a social worker elsewhere would feel justified in wangling every possible advantage for an individual, the union would tolerate no favoritism, especially in such a matter as shipping out of turn. Each man could have only what all could have, unless it could be shown that he was in some special need which would open the door equally to any other union brother.

Secondly, serving an employed group of urgently needed men carries different implications from ministering to people more or less detached, by sickness or other trouble, from contributing to society. In the Union in wartime, men were giving all they had. They came daily to Personal Service with faces gray with fatigue from sleepless weeks of sailing in convoys where at any moment a torpedo might snuff out a ship's life. Often they could not sleep ashore, starting awake from dreams of days and nights on a life raft, their buddies dying around them. Yet they often refused a Personal Service recommendation to see the USS doctor about Rest Home care until their nerves were steadied. They could not let their buddies down, or perhaps they dared not relax, themselves, lest they would never be able to get up their nerve to ship again.[8]

A third difference from social work elsewhere was that it was not a remedial service for disability and failure so much as one geared to responsibility. How do you feel?—which had been a standard question in social work until we laughed about it, was replaced by questions relating to group responsibility. What could a man do, not just for himself but in relation to others in a common task?

An outstanding example was the Union's attitude toward excessive drinking. It assumed that a man's use of alcohol in his leisure time was his own affair, but drinking was not tolerated on ships or ashore when it caused dereliction of duty. A man who missed a ship because he was drunk was as responsible as if he had been sober, much as his friends might try to help him avoid that predicament. The Union insisted that Personal Service was not to be available to men who were intoxicated. The formula was: "I can't talk with you today. Come back when you are sober, Brother." A man had to be responsible for himself to receive help.

We social workers had been trained to treat alcoholism as a symptom, not a moral problem. Undoubtedly it was a symptom in many cases of war neurosis when men drank to forget. However, the man's organized group knew better than any others the needs that drove many to drinking, and the group discipline that worked best in helping them out of it. They were anxious to have men in need of rest and psychatric treatment find these at the USS Rest Centers, and to have Personal Service aid in overcoming their resistance to treatment, but above all they put the moral obligation to do one's duty in wartime.

Fourth, social workers in a hazardous industry in wartime met many emergencies, critical for seamen and their families, which a consulting service could alleviate but not cure. If they were union-conscious, they realized that some of these emergencies could be prevented by collective action. For instance, the union could hold shipping companies to prompt payment of family allotments or injury claims and could insist that the dispatcher know, in assigning jobs, whether a ship was ready to "sleep and feed" its crew or was under repairs so that its stand-by force would be stranded, perhaps over a weekend, without food or lodging.

There were emergencies, however, especially in wartime under pressure of a man's having to sail in a few hours, when money was needed, and there was no other solution. There was no time for debate as to "fostering dependency" or for working out psychological conflicts which might prevent the person's solving the situation in time. Perhaps a family must be saved from eviction, a taxi fare paid to get a sick child to a clinic, a night's lodging provided so that a man need not "carry the banner" (i.e. walk the streets all night) in the last critical twenty-four hours before he sailed into certain danger. Social workers who were union-conscious and sensed what it meant to be homeless and "broke" in a strange city found some other professional qualities more important to cultivate than detachment.

The idea that seamen are creatures of a special kind who choose to go to sea because they are unable to adapt to life ashore like other men has played its part in delaying amelioration of the lot of seamen for many years. Social agencies for seamen have often had a religious motivation, along with a purpose to save men from the hell of alcoholism and, incidentally, stabilize the labor force for shipping companies which gave liberally for their maintenance. We found at the union great bitterness against most seamen's agencies, because their employment services had been used to break strikes, and their lodgings were haunted by company spies.

What we learned from knowing thousands of seamen was that they were a cross section of America, coming from the Great Plains and the Rocky Mountain states as often as from the seacoast towns. In wartime, the industry was flooded with teen-age boys, substituting work in an essential industry for service in the armed forces. Men went to sea as often because they had to have a job as from choice. There were, of course, older men who had sailed from boyhood and could now adapt to no other way of life. What we had impressed upon us was that life at sea was *a way of life,* a "type-situation" which would do certain things to anybody—shape him, condition him, without making him less than human.

A seaman's life is, first of all, marked by deprivations not common ashore: separation for long periods from home comforts, family life, social organizations, churches, the companionship of women under normal conditions, and from sports, the arts, intellectual stimulation. The friendships which sea-

men have with each other may be close while the voyage lasts
and then broken, perhaps forever. Part of the customary making
the rounds of drinking places after a trip was, we found, to
try to meet old friends who might happen to be in port, so that
possibly two friends might ship out together next time. Seamen are chronically lonely men, deprived of the outlets for
emotional tension which are taken for granted ashore.

Secondly, it was only after the CIO unions won increased
wages that seamen earned enough to marry.[9] In wartime the
base pay for an "able-bodied"[10] seaman was around thirty-two
dollars a week, and there was no annual wage. War bonuses for
extra hazards and overtime pay raised the economic level, and
war produced full employment, but intensified every other problem. In normal times, a man's long-anticipated shore leave with
his family was often rendered miserable by the fact that his
income stopped just when he could see most clearly how many
things the family needed.

Seamen lacked protections which are common ashore. There
was no unemployment insurance until coverage was extended to
them after the war, and then with complications due to irregular
employment such that without technical assistance from Personal Service, hardly a man could have proved eligibility.
There was need of accident compensation to take the place of
involved court action for which a man without resources could
not wait. This hazardous industry employed three occupation
groups, each with its own risks: deck workers exposed to
weather and loading and rigging accidents; engine room
workers dealing with machinery and fire; and food workers,
from messmen up to cooks and stewards, all liable to burns and
falls in rough weather.

As a rule, there were no doctors on merchant ships. When
serious injury occurred, someone (the ship's purser perhaps)
had to prop open a first-aid book, take a stiff drink of whiskey
to steady his nerves, give one to the patient, and proceed to do
what he could. It was pointed out to us in Personal Service
that many a man owed his limp to a fractured leg badly set in

this fashion. A brief stay in a Marine Hospital after a voyage could not undo the effects of medical neglect, poor food, and constant exposure to bad weather.

Medical examinations before shipping had come to be distrusted by seamen, because they had been used by company doctors as a device to get rid of active union men. Actually, it was frightening to consider the health hazards which resulted from lack of adequate medical inspection, when men with not-obvious infectious diseases and nervous and mental conditions were thrown together in close quarters aboard ship. It was a long step forward when, on January 1, 1944, the United States Public Health Service set up comprehensive preshipping examinations for seamen. How to get the medical care for what these revealed, was still a complicated problem for seamen who could seldom work and receive medical treatment at the same time.

A feature of life in the Merchant Marine which sometimes baffled social workers was its credit economy, normal in peacetime and accentuated by war conditions. Seamen lived without money concerns aboard ship and were then paid in a lump sum for several months' work. They then went ashore with accumulated tensions and desires to a spending spree which was almost inevitable whether they were single or had families. Most of them first paid their debts to waterfront stores for gear purchased previously and repaid loans from friends to keep their credit good. Many a man lost money or was robbed by crooks who knew where large pickings were to be found. Then he borrowed again for gear for the next voyage. In wartime normal sources of credit dried up as men were stranded in ports far from where they were known, or waterfront stores grew leery of seamen who might not live to return.

Personal Service, then, had to fit into a pattern of life quite different from that on shore where men can plan and secure credit in a stable community. Seamen had their own code of honor about repaying loans (indeed, often embarrassed us by using a loan for food to pay a debt) and were dead set against "charity." For these reasons, USS had no choice but to make its aid in loans, even when capacity to repay seemed dubious because personal illness and family emergencies were almost continuous handicaps to some men. The loans were budgeted for necessities, and we used every resource we could to arrange stays of evictions or repossession of furniture, but we did not hesitate to save a family's home or possessions by a small holding payment if there was no other recourse. If our expenditure for loans was higher at NMU than in other USS units, it was to be understood in part in connection with the fact that more members of NMU than of other unions were family men who had established homes in New York so as to see their families more often.

The social workers at the NMU had, therefore, to shake themselves free from rigidities that develop in any profession and learn to apply in new ways the principle of knowing their community. If we had fears about trusting with money people who might be irresponsible, we reminded ourselves that cash relief rather than ticket orders had become an established principle in our profession, and seamen could be worked with like other people. If we thought one should *never* give a loan to pay debts, we had to ask what happened to a family's morale when their small furnishings, with which they had struggled to make a home, went off in a van, and they were forced into lodging houses where they must live at greater cost. If we thought we did nothing, professionally, unless we used our skills in emotional crises, we found no less challenge when such crises were accompanied by desperate situations in living. For instance, the wartime secrecy about ship movements left husbands and wives without means of communication with each other for weeks. A wife might have no other news than the stopping of her allotment checks, with no way of knowing whether her husband had become separated from his ship in a foreign port, was sick or injured or dead. We had to help women burdened with many family cares to face these agonizing crises, try to get news for them, help them adjust to loss of income, or to get what was due them in cases of confirmed death of the seamen. And we had to counsel with men who had lost everything, including the stability of their family life.

Professionally, then, the experience at the NMU taught us flexibility if nothing else. The handling of large numbers did this for us and challenged our philosophy also. Technically, we learned to sift the needs of a long line of applicants so that cases for information only, or referral to other departments, got attention at once, while those requiring an appointment with an interviewer were given assurance of being seen in turn and with adequate time. Philosophically, we had to give up ideas that we, offering benefits, decide who shall have them. Serving a democratically organized group, we must serve all or none, with all the resources we had.

We had also to learn to use new resources coming from the men's own group. For instance, when the NMU established a Credit Union to which seamen could allot from their pay and have family allowances and foreseen bills taken care of, plus a margin for saving, Personal Service had a potent means of helping a financially disorganized social group to form habits of saving and planning for their future, instead of just dreaming about it. The Women's Auxiliary also helped Personal Service, either with problems discovered perhaps on their visits to hospitals or to families, or in situations we encountered in which union sisters could be of great use. There was no problem here of volunteers who were too far from the way of life of those whom they wanted to help.

Just to enter the NMU hall was an inspiration in those days. First, one would see a modernized building, its cheerful lobby decorated with murals on labor themes, and, at a focal point, a well-lighted little bookstore where, at almost any hour, men would be looking over books and buying packets of them to take to sea. We would see faces from all nations and hear the tongues of innumerable peoples. We would hear the word "Brother" as an accepted designation. The faces of Negro and Puerto Rican seamen glowed as they talked to us at Personal Service about the Union's no-discrimination policy.[11]

In the shipping hall, men would be watching the chart of jobs posted and throwing in their cards at the Dispatcher's window to apply for those for which they had qualifying Coast Guard papers. On the edges of the crowd, there would be corners for games or an art class, provided by USS, where men who had never painted before were eager and absorbed in producing some remarkable work, often sea pictures. At noon one could listen to a USS program, a health talk perhaps, a concert or a film. Everywhere there was a sense of the value of life, as men shipped out to unknown dangers.

A major activity of Personal Service in the last two years was in co-operation with the New York State Rehabilitation program. At first glance, this plan seemed complete in itself: discovery of the patients in hospitals needing and qualified for retraining; consultation of medical and vocational experts to place them in well-selected courses; educational guidance through the training period; placement in work after training. Actually, we found the whole plan could be wrecked unless there was expert personal service at every stage. First, a man would need help to adjust to permanent loss of his familiar vocation and to develop courage to face new challenges just at the time when dependence had been fostered by hopelessness and a long hospitalization. Then there would be periods of crisis in training when discouragement would be inevitable. Someone must be there with whom to talk these over, who would give assurance that the man would not be abandoned if a State allotment was unavoidably delayed. Even after training was completed, there was often a disheartening wait until full employment was achieved. For all this, personal service in the man's own union, which he trusted, was a great advantage. Also, we found some money to be essential for emotional security, if only to pay room rent until a delayed allotment arrived, or to equip with warm clothing a tubercular patient suddenly sent to outdoor work.

The Personal Service department at NMU developed its work considerably in its four years of existence. It had, for instance, enough variety of work to give a challenging training experience to two students of the New York School of Social Work. They were not beginners, but former supervisors in the Department of Welfare, used to dealing with pressures of numbers and time. They brought into the staff discussions fine thinking which the Department of Welfare itself was working out, safeguarding the rights of clients as individuals in a mass program, fostering the role of responsible citizenship in a public service.

There were, of course, many social workers who doubted whether personal service in a union could be classified as casework. If we could satisfy them as to protection of records, as to the validity of short-contact work (which became with us intermittent contacts as seamen returned after trips), and as to the professional qualifications of the social workers, their last bastion was the question of authority. How could a service be professional which was subject to decisions of any group outside its trained personnel? I remember being troubled about this myself, after some union ruling about loans. What we came to realize was that we had never before served clients who had an organized means of expressing the "self-determination of the client" about which we theorized. We had accepted without realizing it a subtle dictation from other groups which influence opinion in the prosperous community, and, in fear of giving offense, we had limited our service to clients when it threatened to expose low wages and wretched health conditions in a prominent industry. We had distrusted group pressures and thought we were free from them when we had never had contact with a client group which could think out the implications of its own situation and constructive ways of dealing with it.[12]

Not least among learning opportunities for social workers was a new experience in being trade unionists ourselves.[13] For me, it was pulling together many threads from the warp and

woof of previous years. I had advocated union organization for
social workers, because there was no alternative if one was to
assume mature responsibility for the service one gave. The
Depression years had banished any illusions we might have had
that philanthropic organizations, just by being such, guaranteed
protection to those whom they employed. Walking a picket line
with grievously exploited fellow union members employed by a
hospital or social agency taught me that getting the most out
of contributed funds is as potent a source of exploitation of
workers who cannot protect themselves as a profit motive can
be. One illusion social workers had left—that if a union was the
employer, and the nearest administrator was a fellow union
member, processes of negotiation would not apply. We found
that while the intent of a union employer might be free from
the motive of personal profit, the purpose to get the most out
of all resources for the service did not, and should not, include
philanthropy toward employees. Union-conscious employees of
a union shared its purpose to serve the interests of the members, but part of their responsibility was the best use of themselves professionally, if they were professional workers. It was
their role, more than that of anyone else, to say when pressures
of work, hampering working conditions, or inadequate pay
would, in the long run, prevent their giving their best. This was
their share in administering a service and was really labor-
management co-operation, which was talked about in war
industries, but, because of basic conflict of interests, never
realized. So, in our experience in the USS-NMU Personal
Service, we negotiated with open-minded employers for a union
contract at the same time that we took full responsibility to
reduce waste of effort and improve the quality of our own
work.

The thrilling thing about social work at the NMU was its new
look at whom we were helping. We social workers had talked
about restoring people to a capacity for doing for themselves,
but we seldom thought of their doing so except as individuals
or small homogeneous groups. We probably feared their acting

as large, organized bodies and doubted if they could. Yet, under peculiar pressures in wartime, an organization of eighty to a hundred thousand men in a single industry did, for a brief time, show what could be done with a united purpose. They were ordinary men, not picked for a demonstration, though they had good leadership developed in their own group. They were unusually handicapped by being scattered over the seven seas[14] on assignments covered by wartime secrecy. They were divided into three occupations with differences of interests and were separated by all the prejudices as to race, creed, and political beliefs which were common ashore. There was not time to educate to union-consciousness all the thousands of recruits who poured into the industry. Yet they showed what creative thinking could go into the amelioration of conditions that had plagued the industry for more than a hundred years. They asked no benefits they could not win by their own united strength and none that did not enhance their responsible contribution as citizens.

The CIO unions, especially, were alert in wartime to community problems of housing, day care for children of working mothers, and health care for everyone, regardless of ability to pay. A Health Council of the unions in New York City dealt with problems of working people as such. Some of the unions set up welfare departments of their own to deal with technical advice to members on industry conditions and better use of community agencies. Some unions, such as the United Electrical Workers and the Fur Workers turned to the NMU Personal Service for help in organizing courses for union officials assigned to welfare counselling. These courses, in which I participated, gave some understanding of community agencies and how to reach them with referrals and some survey of common problems of individuals and families.

There were in the United States some half-dozen projects in which unions shared with professional social workers sponsorship of counselling and referral services.[15] These developments were fostered by two aspects of the climate in wartime. First,

Labor had become important as a "big giver" to community and war funds, and social agencies were thinking seriously of how to interpret their work to labor groups and develop more participation of working people as such in community planning. Secondly, old prejudices in labor circles against "welfare" were dissolving, as it became evident that union aims for economic gains were not an antithesis to concern about personal problems, but intimately related to it.[16]

After the war ended, the USS-NMU staffs did some hard thinking about their continuing function. It was unthinkable that after a wartime demonstration, the urgent needs of a large group employed by a vital industry could be as neglected as they had been for more than a hundred years. On the other hand, the industry was shrinking rapidly from its peak in wartime. In the immediate future, what did we see? A report prepared in August, 1946, stated the case as follows :[17]

"We recognize that the war mobilized resources to an extraordinary degree to keep the ships sailing. . . . After the war, we found ourselves dealing with an employed group, but one subjected to peculiar hazards and difficulties. . . . Men and women had to pick up for themselves the less adequate resources which were left to them after certain war services and war bonuses were discontinued, and at the very time when they were fatigued and perhaps actually disabled by the strain of war years. . . . Personal service is needed more than ever for its educational, morale-building values. . . . Financial aid, when given. . . . must strengthen and not in any way weaken the ability to solve problems, to plan better, and to co-operate better with others in industry-wide solutions for widespread needs. . . .

"How do we see the relation of this general situation to the purposes of USS? . . . Only a superficial view of this service, as *solely* to conserve manpower for war, could consider USS unnecessary as soon as the fighting was over. However, to conceive of USS as cut-down service of the same sort in the confused postwar period would be to deny its essential validity as a service agency."

The report went on to specify certain areas of continuing need, such as medical emergencies against which seamen and their families are singularly unprotected, the service aspect so important to work with rehabilitation cases, and convalescent care after the crowded Marine Hospitals have discharged men too early to fend for themselves in unsuitable lodginghouses.

By October, 1946, the Executive Board of USS voted to continue the service if possible, and received an enthusiastic response from seamen who hated the "Bethel" type of philanthropy. Support was expected from the general public, from the maritime industry, and from the seamen themselves. With reduced financial backing, the USS planned to stimulate community resources in the interest of seamen whose needs ashore had hitherto not been met. There seemed no doubt that the NMU Personal Service Department would continue to integrate its service with all that the Union was doing for its members.

Were we Utopian in our confidence, in 1946? Probably we would have defined a Utopian outlook as one that fails to take account of the human imperfections that so often wreck a good program, or of changing conditions that revolutionize a situation overnight, especially after the dislocations of a great war. We thought we were realistic in seeing a qualitative change from prewar conditions, something new in that Labor was rising to its responsibilities as an essential force in industry and community life. A New Deal might be replaced by another deal of the cards, but, surely, what men did for themselves could not be undone! They had had the strength to do it once and could, if necessary, do it again and yet again.

CHAPTER 17

THE SMOG THICKENS

How did we know when "Keep 'Em Sailing" changed to "Never Mind" and then to "Watch Out, Tie 'Em Up"?

January 2, 1947, was bomb day for USS. In the last week of the old year, it had been expanding its Personal Service staff and two new workers for the NMU hall were to report for orientation to the USS office downtown, the day after the holiday. They never reached their new jobs. On January 2nd the shipping companies announced that they were stopping their contributions to USS for work in United States ports and would continue only to maintain a few strategic centers overseas. A million dollars left from the National War Fund would see the program through a year of tapering off, and after that the USS must itself finance any work it found necessary.[1]

At first, there was some hope of raising the money to meet needs for services demonstrated to be urgent. However, Community Funds in port cities were locality-conscious and not inclined to appeal for the needs of seamen from all over the world. Were not seamen wards of the government, anyway? The unions, faced with declining membership and increasing difficulties with the shipping companies, were not in a position to raise much money for welfare work or to spend it through a co-operating outside agency. The year 1947 was then a year of holding on to serve seamen as long as we could without many of the resources we had had. At its end, I retired from active service, and the two remaining USS caseworkers went over to the payroll of the NMU. Before another year was out, worsening conditions in the Union made any form of personal service impossible.

I remember well the December day in 1946 when the news reached the NMU hall that, without consulting the membership, President Joe Curran had pulled the Union out of the World Federation of Trade Unions. Men were tense in the hall and elevators as they asked, "What next"? They remembered the promising steps toward unity which had been made by a national conference of competing unions in the maritime industry and how that unity had won unprecedented gains for seamen that year. There was hope that the World Federation would be of special advantage to the maritime unions, whose interests crossed national boundaries. In an industry destined to shrink drastically as war-built ships piled up in the "bone yards" of all the coasts, it was high time to consolidate gains by standing firmly together.

Now the words "communist dominated," applied to the World Federation of Trade Unions, took on a sinister meaning in the NMU itself. Factions which had always existed but had been masked by united effort for the war began to fling charges and countercharges of disloyalty at each other. The Taft-Hartley Act,[2] just passed, put government on the side of a purge of union officials and members who could be charged with being communists if they had been militant in the union or had been active supporters of a policy of no-discrimination as to race. Many seamen were thrown out of office, out of union membership, and out of opportunity to ship. The Negro and Puerto Rican seamen and the foreign-born were the first to feel the pressure of petty charges that ruled them out of shipping assignments.

Leaving my personal fortunes to a later chapter, let us trace, through more than a decade, the effects of the smog, the man-made smoke, and creeping fog of the postwar years which became "the period of the cold war."

Adaptation to the climate of community opinion was, of

course, as old as social work itself. The definition of *community* had been shifting from the giving public toward the inclusion of users of services. Working people had come to be counted, in wartime at least, if not actually often consulted. Financing through Community Chests and Councils had been a marked gain. Yet with better-organized support for social agencies, there was a growing possibility that their work might be influenced predominantly by contributing groups, far removed from an understanding of the lives of needy people.

As often happens, it was one incident in a Midwestern city which stabbed me awake to the possibility even as early as 1937. A caseworker in a family agency found that one of her clients could not possibly meet his family's needs on the wages he was earning. When her talk with her supervisor made clear that the agency could not give aid and should not, on principle, supplement low wages, the caseworker wrote the man a nice letter, suggesting that perhaps he could get a raise from his employer or, if not, could find a better job. The man saw in the letter a reinforcement of his plea and took it to his boss in the bakery. The latter angrily took the letter to the Community Fund, threatening to withdraw his contribution if that was what Fund agencies were doing. The Fund executive took the matter up with the president of the Agency Board, and the latter visited in haste, to have the caseworker brought before him and warned of the loss of her job if she did such a thing again. At about the same time, in the same city, a group worker was dismissed for the crime of allowing or stimulating free discussion of a controversial subject.

The lesson which some students of social work drew from the first incident was never to put in writing anything that may be used against you. To me it was obvious that individual workers could not be protected in the use of professional judgment without the backing of organized fellow workers. A year or two later, when I said somewhat timidly to an executive of a children's agency that I feared the influence of financing bodies upon the practice of social work, he replied with unexpected vehemence, "Don't you know that Community Funds already own social agencies, lock, stock, and barrel?" Whether or not his experience was typical, certain trends were causing concern to thoughtful people.

By the time of the National Conference held in Grand Rapids, in 1940, our whole profession was jolted out of any complacency it may have had by the news from California that relief allowances had been cut to starvation levels and denied entirely unless clients would accept labor at starvation wages; that trained social workers in public assistance who protested were replaced by untrained political henchmen; that social workers even suspected of being members of the CIO union were fired; that questioning of workers, on suspicion or on the slanders of paid informers, took place before a legislative committee, and such workers were fired automatically if they refused to answer all its questions about their personal lives and beliefs.

At the Grand Rapids Conference, I was scheduled for a paper on why the social workers are especially concerned about civil rights.[3] My theme was that every form of social work (casework, group work, community organization, and research) depends for its existence upon Article I of the Bill of Rights— freedom of speech and of the press, of assembly and of petition for redress of grievances. Without such a charter, social work could not operate, for it could not remain in healthy contact with its community.

I said: "Civil rights are maintained with most difficulty where bargaining power for economic necessities is low. Social workers deal largely with disadvantaged people whose difficulties. . . . run back to conditions much more widespread than can be attributed to the mistakes of individuals alone. These ills cannot be eradicated until their origin is understood, and social conditions can never be understood unless the people who feel them directly are free to bear testimony about them."[4]

Actually, people who live under economic handicaps are not free to protest. Individually, they are blacklisted as "troublemakers" and ruled out of such essentials as a job, living quarters, and a chance to eat. If working people combine to bargain with the strength of their labor power for better conditions, their leaders are often dismissed and blacklisted. Deprived of their spokesmen and refused opportunity to negotiate with employers, they have also no access to the press (itself, a monopoly controlled by powerful interests). What language is left to workers by which to say to their community that conditions in their industry are intolerable to them? It is a costly language—refusal to work and carrying a message by word of mouth and painted sign through heat and cold and rain and snow, while families hunger at home. For this, workers are replaced not by other workers but by mercenaries, expert in violent breaking of strikes. The workers find not protection but repression from police forces, charged with protection of property and not of citizens without property. So they buy dearly what small freedom of speech they have.

To quote again: "Social workers, then, whose business it is to stimulate people to express their desire to better their condition in all lawful ways, find themselves in the peculiar position of seeing those who do so beaten on picket lines or thrown into jail as evil doers. It becomes almost superfluous to ask, 'Is this their business?'"

I went on to say that social workers may feel that "if people are good they will not be molested. Those who get into conflict with the police must have deserved it somehow. Certainly this could not happen to social workers personally." If we do have such an illusion, the California experience is a rude awakening.

The paper at Grand Rapids did not end without a strong emphasis on the effect of war preparations on civil liberties. After saying that the Bill of Rights breaks down when there is marked economic inequality, I added that the only exception made in its text is "in actual service in time of war or public danger." The United States was not at war. Was it, I asked, in such public danger that being an unnaturalized resident constitutes a crime and automatically condemns a person without trial as a spy or saboteur?[5] "Does belonging to one or another group holding religious or political opinions not shared by all make necessary persecution without redress? . . . Can social workers remain under the illusion that there is a national emergency that cancels the Bill of Rights? Can they not see that there is a national *social* emergency which requires the strictest observance of it?"

It was in 1940, when war preparations were coming to be accepted as an alternative to depression, that the Smith Act was passed to make easier the apprehension of aliens who might be "subversive." Few paid attention to it at the time or dreamed that it would be revived in 1948 in the mass arrest of practically all the leaders of the Communist party, and that political trials and imprisonment would become an accepted part of our national consciousness. In 1940, the American people were resisting strong pressure for universal military training, and only gradually did military service in peacetime become a taken-for-granted break in every boy's life. In 1940, I may have underestimated the danger that our ocean-protected land might be involved in a war, but I did not overestimate, I am sure, the threat of militarism to the American democracy which we were supposed to be defending.

At first, it was possible to believe that social work might go its way comparatively little affected by struggles going on elsewhere for civil liberties. Private social agencies found emotional problems plentiful and their skills in great demand. The Public Assistance Program had had ten years to prove that, inadequate as it was, it made a vast difference to the security of thousands of people in the United States who were caught in economic disaster. We believed, many of us, that no political interest would dare to undermine it or halt its further progress. By 1946, the National Conference of Social Work could have a session on *the right to relief* which featured a scholarly paper[6] by A. Delafield Smith, Assistant General Counsel of the Federal Security Agency. In a paper of mine[7] at that Conference, I

could stress the principle that social workers in a Public Assistance agency were not there only as gatekeepers, to exclude
all whose need did not fit a certain pattern, nor were they
just doing their best to divide up what resources they had
among all who were legally eligible. To administer the program
responsibly, they had to know *why* the planned giving of aid
was necessary. In that spring of 1946, I could confidently assert
that the right to relief rested on the principles which had guided
government aid to seamen in wartime. "We know that men
cannot live without bread and that nations cannot live without
men. We know that the destruction of war must be balanced
by production for peace. . . . War veterans and veterans of
production alike want to throw their energies into needed services. . . . The same powerful forces which deny them jobs,
except at wages which destroy a tolerable standard of living,
would also deny the right to assistance even when there are no
jobs to be had. These workers are the living stuff of which
democracy is made. Unless they can assert their right to assistance on the same basis as their right to work, as part of their
right to live and keep fit to work because their country needs
them, the right to assistance stands every chance of being lost,
along with democracy itself."

In 1947, with unemployment increasing and relief rolls rising,
the mind of the American people was assaulted by a violent
denial of any "right to assistance" and by repudiation of standards of administration of relief which had been built up for
more than ten years under the Federal Security Act. That May,
in city after city, with a timing too close to be accidental, the
Scripps-Howard and Hearst newspapers began a campaign to
discredit public assistance and create a nation-wide scandal. In
New York City, a columnist published stories of clients in mink
coats, of housing in hotels, of "maid service" and laundry
allowances to coddle the lazy, of encouragement to immorality
and neglect of children.[8]

By late June, coinciding with the beginning of a new fiscal
year, the attack shifted from local mismanagement to the

Federal Program itself. Taking credit for exposure of "luxury relief," the columnist of the New York *World-Telegram* subtitled his diatribe, "Aid Is Seen as a Right With No Control Permissible." He quoted out of context A. Delafield Smith's paper at the 1946 National Conference of Social Work, to prove that the Federal spokesman had admitted that relief encourages dependency and that he evidently "rejects theories that persons who accept public assistance should be forced to adhere to certain moral standards or go to work."[9] Thus, local sniping at city welfare departments became a national issue, an attempt to undermine, if not abolish, the whole Federal Public Assistance Program.

The United Public Workers had been active since May with press releases to get the facts before the public. In July, the Joint Committee of Trade Unions in Social Work in New York[10] asked me if I would write a leaflet for distribution. *The Press Lies About Relief* was the angriest piece of writing I ever did. I closed with these words: "Any or all of us may be forced to become relief recipients. Are we ready to become slaves under a Nazi-like conception that relief recipients have no rights which their rulers are bound to respect? If we are not willing. . . . there is no time to lose in organizing protests through every channel open to us. . . . We must expose the attack for what it is, a bomb aimed at the heart of America."

Later that fall, other unions and at least one committee of concerned citizens protested the attacks which had already resulted in serious deterioration in services to clients of the Department of Welfare. The New York Chapter of the American Association of Social Workers appointed a committee, of which I was a member, to see what could be done to protect professional standards. I attended a hearing before the State Commissioner of Social Welfare which I shall never forget.

The pattern of procedure, which later became familiar in political inquisitions, was sufficiently clear that December day. Witnesses who were employees of the Department of Welfare and willing to co-operate with the investigation had been interviewed in a private session beforehand and had given testimony which was recorded. At this hearing, their testimony was read back to them with the question, "Did you say . . . as read?" The only unrehearsed witness was Miss Elizabeth Russell, a casework supervisor with the Department, of high professional standing.[11] She put up a strong defense of casework principles: individualizing of clients; using professional judgment in adapting what could be done under the law to individual circumstances; making use of medical and psychiatric examinations to determine employability. However, everything she said was discredited by the rehearsed witnesses who gave testimony about clients who would not work and those who received special coddling under the guise of professional practice. At intermission, the witnesses were assembled so that the representatives of the press could take their pictures.

Besides Miss Russell's gallant defense of sound principles that day, another incident fired my pride in my discredited profession. It was a rebuke to the chairman of the hearing, delivered in good, round tones in the comparative quiet of intermission, when most of the observers were too stunned to say anything. The speaker was a national leader in social work, with long experience in civic life and welfare administration. She said, in substance, "Mr. Commissioner, I am outraged by the procedings here today. Is it for newspaper sensationalism that they are staged? I cannot blame the newsmen so much, for their trade is sensation. They do not know the awful human suffering that these inquisitions lead to—not honest investigations which we would all welcome. They do not know, but *you* know, Mr. Commissioner, and *you* are culpable." For the remaining hours of the session the Commissioner sat with his head in his hands, and no man ever deserved a headache more.

The attacks on public assistance in the press prepared the way for a new, "economy" administration in New York, which not only cut already inadequate food budgets but also services urgently needed by sick and aged clients and allowances for growing children. It reduced professional staff far below any possibility of adequate service. The staff lost, not only through resignations of those who could no longer endure overwork and harassment, but by dismissals which, if they could be accomplished in no other way, were the result of a device called "below average" evaluations. These were applied to union members and others whose regular ratings were satisfactory, by adding a further note that they were guilty of misconduct or discrediting the Department.

In order to protest this unethical practice to the appropriate committee of the AASW, a complaint had to be made as a grievance by an AASW member. In August, 1950, I took that responsibility. The complaint was: 1) disregard of the AASW Code of Ethics, Personnel Practices, and Civil Rights; 2) tampering with duly made evaluations by addition of unsubstantiated accusations; 3) denial of a fair hearing, punitive transfers, or dismissals, branding employees in the public press as guilty and subjecting them to personal loss and humiliation; 4) assumption by the agency of control of speech and action of employees outside of working hours, so as to deny them their right, as good citizens, to speak in the public interest on behalf of improvement in the public services; 5) singling out for persecution employees engaged in activity in a trade union chosen by a majority of the staff to represent them; 6) penalizing workers (without proof of their responsibility for it) for a brochure, *Welfare in Crisis,* issued by the UPWA, this constituting violation of freedom of the press.

I related this situation to AASW members, most of whom were employed in private social agencies, by saying that the very existence of private agencies in their present form is predicated upon a sound public welfare administration, national in scope. I said further that this situation is "a test of critical urgency of the kind of influence AASW can and should wield. . . . We cannot afford to sink into wordy impotence at a time when our ability to speak for an ethical and vital profession is so challenged." The same letter was sent to both the national AASW and the New York City Chapter. Replies later in the fall indicated that a national committee was studying developments, and the New York City Chapter was watching the situation.

In January, 1952, the AASW published a pamphlet on a serious threat to the cardinal social work principle of confidentiality.[12] Up to the passage of the Jenner Amendment to the Revenue Act of 1951, the Federal Security Agency was empowered to withhold Federal Assistance funds from any state which gave public access to information concerning assistance disbursements. By this amendment, attached to a Revenue Act so that it could not be easily vetoed, the Federal Agency was prohibited from such withholding. Any state could enact legislation to permit publication of names of relief recipients, providing that such lists were not used for commercial or political purposes. The amendment, sponsored by Congressman Jenner of Indiana, had its history in the passage in that state of legislation calling for publication of names of relief recipients. The theory was that, even if the state lost Federal reimbursement, it would save enough by reducing relief rolls through shaming clients and their relatives to be as well off without Federal funds. Of course the passage of the Federal amendment saved them even that hazard. Such an outcome would hardly have been possible without the five-year barrage of newspaper publicity throughout the country, in which the "secrecy" of relief grants had been deplored.

The AASW pamphlet called attention to serious implications, such as the impossibility of enforcing the provision against commercial or political use, once the relief rolls were made public, the avowed purpose of shaming the clients, and the difficulty of protecting other types of confidential information, including health records and family data. It made clear that this was an attack on the basic principles of the Public Assistance program. It urged action directed to state legislatures where proposals for such legislation were pending, to Congress for repeal of the Jenner amendment, to candidates for public office, and to the press. It stressed the importance of the issue of confidentiality to the whole philosophy and practice of social work.

None of us who watched with deep concern the downward trend in public services had any illusions that a small group of professional people could, by themselves, affect the outcome in favor of decent standards. The backing of millions of people was necessary and could only be secured by reaching them with the truth through their own organizations. Labor unions had demanded free public education and had saved it from destruction a century ago. If labor leaders now thought public assistance no concern of theirs (provided they succeeded in their wage struggles), the large users of labor knew better. If public assistance could be destroyed, Labor could be forced to accept wages below subsistence levels, and without recourse. If protests of organized Labor could be eliminated, public assistance itself could be reduced to legalized starvation under controls approximating slavery. It was one attack on two fronts.

Back of it all was fear. It was not, this time, fear of starving beggars like those who haunted the roads of England in the Middle Ages and whose presence gave rise to the Poor Laws with teeth. Now it was fear that free men, whom war had set in motion, would defend their own living standards. They could be rendered impotent only through fear, the ingredients of which were at hand.

Thirty years of violent propaganda against the USSR had had their effect. Even though most people now knew that the working-men of the Red Army (whom we had branded as slaves eager for liberation from despotism) had indeed fought like free men and saved the Allied cause in the war, it was easy to revert to the old hatreds. It was really the wrong war we had fought against the Nazis, who now began to be wooed as allies. The USSR was the real enemy, most treacherous when it seemed most anxious for peace. If a "cold war" of nerves was the only war possible in a world weary of slaughter, it could still be immensely profitable. Government spending for "defense" could take the place of depression palliatives. Labor could see its own stake in full employment. The mind of the public was prepared to believe that our country was in acute danger, even while we brandished an atomic bomb to terrify the rest of mankind.

Certain events and their dramatization in the press and on radio and screen fairly well established a set of concepts which were interwoven but showed a discernible chronological development.

From 1947 on, loyalty oaths, required from a widening range of public officials and employees, warned the public that we must be alert to danger from within.

In August, 1948, when the mushroom growth of the Progressive Party threatened the expected two-party domination of the fall elections, the officers of the Communist Party in the United States were suddenly arrested under the Smith Act, as having organized to teach the overthrow of the government by force and violence. Their trials, continuing through most of 1949, were played up in the press to establish that they were dominated by International Communism and to prove their deceit in affirming that they did not advocate violence.[13] Here was the enemy, both from without and within.

The Walter-McCarran Act in 1950 added a long list of organizations to the active Communist Party itself, under the title of "Communist-front organizations."[14] These were organizations for civil liberties, protection of the foreign-born, and organizations against racial discrimination and for social justice.[15] Guilt by association became admissible as evidence that a person was a menace to his country.

Assuming that the USSR was uncivilized and backward, the announcement in 1949 that it had the atom bomb could be interpreted to the American people in only one way—it had stolen the secrets from us through the treachery of spies! A succession of trials of accused "spies" culminated in 1953 in the execution of Julius and Ethel Rosenberg, a young New York engineer and his wife, charged with responsibility for the Korean war because of the assumption that the USSR had started it and could not have done so without the secrets stolen from us. A sinister feature of their case was that they were offered immunity up to the last hour of their lives, if they would testify that they were involved in a Communist conspiracy and name others. They refused and went to their death affirming their innocence.[16]

All of these developments and more contributed to a creeping fog of fear throughout the whole of American life. For such offenses as signing a petition for peace, attending a meeting perhaps years before, or mailing letters, people lost their jobs, were driven from public office, and were sent to jail.[17] It sounds like the understatement of the year to say that communication with one's fellows became difficult. Meetings were suspect and the press closed to any but approved ideas. Even the give-and-take of private conversation suffered, for who could tell when the next person might be an informer. Perhaps he literally was or, if not, the fear of informers stifled free speech quite as effectively.[18] We lost our Social Service Employees Union after no social agencies would sign contracts. It had been, as part of the UOPWA, expelled from the CIO on a charge of being "Communist-dominated." This had happened to some eleven unions which had been most active in winning gains for their members. So our channels of communication were closed one after the other, not only with our outer world but among people who had been accustomed to think and work together.

However, the spark of life will not be quenched. Small groups of people came together as they could, around certain vital issues. There were the Social Service Volunteers for Peace and the National Council of the Arts, Sciences and Professions, gathering data on what atomic war would mean to mankind and making it known. These groups and others made it possible for me, isolated individual as I was, to speak to my generation a few times more. I remember most vividly four such opportunities.

First, there was a book which I wrote to convey to fellow social workers the immense enrichment of the experience we

had had at the NMU.[19] It was not approved by leaders in
social work. One of them said to me, "You write as if you were
outside social work." So I did, for it seemed to me that we
needed nothing so much just then as to "stand off and look at
ourselves." The publication of this book was difficult but not
impossible with the help of friends who refused to accept
defeat.[20] It evaluated our philosophy of social work in the light
of an experience with ordinary people who were doing what
they could for themselves.

On January 30, 1952, there was a meeting in New York in
celebration of Franklin Roosevelt's birthday—a time for remembering his objectives of social welfare and peace. My talk
on that evening asked the old question of how the struggles
going on around the world touched us as social workers.[21] The
picture was not a pretty one.

"As professional workers, we are frustrated and restless,
changing jobs or perhaps feeling trapped because we cannot
change. In public agencies, the services are crippled. . . . When
public services deteriorate, private social work becomes more
and more unreal. How can caseworkers discuss choices with
people who have no choice? How can they treat anxiety in
people who know nothing else in their daily lives? How can
group agencies offer cultural opportunities which mean something creative to young people who are soon to be swallowed
up by a war machine? How can adult education stimulate discussion of vital issues when people are being jailed for thinking
and speaking outside the patterns set by official propaganda?

"We may have felt that we could escape turmoil by becoming
absorbed in technical skills which have been successful in solving
conflicts within individuals and between individuals and groups.
Now we are confronted with conflicts beyond the reach of any
technical skill. Naked greed and oppression are opposed to the
demands of everyday people to be able to live, to be free, and
to be happy. . . . Never so much as in our day have people everywhere been stirred into movement to win these goals for themselves. Are we ready to go with them?"

The question was not an empty one. In 1952, there were still peoples' organizations one could join, there were letters to be written, petitions to be signed, delegations and rallies in which to speak out. Were not these dangerous activities? Of course. But it is dangerous to be alive and far more dangerous to be dead while one is supposed to be living.

The next year, 1953, I contributed a paper, "Fear in Our Culture," at a meeting during the National Conference of Social Work at Cleveland.[22] Discussing the fears of the unknown which plague primitive peoples and which an age of science has largely overcome, I found an alarming group of new fears in our culture—fears of destruction from the enormous powers that science itself has created. Then there are fears engendered by living in an interdependent world, where an individual's survival and opportunity to work for a living depend upon others, unknown to him and uncounted miles away. Surpluses of goods to which he has no access, depressions of which he knows not the cause, the blood-letting of wars he never made— all these are beyond an individual's power either to escape by flight or to overcome by struggle.

So we ask ourselves, "What is it *ever* possible to do about a fear?" Of the three alternatives offered us by the psychologists, "freeze, flee, or fight," which ones are available to us in these tense days?

"Man, who is physically weak and not fleet of foot, by animal standards, has an intelligence which is more than individual cleverness. Man has the power, not found among animals, to communicate with his fellows by speech, and hence to co-operate intelligently and planfully for mutually desired ends. The challenge to us all, then, in this age of fear, is to use our intelligence in social co-operation with others to overcome the dangers that threaten us. We are confident that we can overcome them. The unknown in climatic conditions, plant and animal diseases and those that afflict man, is being systematically attacked by scientific research. We have no reason to believe that we cannot learn to use our own inventions wisely, or that we cannot, if we will, find some way to overcome economic crises. Is the only danger left, which we consider unreachable by science, our danger from each other?

"The startling thing about our present fears is that they are precisely the kind of fears which would deter us from using the remedy of intelligent co-operation with other human beings.

"First, the fear of using intelligence itself. The idea is inculcated that questioning the propaganda fed to us is disloyal and subversive. Then we are prevented from using the intelligence we have by fear of the unknown. Communism is represented as something so insidious and utterly evil that to study it, to find out what it is, is the mark of a perverted mind. Since those who teach it are jailed as criminals, those who try to learn can only be accomplices.

"Furthermore, people are prevented from seeing their own stake in association for mutual self-protection by the divisive effect of the choice of victims. If it is a Negro who is accused, it is assumed that white people will not feel personally threatened or, if they do, they too may be accused on the ground that they must be communists. If it is a Jew, the whisper among the well-to-do is that 'All Jews are radicals, you know,' and among the poor it is that 'Of course, we know that wars and depressions are caused by the international Jewish bankers.' If a person is foreign-born or active in a labor union or an outstanding intellectual, there is always a portion of the population that would tend to be against him for that reason and believe him a public enemy. If the accused is of exemplary character and public spirit, that is expected to be proof that you can trust absolutely nobody. It only shows how deceitful the communists are when they clothe themselves with the words and deeds of citizens concerned with the public good. The pattern of all this incitement to fear is to create a firm public opinion against joining anything, signing anything, protesting anything.

"The choice is before us. What kind of country will we have? What kind of people will we be, as we live in this most critical time of all history? Once we get into motion with other

courageous men and women, fear will dissolve in the out-
pouring of living energies. The point is to get to work with
others, where we are and now."

On the fourth occasion, I spoke in defense of our profession
against destruction of trained and qualified personnel by the
current witch-hunts and gave examples of social agencies so
blighted.[23] I told of a shocking example of violation of ethical
professional principles in which both a public and a private
social agency were involved in devastating political persecution
of two innocent children.[24] I closed as follows:

"Our profession exists for human welfare, for happy homes,
healthy bodies and minds, the right to work as free men and
women and to enjoy the fruits of labor. We can do no less
than to stand, without equivocation, for these goals of a mature
profession, prepared to protect any of our number who suffer
in defense of just such goals and standards. When we recover
from the fright which has isolated many of us, enough to get
together even in small groups, to take counsel how we can
implement our professional principles, we shall have taken an
important step toward a mature acceptance of the responsibility
and the honor of living in this day."

The theme of that paper, that fear reached into every corner
of our life, was illustrated by what happened to me as a result
of delivering it. I was suddenly barred from study at a summer
seminar at a school of social work, for which I had been accepted and welcomed. The reason given was that the school had
just remembered that my distinguished attainments would em-
barrass the leader of the course. At that time, the paper had
not been delivered, and no eye but mine had seen it, but fliers
advertising the meeting had been circulated at the National
Conference, bearing the fearsome words, "McCarthyism vs.
Social Work." The pressure which the school was unable to
withstand boded ill for academic freedom of teaching.

In all the turmoil of war and domestic strife, what was happening to the voluntary social agencies which had a tradition
of defending standards of service and of moving social work

toward the status of a profession? We have tried to appraise at intervals the progress of this young profession: the great changes, amounting to a revolution, after the First World War; the beginnings of formation of a generic content underneath a group of specialties; the breaking up of old forms and reorganization under the impact of a major depression; the marked changes instituted by the passage of the Social Security Act. Had private social agencies continued to lead in the forward march of this growing profession?

This question took a number of forms in the years under review. Could private social work justify its existence when economic need was removed from its area of concern? Could it operate by its own standards while community pressures increased? Could it grow in breadth and depth in a world of fear and frustration which needed it beyond any reckoning?

CHAPTER 18

EDDIES OF CONTROVERSY

A spring wind was blowing from the ocean when the National Conference of Social Work met at Atlantic City in 1948. How many of us remembered the prairie wind at the Conference at Kansas City? Was it only fourteen years ago? What changes had come! Then, a great depression and people's organizations in motion to do something about it; after that, war clouds and war itself; then fear and repression and more fear. Now another depression was threatening, and what had seemed like a permanent gain (acceptance by the government of a democracy of some responsibility for the survival of people who were helpless in the grip of economic disaster) was grievously attacked.

The meaning of this critical situation for social work was brought to this Conference by the Joint Committee of Trade Unions in Social Work. One afternoon of its program was given to a meeting on "Storm Clouds Over Welfare," at which the President of the AASW and the Regional Director of the UPWA were speakers. I read a paper on "Are Private Agencies Meeting Their Responsibilities?" Later that year, it was enlarged into a pamphlet related specifically to Family Service, once the "general practice" of social work.[1]

Trying to find bench marks by which to measure the progress of Family Service, I went back to the reports of the Milford Conference and to two studies published in 1934, that of the American Association of Medical Social Workers and one by

279

Linton B. Swift, General Director of the Family Welfare Association of America.[2]

All of these studies agreed upon a concept of generic casework which centers on the client as a person in a social situation in which he needs help. All agreed upon the importance to the client of a professional relationship to an understanding person and upon the goal of helping the client to use in his own way all the resources available in himself and in society toward the solution of his problem. In 1934, there was a strong hope that social casework would soon mature to the point of demonstrating its usefulness in all sorts of social institutions, including churches, schools, courts, and recreation centers. I asked, "Has this expectation been realized?"

Mr. Swift's monograph was my point of departure. He saw private family service as occupying a frontier which is especially important in a transition period, adapting flexibly to "changing conditions in the social fabric." He believed it would always be backed by a smaller group of socially aware people than the majority who are ready to support services for well-recognized needs. He thought relief-giving should be limited, and a private agency should instead give leadership to the community in developing new resources. It should extend its service to economically secure families which have problems in social relationships and should contribute research and provide centers for training professional workers for both private and public agencies.

In my pamphlet, *Advance Or Retreat,* I tried to measure the present status of private services, particularly those to families, by use of four sources of information, inconclusive though each alone might be.

1. What social agencies say about themselves when they appeal for funds. A brief survey of campaign literature showed a prevalent appeal to fear—the community's fear of poverty, disease, and crime.

2. The response to fund appeals from the community. This showed a marked increase through the years, but with some

question of the voluntary nature of giving, since collections were increasingly made through industries where a man's job might be jeopardized by refusal to give.

3. Statements of the profession about itself in its literature. These revealed two concepts of the role of family service, known as the diagnostic and the functional points of view. Of these we shall say more presently, but here only that the profession itself had no unified concept of its role and aims.

4. How clients respond to the service they are getting. This source was especially inconclusive because of a doubt whether clients are free to say what they think about a service upon which they may have to depend. However, experience of the Personal Service at the NMU, where clients were as free as they ever are, tended to show that private family services had scarcely touched the lives of the cross section of the American people represented by some thousands of seamen and their families, and that when attempts were made to use these voluntary agencies for seamen's families they were seldom successful.

Assuming that family service had not stood still since 1934, in what direction had it moved? Mr. Swift's recommendation that relief-giving be limited had been followed, as had that of extending services to economically secure groups. There was marked increase in attention to personality problems, regardless of economic status. Under both of the prevailing schools of thought in casework, a high degree of psychological competence was required in the caseworkers, and both used a closely controlled process in counselling. The "supportive" casework treatment that family agencies in the past had given to "families whose situation or personality patterns did not admit of much change" had almost disappeared by 1948. It seemed to me that flexibility was decreasing, as agencies came to rely either on "the fixed social reality to which the client must adjust himself" or to "escape contact with the cases in which the most acute problems occur."[3]

As to the role of community leadership, this could not be appraised without taking into account the community upsurge for better living standards which had characterized this four-teen-year period. There had been wage struggles of a rising labor movement and nation-wide pressure on government for some protection in social insurance against the disaster of un-employment and the oncoming of old age. Private social work seemed more and more apart from these movements, even as they increasingly relieved it of responsibility for economic problems. It turned more often to needs connected with mental health, recreation, and culture. These were important, but most of the people in American communities were most deeply con-cerned in this period with survival itself.

Was the community leading in determining the direction of private social agencies, for which it pays as truly as for tax-supported services? Was it receiving leadership from them as to desirably sound social policies? I did not feel with Mr. Swift that voluntary social agencies are the private preserve of any group, no matter how socially conscious or sincere, or that they exist to be an outlet for the generous impulses of their sponsors. Leadership can only be based on a close relationship to those who are led and to their needs.

I had some words to say about the role of private social agencies as guardians of a high quality of trained professional service. Have they led in professional education and in per-sonnel practices? In the latter, they seemed to me to have clung to a paternalistic relationship to employees longer than agencies elsewhere, in which workers had accepted a more mature re-sponsibility in organizing into unions. In education, the use of private agencies in the main, as training centers, and their con-centration on a type of counselling allied to psychotherapy, had limited the usefulness of schools of social work to the public welfare and medical agencies in which the bulk of social work was done. Where could training be found that would develop the workers in these strategic fields as they had a right to demand?

In research, I did not find that private agencies had followed

Mr. Swift's recommendation that they find out what becomes of people when social conditions change rapidly.

"They sift out people who are in acute need and their problems with them too quickly to know."[4] In my work as consultant, I had seen a dynamic growth of practice in public agencies without time for research, but in private agencies, research seemed preoccupied with what caseworkers were doing in a controlled, carefully recorded "process." I found less and less interest in the very poor and very sick, and even in broad programs of prevention of social ills.[5] There was increasing interest in emotional adjustment, to deal with which psychological training was equipping caseworkers more adequately. Even here was a "no man's land," since caseworkers were confused, on the one hand, about trespassing on the domain of the psychiatrist, and on the other, unable to deal with problems of social and economic origin. I asked, "Is there anywhere, for most people today, any organization that will accept them as human beings who have a right to be there without having to *prove* it, any agency which will listen to them and begin to move with them from the point where they are toward what they can do about their situation? Is there any agency that will bring to bear on the situation as much knowledge of, and interest in, the social dynamics of it as of the psychological mechanism the person is using? Is there any which will fight for the community resources necessary to make a rational solution possible? If there is, I dare to predict that it will not have to worry about its field or its professional growth. Under what circumstances can we hope for such an advance in private work?

"Advance is only possible today through a determined struggle for the most elementary rights: to earn a living; to express one's opinions honestly and without fear; to be treated like a human being, not a beast of burden or cannon fodder.

"The way we do our professional work contributes inescapably to the outcome of that struggle. If we think social work is not a force in the battle of ideas, the enemies of the people know better. Either we serve the people's needs or we evade them. Either we make democracy real or we reduce it to an abstraction which the foes of democracy do not object to at all. Either we use all that science can teach to help people to build a genuinely good life for themselves, or we build a professional cult that takes the place of interrelations with other advances in human knowledge."[6]

This was hot stuff, and did not add to my popularity either with leaders in social work or with some of my colleagues who were personal friends. The next kettle of hot water into which I plunged was foreshadowed by my remarks in *Advance or Retreat* about the diagnostic and functional schools of thought —a burning subject in social work. What were these two approaches, and how did they originate?

What is our function? This question had become terribly important to us in a disturbed period when need for security had left its mark upon us all. The psychological era of the 1920's had brought no satisfactory answer. We psychiatric social workers were aides to the psychiatrists, securing prideful histories of patients, carrying out recommendations, and sometimes honored by being asked to take part in therapy. In family agencies, we dealt with cases of emotional disturbance scarcely matched for difficulty by those in psychiatric clinics. Professional prestige depended upon how much psychiatry we could learn, but it came to us from psychiatrists, not from a melting pot in our own theory and practice.

The Pennsylvania School of Social Work, following the psychology of Otto Rank rather than that of Freud, developed new emphases that psychiatric social work needed badly. First, Virginia Robinson's stress on the client and the relationship of a client to a professional person. Then, emphasis on the function of a social agency was learned in the emergency relief administration and was expanded in the practice of agencies offering other specific services, like child-placing. The School at Smith College welcomed these new emphases, and, as it placed some of its students in Philadelphia agencies where they were applied in practice, found its whole curriculum enriched thereby.

There came a day when the Philadelphia agencies felt that students of Smith had "too much to unlearn" and did not have sufficient "conviction" about what they were doing to work well in field practice there. By the late 1930's, teachers of the "functional" approach were giving institutes in many other cities, and experienced caseworkers were commuting to Philadelphia to learn the new thinking which gave them confidence by its sure-footed dealing with all sorts of problems. By that time, books and papers had crystalized a body of theory in which students could be trained and which some agencies adopted as an official position.[7] The term *functional* came to be used to distinguish this philosophy and practice from that based on the Freudian psychology which was called *diagnostic* and which still had the backing of most psychiatrists and a position of high prestige.

By the 1939 National Conference, the Association of Psychiatric Social Workers held a symposium on "Function and Process," and published in their newsletter the five papers given.[8] I reviewed them for *The Family,* with a criticism I had not publicly expressed before, that to focus not on the client but on the function of the social agency, "the most man-made and temporary of all the social forces within which we operate," is to distort the casework process instead of clarifying it.[9] Where Dr. Jessie Taft, in her paper in the symposium, found it a happy accident that a public assistance worker revived the crushed spirit of a man in line before her and thought the relief function primary, I considered the relief-giving both an opportunity and a limitation on the worker's time, and the "accident" an instance of superb casework under difficult conditions.[10]

In 1949, my reference to diagnostic and functional casework generated enough heat almost to stop the publication of *Advance or Retreat,* lest, as a union pamphlet, it inject a professional controversy into union solidarity. By 1952, the practical repercussions of the conflict were so serious that agencies were labelled either diagnostic or functional, and there was difficulty in referring clients between the two. Schools were not placing students for field work in agencies of the wrong "faith." Applicants for employment were asked to which school they belonged and were not considered by some agencies if they said, "To neither." I had taken the position that both approaches should be used for all the good that was in them, and this probably satisfied no one.

In the hope of reconciling these hampering differences, the Family Service Association of America appointed a committee to study the basic concepts in casework practice. It published its report in 1950, finding the differences to be irreconcilable and stemming from the opposing psychological theories of Freud and Rank.[11] A new magazine of opinion in social work, called *Trends*, asked me to review the study.[12]

I did not consider it my business to challenge the conclusion of the study committee that (after a careful review of a few cases worked with under each theory) they found the two approaches about equally successful. People are helped under a variety of theories or by no theory but "dumb intuition," and that proves nothing. What I did question was whether the real opposition was between Freud and Rank.

I found the basic conflict to be between two world philosophies, with Freud and Rank examples of *one* of them. These were the idealist vs. the materialist or scientific approach.[13] Freud began his work as a scientist, observing facts and trying to deduce principles from them. He ended by building a world view according to his experience in his practice with upper-class patients in Vienna, feeling that he had arrived at concepts universally true of the nature of man. Rank, his dissenting disciple, built also a philosophy, based on his sense of the uniqueness of the individual, which demanded something *given*, a creative will which cannot be studied or known, but is the organizing force by which life grows. Neither Freud nor Rank was able to maintain a scientific attitude toward the objective world, apart from his own ideas about it.

My conclusions, which some of my friends found hard to

take, were that the diagnostic school had the possibility of developing a scientific base for the practice of its art, but had lost its way in Freud's generalizations about the nature of man, which he thought valid for all times and places. Of the functional school I said: "The value which it has in helping people, if its teaching is accepted and applied with conviction, is a value to be judged by the criteria of a philosophical or religious belief, not the criteria of scientific testing and comparison of cases, one with another." I did not think that the functional theory of casework had the possibility of becoming a scientific discipline. Unpopular or not, I had no other choice than to state my opinion honestly. I would be glad to see a different opinion published.[14]

The cost of private social work was a fearsome subject always. Especially vulnerable was the mounting expense of case recording. Among ourselves it could be said that nobody wanted long records, but agencies had to produce them because schools demanded them for training. Schools, likewise, had to teach recording that would show the *process* of how casework was done, because, without such records, agencies could not match prestige with their neighbors. Long psychiatric histories had been modified in favor of better focussed records, but recording of interviews continued to show who said what and how. Add to this that no agency allotted to recording as much time as it took, and workers lived in such a state of guilt that if they were drowning their last thought would be, "What about my unfinished dictation?"

It was a fine discharge of emotion to tackle this subject as I did in 1941 when the Council of Social Agencies of Dayton, Ohio asked me to give a two-day institute on records. For once, we all spoke our minds. We came up with an analysis which separated the client's record (which could be relevant to the problem and brief) from a record for teaching purposes (which tries to capture the process of interviewing, although heaven knows that what we remembered to put down was little

like what really happened). Also we recommended that use of
records for evaluation of the skill of the caseworker should be
limited to examples prepared by the caseworker for this purpose
and should not reduce every client's record to an agonizing
"How am I doing?" Our query about the possible misuse of
files of stored records under an unfavorable political climate,
proved to be prophetic of what happened in the legislation of
ten years later.

The concern of fund-raising bodies and agency boards about
the cost of social work came out frequently in plans for reduction of waste, for cost accounting and for showing results
which would appeal to businessmen. The "Social Breakdown"
plan of 1940 drew also upon interest in sociological research
and community planning.

I met it unexpectedly when I stepped off a train, in February
of that year, to give an institute for a Psychiatric Round Table
in a New England city. The welcoming committee asked me
to discuss it because the plan was proposed for their community,
and they were uneasy about it without quite knowing why.
Settled in an easy chair with a few hours to prepare for the
first session, I was shocked and incredulous at what I read in
the monograph the committee gave me.[15]

The substance of it was that most of the time of social
agencies is taken up with relatively few families who are "re-
peaters" in social maladjustment. Research should define these
maladjustments in measurable terms, establish a "rate" for
them in a given community, and use existing social resources
to control that rate. A community could take the first step of
a study which would set up a central file of "breakdown"
families, and then, if it desired, go on to use some modification
of a plan of control already tried out in Stamford, Connecticut.

Categories of social breakdown had to be *officially* recognized
by the community, as evidenced by arrests, commitments to
institutions, relief rolls, etc., of which written records were
kept. Seven categories were selected: Crime, delinquency,
serious mental disease, divorce, neglect of children, unemploy-

ability, and mental deficiency. A family unit was employed for statistical purposes, as showing that while individual deviations from community standards might be "symptoms," the underlying social pathology would come out in the piling up of "breakdowns" in certain families.

Once a file of such families was established, the plan of control would call for a committee, representing the main types of social agencies in the city, which would assign each of the families to *one* agency of major responsibility, no matter how many might be working on various problems with family individuals. Thus, there would be co-ordination of effort. The committee would meet weekly and deal with reallocations of responsibility as well as assess new cases. They were not supposed to take too much time on each case but to use brief prepared summaries instead of full case studies. The possibilities for research and for prevention were stressed, although it was not estimated how much time would be left for agency work with nonbreakdown families.

That afternoon at the Round Table, I discussed two cases *as if* the Social Breakdown plan were in operation and then, in the evening, voiced my seething indignation at such a travesty of what we would call social work.

We believed in research, of course. But statistics based on the categories set up could only be false and misleading. Arrests are as likely to vary with the policies of a police department, prejudice against certain groups of citizens, or political influence, as commitments are to respond to changes in state laws and in facilities for care of the mentally disturbed. To assume that all people on relief, including Mothers' Aid, were unemployable, when millions in the nation could find no work, was as absurd as to exclude breadwinners over sixty-five but not widowed mothers from a "social breakdown" category.

I found a disturbing class selection in most of the categories. These "objective" tests were supposed to show social breakdown in families victimized by unemployment, bad housing, and lack of medical care. No such breakdown was recorded in families able to settle out-of-court law violations of their members, to send their mentally sick to private hospitals, to go to Reno for divorce, to neglect their children, or to be unemployed in pleasant surroundings. Motor vehicle law violations and gambling were excluded from the categories. Thus it was poor families who furnished the examples of breakdown and incidentally received the stigma of being listed as such. The Social Service Index, instead of being a confidential file for the sole use of professional persons interested in helping, now became a keeper of a potential rogues gallery of families which, if more than one social deviation came to attention, were expected to become "recidivist" families.

The importance of the issues raised by this plan was registered in the casework magazine, *The Family,* which devoted a whole number to a symposium upon it.[16] My review in *Social Work Today* emphasized that the control features of the plan were a reversal of the gains of the last decades in casework history: respect for the client's self-determination and choice; and a growing inclusion of the clients of social agencies in the total community, not their isolation in a stigmatized group. I ended with this question: "If a program of prevention is set up in terms of control rather than of serious study of social causation and individual treatment, could not control be exercised much more economically in a concentration camp?"[17]

If I remember correctly, there was sufficient opposition in the city to prevent the adoption of the social breakdown plan. Seven years later, some of the same workers asked me to come to them again to help them think through a new "economy" proposal for a merger of a family agency with two for children. The workers were not opposed to a merger, if it was found to contribute to better service, nor to serious study of how to meet rising costs and increased need for social services. The plan proposed, however, severely limited use of social agencies for training and advocated employment of fewer "well-qualified" caseworkers to carry larger case loads under less supervision. As proposed, the plan was to be put into effect

in time for the next budget year.[18] The conclusion reached in
our discussion was that the community's stake in private social
agencies demanded a thorough appraisal, not the hasty adoption
of a scheme which would save very little and cost a great deal
in quality of service.

The 1948 National Conference in Atlantic City was really
memorable for the most controversial event in all our history,
the entrance of social work into a political campaign. We came
to it naturally enough and not without precedent. Theodore
Roosevelt's campaign in 1912 had adopted as part of its platform the program set forth at the Cleveland National Conference of that year. Another Roosevelt, twenty years later,
had brought about the conditions for the implementation of
some of it. Now, in 1948, with President Roosevelt gone,
many of his goals of peace and social welfare were slipping
away. That winter saw a political upsurge such as had not
shaken America since the Populist movement of the 1880's. It
brought suddenly to the stage of history a new political party,
called Progressive. Its presidential candidate, Henry Wallace,
became the spokesman of millions of plain Americans who
wanted government to mean real attention to the critical problems they were facing. That upsurge, abortive though it proved
to be, had the astonishing effect upon social work of sweeping
it into the arena of political action.[19]

First, early in 1948, more than twenty leaders in all fields of
social work drew up a statement to submit to all presidential
candidates, asserting opposition to threats of war and to foreign
aid programs administered with discrimination as to race, creed,
or political belief, or associated with demonstrations of military
strength.[20] The statement upheld the right of all peoples to
organize for betterment of social and economic conditions. It
offered support to those candidates in the United States election who would, if elected, work within the United Nations for
peace and for living conditions throughout the world, corresponding to the current high productive capacity which science

had made a world possession. There was special stress on out-
lawing the atomic bomb and upon developing atomic energy
"to enlarge the people's opportunity for the abundant life."

Henry Wallace responded to the statement and accepted an
invitation to speak at a meeting of the Joint Committee of
Trade Unions in Social Work at the Atlantic City Conference.
I shall never forget his stirring address in the Auditorium building that day, his concise, down-to-earth discussion of the
objectives of social welfare and peace for which we all stood.
He did not hesitate to say that billions for guns would not
bring butter to undernourished children, nor Red-baiting stop
a world-wide demand for decent security.[21]

After the meeting in the crowded hall was over, a long procession of us followed Mr. Wallace's tall figure down the boardwalk to the hotel where a reception in his honor was held for
the whole Conference. I was convinced that day, for all time,
that politics need not be something dirty to be shunned but
could be a genuine expression of a people's will and right.

This chapter has been a record of controversies. I see them
not as unfortunate interruptions in an ongoing development
of social work, negative incidents to be forgotten as soon as
possible in favor of plaudits for positive gains. I see them as
evidence of what might be the theme of this whole record of
more than forty years—is social work a part of the life of its
time and place? *The answer is yes.*

If it is one with the life of a period, social work shares the
controversies by which a people determines its destiny. Which
are more important, people or things? How do people who are
distinguished by *having* settle their differences with people who
create wealth but do not have it? How do these last, who are
in the majority, claim their heritage of the resources of this
earth? In the meantime, while world-shaking battles for human
welfare are shaping and being fought out, how are the logistics
of survival carried on, corresponding to the food, shelter, and
medical services of a fighting army?

We have seen instances of such services being captured by enemies of the people's welfare, ambushed though they may be behind the "public relations" of philanthropy. We have seen more important instances of democratic forces breaking through into occasional expressions of a people's will. In such a titanic world struggle for human welfare, it is vastly important how we do our work, ministering to individuals and groups while the battle for social justice goes on.

It is in seemingly small things that we learn how to serve democracy and the good life through our profession. We are defeated and rise again to fight the harder. We gain, but rest not on any laurels. We hope to be part of the life of a better time which we will help to build.

We hope. Are we sure, now that man has discovered how to exterminate all life on this planet, but not yet how to keep that awful power solely for man's good? Building democracy in our small tasks seems so futile when man rockets to the stars and weighs the risks of annihilation from his own hatreds.

Nevertheless, it is precisely in human relationships that our world needs intelligent building most. It is precisely in man's heritage of co-operation with other men for common goals that he has found means of survival and will find means of social advance. If we are now living in one world (not in isolated islands and valleys), if we are now wracked by the pain and hunger of millions of whom, in past centuries, we would never have heard, so much the more must our new powers and abundance guarantee that our new world live in health. And the role of persons skillfully dedicated to human welfare is not inconsiderable.

CHAPTER 19

TIME TO REFLECT

What happened to me when the good ship USS went down? Did I ship out again, or find a safe harbor and think things over?

Being sixty-two was one inescapable fact. Growing old was a prospect I had evaded all through my fifties for I intended to keep on working—always. After sixty, however, one crosses an invisible line. It is possible to keep a full-time job, but usually at the price of doing almost nothing else. I wanted to live as a person, not exist only as a working machine. Already, when pressures had relaxed after the war, I had obtained from USS a twenty-hour work week at reduced salary. When I went to lunch at one o'clock, I was free to rest and then, in late afternoon or evening, to enjoy social life or perhaps to do some seminar or consulting work. During my last year at the NMU, I had built up a satisfying amount of such informal teaching. This was not, however, sufficient to provide a living in New York City.

I was extraordinarily rich in friends, many in New York but more of them scattered all over the United States. If I stayed in New York as a retired person, I would be like a child out of school with no playmates. Anyway, I was a bird in a cage in a big city. I loved the rhythm of day and night and the seasons in the country, its woods and meadows, its bird songs and chirping insects. The old home in Stoughton, Massachusetts was still there, though my mother had recently ended a serene old age at the age of ninety-four. My brother was living alone in the homestead which had, for a hundred years, been adapted for two homes. Why not go there?

At first, I was afraid. I had once beaten my wings on the bars of that comfortable cage, longing to fly and be myself. I had been freed to fly. Could I take that release of spirit back to the old setting, or would I find myself in a cage again? I thought I might take with me a sense of being one with other people which I hoped never to lose. After all, there were people in Stoughton, too.

The decision to make a home there was strengthened in a strange way, even in 1946, before Mother's death. Over that New Year holiday, there was held in New York a conference of supporters of Claude Williams' People's Institute of Applied Religion. "Rev. Claude" had just finished his work as labor chaplain in Detroit and was moving back to the rural South, convinced that unless a strong educational force against racism was created in that area, the South would become the breeding ground of an American brand of fascism. He saw the potential of a force for changing the mind-set of his home country in the Negro and white rural preachers, who might, unaided, be destroyed by racial and religious animosities, but who were utterly sincere and extremely influential among the poorest working people of the South.

For me, personally, that conference bridged a chasm that had lain across my life since liberation and with which I had learned to live without thinking much about it—a gap between the religion of my youth and the vital but unorthodox beliefs of mature years. Why expect to bridge it? Perhaps it did not matter in a large city where spiritual companionship could be found in many forms and places.[1] In Stoughton there would be just one place open to me—the church. Could I, in all honesty, fit into that setting?

The New Year conference "knit me up," as I said then, and gathered some ravelled leavings of old days into a new wholeness. "Rev. Claude" placed the Bible in the context of history, as courses at Smith College had only begun to do. It was the history, from the earliest times, of peoples' struggles to live: of the Hebrew brickmakers of Egypt and the slaves of the Mediterranean; of the Hebrew prophets crying out for justice and the great ones who built temples but forgot the poor; of the Carpenter of Nazareth and the surging life of the early Christian centuries; of the laborers on the land and in the mills of the South today, opening their union meetings with prayer and standing by each other through this present hell. Claude could translate Biblical language into today's tongues. If he could in the South, I believed I could even in a conservative New England town.

When it came to planning, I insisted on one thing—my own home in the ell of the family house. My brother agreed. I spent my substance gaily in modernizing five rooms, of which the "summer kitchen" became a living room, and an electrified kitchen moved into Grandpa's little bedroom. A small dining room nestled in a cosy corner. A many-windowed room upstairs became my workshop and retreat. Two coveted luxuries took shape in a guest room and a fireplace, the latter built with gift money from my friends in the Social Service Employees Union in New York and inscribed: "From Friends Whose Love Makes Warm This Hearth."

The living arrangement we worked out is a co-operative in which some activities are shared, while I specialize in cooking and mending and my brother Frank tends gardens, provides a car for needed transportation, and cuts wood for the fireplace (which is only a pleasure-supplement to comfortable central heating). In our separate apartments, we are free to have guests or not as we please, or to let little homely details express our real selves. We have each other when many people of our age have no one.

Stoughton is a good town to live in. Once rural-industrial, it has in the last decades become industrial-suburban, with enough industry to keep it from being a detached bedroom for

Boston. Its factories are relatively small, past the stage of calling the boss by a nickname and not yet routinely impersonal. Stoughton has never had a wide variation of economic status nor developed a snobbish mind-set, even though it has had its share of cliques and prejudices. It is a town where people generally speak their mind and fraternize with their neighbors cheerfully.

I think of myself as extremely fortunate. Economically, what could be better than to have enough for all needs and for some giving, yet not enough money to create worry over what to do with it or to stifle effort? It is good to be able to work without thought of pay and still to be one with working people in the common problems of daily living. Added to this, I have excellent sight and hearing and a working degree of physical mobility. I can roam the world in books, listen to the world's best music on records, enjoy nature, and work to maintain a home. What more could one ask?

If the innkeeper in this house of life where I am now a guest should inquire: "Have you any complaints, Madame, about the service?" I can think of only one, the same as that which sent me packing from Danvers so long ago, a complaint of being too comfortable. A Smith student said it in a delightful drawl when she was asked why she did not study in the "browsing room" of the library where there were easy chairs. "I have found out," she said, "that you can't be too comfortable in this world and keep your wits about you at the same time." It is not that one would ask to be uncomfortable, but one has to make real effort to get rid of barnacles on the spirit if one is sheltered from the buffetings of thought and feeling which are part of our common humanity.

There are new things to be learned in any situation—unpredictable things in growing old, because one never has the experience ahead of time and tends to disbelieve those who reach that state first. About the first thing that struck me was that it is impossible to plan and then, forthwith, do. I was brought up to believe that the only safeguard against disaster was to prepare for every contingency. No child in my family dared to offer the excuse when something went wrong, "I didn't think." "It is your business to think," was what we heard. However, after sixty, such matters as eyes, ears, joints, blood pressure, energy, income, and transportation decide for the ambitious planner.

It may dawn upon a reflecting person that perhaps it was not a good thing anyway to be so confident of controlling one's destiny. Did that sometimes mean a Jehovah complex in miniature, an urge to move other people, whose destinies were as important, into fulfillment of one's plans? If man's best achievement in being human is to become a social being, is it a calamity if one is linked more closely, even by receding powers, to the lives of other people? Too often we see the reverse side, when an older person exploits the chance to make others stand around or becomes miserable through not claiming the consideration really needed. The lesson to learn, however, is the ever-useful one of balance, the interplay of interests of old and young which may not have been searched for when life was running fast.

Another important lesson is the necessity for health of mind and body and of full movement through what we used to call in psychology "the sensory-motor arc." We need mental stimulation to live as much as we need food; we must digest experience and make it our own; we must give it out in some form of action. This may be in communication to others who can carry the action to a wider impact upon the life of our time, but communicate we must, or thought grows stale and interest in new ideas recedes.

It is precisely in opportunity to communicate that an older person may be blocked. Perhaps the catch is in getting where people are. Perhaps, in a time of rapid change, the *way* of communicating becomes different—pictures instead of speech, wholesale transmission by radio and television instead of the personal touch, other media than the written word. Perhaps, for all one's eagerness to absorb new ideas, fresh experiences are not available, and one gets to be just a little behind the times. In my geriatric studies, however, I was sometimes forgetting the smog to which we had gradually become accustomed, and I needed to be reminded that just then nobody, at any age, could communicate freely.

I used to sit in church in the first years and drink in the look of the people around me. I had ceased to be disturbed by my own unorthodox beliefs, for I could be sure that many of the heads in the pews contained ideas as divergent as mine. I felt, however, like a person in a library, forbidden to read. What human stories were hidden beneath those covers? How could I get beyond the customary handshaking and really know people? After all, in a motor age, people do not respond to invitations to "drop in" at one's home. They just whiz by on urgent errands.

Fellowship by age groups was then at its height. I was assigned to what I called "the grandmothers club," but I had no grandchildren to talk about—only a cat. These were also women whose interests centered in expert housekeeping, and I was an amateur. I learned some facility in making aprons for the annual fair but could not find them very important. The picture has changed with the years. I find joy in choir singing, in leading study groups about near and far peoples (for which I had to stimulate a demand), in being a roving pianist in religious education and seeing the smallest children each week at their gay pursuits, in coming to feel close to other women because, in homemaking, we all have a way of life in common.

If these activities and this fellowship have seemed sometimes to be of limited significance, I have found friends who could think and feel deeply with me, even though distance may make meeting a rare experience. I have found rewarding communication with many friends through correspondence. Even out of contacts which have largely been by letter have grown relationships of the quality to give me three "daughters," who, with their families, have gladdened my life.

Disposing of an overgrown sense of mission, however, is as difficult as getting rid of radioactive residues. I wanted to reach out to people I knew I could help, not just to wait, hoping some would come my way. People did find a path to my door, coming for consultation in personal trouble, and calls still came from far places for my kind of teaching. These were as unpredictable as the ravens who fed the prophet Elijah in the wilderness. When drought threatened to become severe, however, those friendly birds never failed to come to me with something in their beaks. So I slowly learned that living is responding to what comes, whether or not one is in a position to help to bring it.

I cannot stop to list the places into which I was called in the first seven years in Stoughton. They ranged from great industrial cities like Pittsburgh and Detroit to a Veterans' Hospital and a psychiatric center in the wheat fields of Kansas; from Montreal to Nashville; from Philadelphia to Cleveland. Twice I renewed rich friendships in both northern and southern California, when individuals, if not organized groups, sponsored teaching institutes. Once the School of Social Work of the University of California at Berkeley offered six weeks of summer school teaching, and once the State Department of Welfare of Oregon made possible several institute sessions. One unforgettable September, I met with the Child Welfare workers of Colorado at a resort in the mountains, in glorious view of Pike's Peak. It was at that conference that I added another quality to the versatility of social workers—ability to drive a car on mountain roads and cope with the worst in weather emergencies. Just then it was aspen time, and as we rode over the pass back to Denver, the litle golden trees, emerging in groups from the dark evergreens, looked like fluttering and dancing children coming out to see the cars pass.

Two teaching experiences will round out the record of the growth of social work in the years in which I knew it. One was a series of seminars given with a psychiatrist at the William

Alanson White Institute of Psychiatry in New York, and one was a last trip to California in 1957.

In the fall of 1948, I was called to a conference with the Directors of the White Institute to explore whether I could give a course for the social workers who enrolled for training in psychotherapy. In collaboration with a psychiatrist, I was to try to clarify just what made the two disciplines distinguishable. I laughingly said that I supposed they picked me because I was the only social worker who claimed to know that they *were* different, and maybe I only thought I knew. The Directors made clear that they did not want this course to be a repetition for social workers of what they were getting from psychiatrists. I thought a valuable series of sessions could be built on discussion of cases by the two leaders, each from his own point of view. The psychiatric thinking differed in some ways from the more Freudian approach with which I had worked before, but in a favorable direction, that is, introducing more consideration of social conditions and of interpersonal relationships. As I stated my psychiatric outlook, the Directors thought there would be no problem of too great divergence.

After two preliminary seminars in supervision and administration, the succeeding years until 1954 took me to New York each year for a series of ten seminar sessions, two weeks apart, in which were discussed cases which showed both co-operation with psychiatrists in various clinic relationships and social casework with clients who were not under psychiatric treatment.

The cases were supplied by members of the group who were able people of considerable experience. I found the records long and usually reduced them to summaries of two or three pages, so arranged as to answer questions as to social diagnosis, relation to psychotherapy, plan of treatment, and outcome. Here again, I was a maverick. Almost invariably, the facts on which to form a social diagnosis were lacking, except for some information on interpersonal relations. People were all tangled up in their emotions, but there was little to give clues as to how they got that way or what they could do about it. Once a case was accepted, there seemed to be a compelling pattern—to schedule a series of weekly appointments to explore partly-conscious psychological reactions. In many cases, once the caseworker present furnished more diagnostic data, or I brought out enough that could be inferred from what was known, it seemed to me that a good social diagnosis could have pointed the way to a tentative treatment plan and perhaps to clearing up the present difficulty within a few weeks. Instead, the process of weekly interviews went on and on for perhaps a year or more. I could not see that a person with employment difficulties need necessarily be treated as a psychopathic individual, any more than that the last resort of long and expensive psychotherapy should be neglected when it was indicated. Our groups did find use for every bit of psychiatric knowledge all of us had as we discussed these cases with the psychiatrist from his own point of view. The conclusion to be drawn from these experimental discussions was, I believe, that our profession has rich resources in social diagnosis and methods of treatment, even of problems of personal maladjustment, which are being neglected while we are trying to work by the methods and thinking of another, important but different, profession.[2]

After 1954, seven years of retirement had made a gap in my direct experience with social casework which could hardly be bridged by the cases brought by seminar groups. So the ravens stopped coming. Then, to my utter surprise, a telephone call from San Francisco one evening in 1957, greeted me with an urgent invitation to come there for a series of institutes. The Los Angeles area soon joined in the plea. Of course, there was nothing on earth I wanted more. So it was that an April sunset found me boarding my first plane in Boston for an enchanting journey through the night. I saw the jewelled carpet which was Chicago and at dawn among the peaks of the Sierras could recognize the Half-Dome of Yosemite. Sunrise was on the Bay when we came to earth in San Francisco.

That trip to California was complicated by my fracturing an ankle after the first week, but I did not miss any engagements except one (which was at State Conference and could not be postponed), and to that I sent a paper for discussion. Meetings in both San Francisco and Los Angeles were crowded and enthusiastic. Did ever a Rip Van Winkle wake up and return to a more heartening reception!

There was great agitation among social workers in that spring of 1957 over an article in the March number of *Harper's Magazine* entitled, "Social Work: A Profession Chasing its Tail."[3] Every planning committee asked me to discuss it. I was reluctant at first, for while it posed pertinent questions as to whether social workers were losing themselves in pursuit of their own prestige, the article seemed to me only partly serious and full of half-truths that one could waste a lot of time trying to answer. I could do nothing else, however, than to take its main drift seriously: Where are we going in social work?

I retraced for the California groups some of the history which has been unfolding in these pages, which, I suddenly realized, a new generation did not know. I traced unmistakable gains for a more democratic spirit and practice and the revolutionary advance made by psychological understanding of people and their behavior. I could pick out signs of a return from extreme individualism to a better appreciation of group relationships and the broad sweep of social forces. In our discussions, we could see that this process had not gone far enough, and too often we were isolated by our preoccupation with our own techniques and prestige. The strong, health-giving currents of social change moving around the world were not reaching as they should our little pool which was becoming both stagnant and restless.

I found that social workers *were* restless, and they fastened on one complaint: What other profession keeps its practitioners under perpetual supervision? Why could not qualified workers, as soon as they acquire some experience, gain in consultation with each other all the help they need? I was asked to join in an all-day workshop in Los Angeles on this subject and had time to review a considerable body of literature dealing with it.

Traditionally, supervision in social work had meant control

to see that the work was so carried out as to meet with the approval of agency boards, representing supporting community groups. As social workers came to be professionally trained and sought continuing growth, supervision added an educational function but did not lose its security role. Senior workers did not graduate from supervision regardless of years of practice of their art. They might be thrust into being supervisors themselves, but usually at the price of relinquishing their practice for more prestige. Over the years, while social agencies became more democratic in relationship to clients, they tended to remain paternalistic in their dealings with staff. As one group worker said to me in the late 1930's, "Nowhere, even in group work agencies with the best practice, do we begin to apply what we know about group relationships in our own staff groups."

Today, the paternalistic social agency which was typical when I entered social work is rarely found except in small communities. Instead, central financing has tended to limit the functions of the board of a single social agency to administering funds collected and allocated by much larger bodies, community-wide, state, or national. Social work dispenses millions and is influenced by powerful forces. Its employed staffs, whether professionally trained or not, are increasingly judged by their production, measured in quantitative terms, to demonstrate that the community is getting full value for its welfare dollars. Supervisors in many agencies are torn between being educators and production managers, and in a system of accounting that measures costs per interview and per capita for workers and clients served, staff education tends to become a liability.[4] In my years since retirement, I had seen this trend growing in places as far apart as Michigan and California. I saw executives chosen not for interest in work of a professional quality to meet human needs (which might be labelled sentimental and impractical), but for ability to give a social agency a "business administration."

Wherever I met them, social workers were insecure, often shifting from job to job and not always (as was implied by the article in *Harper's*) to increase their own prestige. If they were really concerned about skillful practice in aid of troubled people, they felt stifled in agencies where quality of work became almost irrelevant, staff education an expensive luxury, and staff participation considered a waste of time and replaced by executive decisions.

That afternoon, in the workshop in Los Angeles (when I sat with my leg in a cast and rested irreverently on a lectern), I ended my career as I had begun it—a maverick. I said some of these shocking things and maintained that we had misplaced upon supervision, which touched us personally, a dissatisfaction which went much deeper to the unhealthy administrative structure of many social agencies. We were prevented from questioning this by the tradition that administration is the business of nobody except administrators and boards. I said it was everybody's business in social work, the community's, first of all, and ours as part of the community.

To the objection that we, as employed workers, cannot do anything about policies, I spoke of our taken-for-granted interest in our own future. In the accepted line of professional advancement, even a beginner who will be an administrator some day has a stake in understanding administration in the lower levels of responsibility. Certainly it cannot be healthy to leave all such responsibility to parent-like persons up above. If a young worker hopes to advance through teaching or research, it is still a maturing experience to understand how an agency goes beyond technical help to a few people, to gear into community planning for welfare needs.[5]

I did not share the feeling expressed at the meeting that supervision should be replaced by voluntary consultation after the first years of professional practice. Even use of well-qualified consultants is apt to degenerate into rambling shoptalk if time is not set aside, and staff education is not made a conscious part of an agency's program. A worker who needs help most may be least able to seek it and organize it.

It seemed to me that an agency which is a healthy working

team (and this includes clear allocation of administrative responsibility) has a life of its own, which is something much more than being a housing project for a number of independent practitioners. It has a group spirit and goals which inspire and develop individual workers, and this enrichment has to have some structure to carry it, call it what you will. My word of counsel in this critical time was to *pay attention to administration,* for upon it depends the kind of service to people which a social agency can offer to a community.

I knew well in the golden days in California that this return to be with the workers in my beloved profession was a privilege not to be repeated. For some three years before that, I had realized that my connection with social work was ended and had been working on the different problem of how to build a meaningful life with the materials available in Stoughton. "Transportation decides everything" took on literal significance while the family car grew old like its drivers and was limited to the immediate locality.

In Stoughton, as I have related, there was just one organized group of people to which, even with reservation, I could belong —the Methodist church of my childhood, greatly liberalized though it had become in the intervening years. There are various ways of belonging in a group: One, for instance, is the surface fellowship of *having* the same things, like gardens or motorboats; and another of *doing things together,* which may or may not be meaningful to a particular person. (Making aprons, though pleasant, was not an adequate bond of fellowship for me.) The essence of a significant relationship was an opportunity to communicate thought and feeling while pursuing common tasks. While I could not expect to find others holding my world view, I did begin to find, as a basis for fellowship, a consistent purpose to become better people.

How do we become better people? Is effort to that end as useless as trying to grow tall and as pathetic as Benjamin Franklin marking himself each day on his chart of all the virtues? On this point there is a curious meeting of opposites between certain religious beliefs and some very modern theories. Set over against the teaching that one must simply trust in the mercy of God for a salvation from our sinfulness that we could never earn, is the psychological theory that one must find the springs of conduct in the unconscious and that our conscious intelligence can do little more than understand the workings of our nature. By this latter viewpoint, which grew to great acceptance in my day, behavior expresses all that a person is— a delicate equilibrium of all the forces that have made him. If he faces honestly the facts about himself, while trying to meet the demands of his social situation, he will become as good a person as his essential nature allows him to be.

By contrast, I encountered among Marxist scientists an outlook which placed similar emphasis upon understanding natural forces and living in harmony with them but found those determinative forces not so much in biological inheritance as in man's social evolution. Man is a creature unique in being able to produce his livelihood and become a *social* being in the very process of working with others to live. By this view, the demands of social living are not hindrances to individual development, but the very dynamics of growth. Conscious intelligence is our means of understanding the forces working in human society and co-operating with them. The outreaching emotions, love and compassion and loyalty, are most important for social living, but should not be cultivated by denying and repressing those of self-protection.

Since I had been immersed for a lifetime in these varied interpretations of how people become better able to share the struggles of folk in trouble, I came out, not surprisingly, with a blend of old and new. Basically, the guiding light was to live in harmony with nature, but nature expressed for man in terms of social living. Such a merging of an infinitely small person with the great whole of the universe meant relaxation and inner peace, in which one could find fellowship with religious people. Religion, however, means more than a tie to the great whole.

It means obligation (from the same root word), responsibility to grow and create, and especially to create better conditions for human life to grow on this earth. So, again, there is the possibility of fellowship among those who, under various beliefs, give their lives to something greater than themselves.

The greatest personal gain of these years is perhaps a lessening of distance from people who think differently than I do (a distance fostered by too great a sense of mission), and a growing feeling of belonging to the universe of all living things. In this, there is fellowship with a host of others who seek what is true and beautiful and good. These are not only people who live now in all lands, but the great dead who gave freely what they had and hoped that later ones would gain the rewards they could not live to see. There is cultivation of a sense of the universe, the wonder and awe it inspires, and grateful reverence.

I wish I could say that I came unscathed through the period of choking smog which is not over at this writing. On reflection, I wish no such thing. I do not really believe that it is desirable, even if it were possible, to be unaffected by conditions which block healthy activity, as if one were something special, outside the laws of nature. There was never a doubt that the onrushing stream of humanity's search for betterment would become visible again after its underground course. I did wonder if it would in my time. I would not give up holding my end of a bridge over to the best I knew, but did it stop in midair, unattached to the reality which is created by active people working for specific goals? For some two or three years my friends were as lost as I was. We could keep our bridgehead stubbornly and keep faith with the multitudes who had gone before, but we could not go forward.

One small event was a turning point, and incidentally taught me never to say that effort is lost. Thirty years ago, in one of Mussolini's jails, an Italian patriot was eking out years of miserable existence. He was dying of tuberculosis, but he forced himself to write as long as he could hold a pen. Somehow his notebooks were preserved, and extracts from them were translated by an American patriot who had himself suffered persecution for his beliefs.[6] This little book came into my hands when I had almost concluded that systematic study was futile as long as it could not be used in action. The man in prison thirty years ago spoke to me with the freshness of today. He sent me back to the habit of early-morning study of the science of society with renewed faith that there would be a future in which to use it even in my time.

Time to reflect can mean two things: vacancy of other pursuits such that one reflects because there is nothing else to do; or "high time" to reflect, urgent time, time for which the future waits. This second meaning I began to grasp again with courage.

CHAPTER 20

WE HOLD THESE TRUTHS

It is fifty years now since I embarked on an uncharted journey and wrecked my little boat almost at the harbor's mouth. Getting off to a fresh start, the voyage proceeded with what I thought was a clear direction—a mission to serve people and a search for the most significant ways of doing so. I can see now that I could not possibly have planned the significant contacts that actually came to me. The most I can say is that, ready for them or not, I somehow responded.

How could I have known, for instance, that the titanic struggle of humanity in the twentieth century would center around the liberation of people of darker skin? These folk, comprising three quarters of the human race, are now claiming their own after more than three centuries of colonial bondage to the dominant powers of Europe and North America. Fifty years ago when I went to Atlanta University because I needed a job and wanted to "do good," I little dreamed that I would become acquainted there with one most significant aspect of the growing, world-wide liberation struggle. The grandchildren of Negro slaves were asking education from their country, and there was a strong trend toward offering them only so much as would make them efficient laborers. Atlanta University was the center of resistance to this trend, which was also linked with denial of full rights as citizens. There, Dr. W. E. B. DuBois, then in his young manhood, was waging a battle (which he gloriously continues in his ninety-third year) for full equality

of the Negro and an education to match its responsibilities, including those of leadership.[1] Since that experience in Atlanta,
for which I was so unprepared, the racial aspect of the perennial
struggle for human rights has never been remote from me nor
out of my concern.

How could I have known, also, that the American frontier
which had pushed as far as it could go to the Pacific was,
about 1910, shifting to frontiers of the mind—the discovery
of springs of conduct in unconscious mental activity beyond the
reach of introspection.[2] I was soon lifted on a wave of new
awareness of personality which we had not had (to our sorrow)
in the first years of my vocation in social work. It was exhilarating to see human behavior not as something to be approved or
condemned but to be understood. No wonder it seemed to us
then that in tapping the secrets of individual behavior, we had
found the dynamic of human progress.

Could I possibly have guessed in the burgeoning 1920's that
well-adjusted individuals were not to be the salvation of our
world? *Adjusted to what?* took on sinister meaning in the 1930's
when the economic substratum of our life turned up in a mighty
earthquake, grotesque examples of an underworld of human
misery which we had thought only incidental to a well-ordered
civilization. Now we began to wonder if there was something
wrong with what we called civilization itself. Again, I was
living at a point of significant change in history.

At the midpoint of the Depression decade I was fortunate in
coming in contact with a science of society that made sense of
what seemed like a chaos of disaster. Even so, theory might
have remained detached from the real world of conflict were it
not that I lived to see the transformation of nation after nation
under the guidance of a scientific outlook, derived from Karl
Marx and those who had followed him in a hundred years of
rapid change. These nations not only survived economic ruin
and wars of invasion but made the most astounding economic
and cultural advances in history. One, the first to try out
socialism as an economic system in a huge multinational state,

rose in forty years from extreme backwardness to become a world power. To what competition did the first socialist state, and others following, challenge the world? To competition in precisely the things that dictators have never bothered about or dared to permit. These features, characteristic of each new socialist state as it arose, were: consistent raising of the standard of living of entire peoples; underwriting health care as a necessity, without reference to ability to pay for it; education of hand and brain for all, not just for a privileged few; use of natural resources for the people instead of for waste in profit-taking and aggressive wars. Now close to half the population of the world is either living under a socialist system or moving toward it in ways varying with national traditions and resources—substituting planning instead of a scramble for profits and usefulness to a people's well-being rather than competitive looting of the earth's natural wealth. It was my unplanned good fortune to be living to see all this.[3]

I certainly would not have chosen another significant feature of my life's journey—a connection with the world-wide labor movement. In my farm childhood, to combine with others to better our condition was farthest from our thoughts. I was in my late forties before I began to sense how indispensable to any improvement in the lot of working people is the organized striving of workers for themselves. It was grueling experience in my own profession that taught me this, and a fortuitous circumstance that threw me into association with a labor organization in a major industry with world-wide connections.

Equally enlightening was living through the period of disintegration of labor forces. Unions which had fought company spies, intimidation, and blacklisting and had held together through costly strikes, were weakened from within by their own leaders. These were persuaded that a war program which would produce employment was in the interest of American workers and that "defense" was so crucial that a union's primary function was to purge itself of "Reds" and make concessions to employing corporations. So union strength was dissipated by compromise, Red-baiting, racial discrimination, and interunion rivalries, while wage cuts, speed-up, and loss of bargaining power made a Roman holiday of workers' living standards and rights as citizens. If I had not known the depths of labor disorganization and defeat during the postwar period, I could not now so fully appreciate signs of movement toward labor's use of its real strength.

In my lifetime, then, I have been in touch with four movements significant in human history—the struggle of colored peoples for their full rights as men and women, the psychological revolution, the economic transformation of half the world (with an opportunity to understand the science under which it was carried out), and the gropings of working people in the United States toward being active, responsible participants in shaping their own destiny. If I could not have planned these contacts with significant movements, I could at least relate myself to them and try to understand them.

If one word is needed, then, to begin to sum up what fifty years of living have taught me, that word is *relatedness*. It is possible to become absorbed in a personal struggle for survival and for the capture of individual enjoyment, but, if that is all, deterioration is inevitable and sets in early. It is relationships with other people that make us human and give us immortality in the heritage we leave (however small or obscure) to future generations.

As we have noted in my case, an individual has only a limited range of choice and little foresight in knowing to what to respond out of the immeasurably rich heritage we have from the past. We are heirs not only to the technical knowledge for which others have given their lives and which lifts us out of unending drudgery, but of evolving ideals of what is true and good and beautiful. Choice is not easy because there is so much to respond to and because our legacy of good is so mixed with debris from the past—superstitions (which are easy to see in others but not in ourselves), old hatreds, and hardened ways of dealing with each other.

Inevitably our choices are conditioned not only by the time and location of our birth but by our position in organized society. How we get on in the struggle for survival tends to channel our choice of relationships to people in the same general situation. Life looks different from the windows of a palace or the doorway of a field laborer's shack, from one or the other side of a color line, or a collective-bargaining table. Obvious as this seems, it is nonetheless true that many people do not know that they stand in any particular place in society, and so they judge their viewpoint to be the only one possible for anybody. I believe it indispensable to a sound relatedness to others to know where one is to start with, for what biases and blind spots to make allowance, and to know that there exist other and quite different viewpoints.

First in importance, after the initial responsiveness which makes us socially alive, I would place relatedness to what is true. When, in 1940, I tried to express a social *credo* which would be "fireproof and durable" in the face of a menacing fascism,[4] I put this first:

"*I believe* that it is possible to understand scientifically the movement of social and economic forces and to apply our strength in co-operation with them."

At first glance it seems unnecessary to state that, if we believe in a noncapricious and objectively reliable universe, such belief includes also social and economic forces with which we can co-operate. Actually, in our society, we constantly deny this reliance on objective reality in favor of wishful fantasies. For example, we repeat that the economic and political system we have is the highest achievement of mankind, permanent and unchangeable. The will to succeed can overcome all obstacles. There is nothing to fear but fear itself. Riches and poverty, sickness and health are in our minds. We cannot really know the truth, only what is true for us and works in our experience.

In this way of thinking, ideas (whose truth we cannot really know) are powerful explosives. It is, therefore, imperative that people should not get undesirable ideas that may erupt into unwanted acts. So we have seen socialism denounced lest it infect the world like a plague, socialist countries put out of existence (in words) a thousand times, and finally (when their existence can no longer be denied as is the existence of a government of six hundred million people in China even today) we have seen it made a crime to investigate or teach "dangerous thoughts." What enslavement of the mind is this? How does it compare with freedom to learn and to follow objective truth wherever it may lead? If it is freedom we want, is there not all we can use within the reality which presses upon us like the atmosphere but supports us and gives us breath?

There is a similar straitjacket put upon feeling and for the same wishful reasons. Our society fears the emotions which are generated by its frustrations. It marshals all the forces of religion and culture to teach that it is love that should determine all relations among men and that love will overcome all the wrongs that are so apparent today. If we have the right emotions, justice will prevail. It obviously hasn't. As frustrations pile up, there are more and more "wrong emotions" to suppress or to act out with unutterably dangerous results both to mental health and to social stability. Many good people, however, are more concerned about the "wrong emotions" manifested in spontaneous revolts against impossible conditions than about the evil conditions themselves.[5]

I was predisposed, both by temperament and training, to a philosophy of nonresistance. Psychiatry, however, impelled me to the viewpoint that aggression is as much a reality as submission, and that neither love nor hostility can be turned on at will or erased from existence when they are repressed from consciousness.[6] Love is a natural feeling when reaching out to others meets with response. Hostility is a normal reaction to frustration. If it is true that any society needs at the very least relations of mutual trust to bind it together, it must create conditions in which love and trust can grow. No society can survive which tolerates conditions that produce hatreds of such magnitude that people torture and kill each other. Nor is it a defense for a nation to claim that it is impotent to protect its citizens, and they have no recourse but to love their enemies and have patience. If some frustrations are inevitable in any society, so are the feelings they generate. A healthy society gives outlet to these feelings in open criticism and constructive action to reduce the actual causes of frustration.

Following my immersion in psychiatry, the Marxist science of society gave me a profound respect for facts and for feelings as important facts in themselves. Above all, I learned the necessity of relating myself to what is true, rather than to what I may wish to be true. Increasingly over the years I have seen the incalculable harm wrought by false beliefs, no matter how beautiful or useful they may at first seem. Our society spends millions every year propagating what seems most desirable for the public to think, rather than searching for and proclaiming what is true. The resulting ill-conceived actions may eventuate in a war of extermination for all mankind. Truth is on the scaffold, but not forever. I devoutly believe there is no other star to follow.[7]

What place is there for individuals in a world of titanic forces? I grew up with a profession that first found its identity when it reached into the masses of people displaced by the industrial revolution and found individuals. It found them first in families, as economic units, and its mission was to restore them to self-maintenance. Then it discovered what the personal touch could do. When I first met the still-new thing called social casework, it was a cultivated personal touch between privileged people who gave of their time and interest and underprivileged folk who received guidance as well as financial help. Even then, fifty years ago, the "retail' method of helping was challenged by reform movements that actually did wipe out important sources of human misery by legislative action.

Alongside a profession dealing with individuals in trouble grew a sister profession, stimulating and guiding group associations, organized by neighborhoods and by age, sex, and interest groupings. Social group work and community organization may have had their inception, as did social casework, in community fear of the people in poor neighborhoods, but group work was a step ahead in feeling that, once deprivations were levelled off a bit, people anywhere would respond to the finer things of life and act together for civic improvement.

To me, conditioned by intense study of individuals, it was a revelation to discover that social casework and group work were not just parallel methods of helping people but were interwoven, even while the structure of social agencies kept them apart. Individuals receiving therapy lived in families and communities, and we forgot that to our peril. Educational work in physical and mental health found it silly to engage solely in individual guidance when groups learned faster and helped each other. Groups were composed of individuals who sometimes did need to be picked out for special treatment. So we began to know each other to the immense advantage of our service to essentially the same people.

It was a painful surprise to me to find that influential people in our society, including some of the backers of social casework, were actually afraid of groups. It was all right to give young people opportunities for recreation and culture to counteract commercial exploitation of their needs, but the young must be protected from controversial ideas which might tempt them to act in unapproved ways. So, while the early social settlements had made a glorious record of relatedness to the life of their communities, there was in my lifetime a growing restriction upon free discussion and group action. Freudian concepts also reinforced the feeling among caseworkers that individuals are apt to be hampered in their unique development by joining groups, that groups too easily become "pressure groups" dominated by individuals with a need for power, and that the mature person should remain free to develop his individual love-life without relying too much on group relationships. It was in the setting of such ideas that another statement of my 1940 *credo* was evolved:

"*I believe* that the fulfillment of individual life is in belonging with others who share the same purposes. In this relatedness an individual finds use for what is unique in him, responsibility which develops him, and a sharing which gives both glory and meaning to life."

In all these years, there has been in social work an amazing growth of belief in people and in what they can do for themselves. We may measure how far we have traveled by the uneasiness with which we react to the overtones of the skit, *Simple Simon,* with which we started this record.[8] Briefly, the play seems to be saying that people who want what they cannot pay for may be treated crustily, identified as pathological (though we still can't find out just what is wrong with them), or considered likely to thwart our good intentions by resisting us. There is no hint in *Simple Simon*[12] of the wonder with which, in the Depression period, we learned to greet instances of amazing resources in people who, we thought, should have been utterly defeated. By the war years we were beyond surprise. We expected simple, unproclaimed heroism. We turned to the people we had thought helpless without us for their help in working out the difficulties not of inferior people, but human beings with problems common to us all.

To be sure, we saw the depths of defeat for them as for us all. We saw energies tied up in fear or dissipated in false solutions like feathering individual nests or protecting individual plumage. Yet with a little wait for forces to regroup themselves, common folk have again been presenting (here and there and soon in larger numbers) amazing instances of courage and ability to work together "come hell or high water."

It is a common accusation against class-conscious thinkers that they believe that working people have extraordinary virtues and "exploiters" are all heartless and cruel. To me, it is not a question of good people *vs.* bad people, however one defines the good.[9] The social picture which I see today from my many-windowed study is that of a system which victimizes everybody, rich and poor alike. Those who are considered fortunate within it are haunted by fear (perhaps only partly conscious) that the labor of others on which they are terrifyingly dependent for their way of life, may be withdrawn. Control of mechanical power or command of financial resources must be supplemented by control over men—men all over the world whose votes (if permitted) may wipe out the superprofits which have been made from their labor. Fear makes potentially decent people do terrible things, such as rigging elections, torturing dissidents, and promoting wars.

Working people have fears of such real things as want and disease and violent attack, but these can be overcome by intelligent effort, if not by individuals then by organized strength. Working men are not inherently better than other men, but it seems to me that their situation does something different to them, something healthier, than does the situation of exploiting other people. Poverty and disease are remediable and can be dealt with to the greater health of society.

Belief in people, growing with the years, translated itself into an article of the *credo* which was written in a dark time when democracy itself seemed unlikely to survive:

"*I believe* that the needs and desires, the feelings and the will to act, the strength to endure and the power to change the conditions of their life are in people not only real but indestructible."

When I wrote these words, fascism was in the ascendency. We have lived to see it defeated but only partially, and even reaccepted by nations which were once prostrate before its total destructiveness. We have lived to see developed, bombs of a power then unthinkable. To that is being added the threat of the fiendish device of bacterial warfare, which is called a "humane" way of making war because it destroys only people, not property!

Why has the march of history demonstrated to me the indestructibility of people who can be so easily destroyed physically? First, because their needs and desires have not lessened, including a demand for freedom and dignity which no oppression has been able to kill. Second, because working people are indispensable to the survival of the human race, and they cannot be pushed off the stage of history. Third, because the challenge to struggle against and overcome obstacles and natural enemies is built into man's history as the dynamic of his development. Living by exploitation of the labor of others may temporarily produce power over other men, but not the virility of a strong people.

In our time, in the United States of America, an economy of abundance is so new to our pioneer tradition that we tend to strive only for *having things,* and have almost deprived our machine-nurtured children of the essential challenge of exertion of muscle and brain. When the young, with a sure instinct, try to put back danger and daring into sterile lives, we call it juvenile delinquency but are helpless to offer them a valid equivalent. No one can make me believe that, though the labor of man's hand and brain has brought him up from an animal existence to become a social being, man cannot find new challenges for each generation in our intricate modern life.

In 1940 I wrote these words:

"*I believe* that common experiences, common needs and aims make certain that in the long run men will work together instead of in competition to achieve their goals—theirs, not the goals of others for them."

Is it a calamity that people will eventually choose the form of government and economic system they want, even if it turns out to be something different from what we now have?

The world is entering a period of technological change vastly more revolutionary than anything known in history. The earliest machines were only more efficient tools, adding strength to man's arm and agility to woman's fingers. Now machines can produce not only unlimited power but *control* of power, such that they almost tend themselves. They count and select and sort until man's brain seems useless except to invent and service ever more intricate machines.

A century ago social work was turned to, to find better ways of dealing with displaced, unwanted laborers than to let them starve or to feed their strength only to fear their menace. Today, if the trend toward automation goes on as it must, social work cannot be even *imagined* to be a sufficient answer. What shall be done with millions of people whose skilled hands are now too slow and whose brain power (if production of goods is all that is wanted of men) is becoming superfluous?

There is one answer which the civilized world rejects and yet toys with—extermination. The Nazis were blatant about it with their crematoria—and we dare to honor Nazis today! We say the same thing, but more obscurely, when we segregate people for their skin color or beliefs and contract unbearably their living space. What is this but saying, "Get off the earth"? It seems to us a mark of progress for great cities to embark upon slum clearance to make room for luxury apartments and office buildings. There is no room for people who are not profitable, slum dwellers who are driven from horrible to still more horrible and crowded slums.

Socialist countries have another answer. They have un-limited use for people and welcome automation to banish brainless toil from the earth. First, the hunger of the whole world for goods is to be satisfied. And what a vast hunger that is! Then, planned production stops when demand is fulfilled and does not insanely pile up surpluses to rot in storehouses in order to keep up prices. As less of their labor is needed for making goods, the workers find a new kind of leisure—not dragging idleness, but satisfaction of an insatiable longing to know and to enjoy. Workers displaced from machines become teachers, scientists, explorers, leaders in sports, artists, writers, musicians.[16] The possibilities are endless, once the roadblock of profit-making is removed, the roadblock which stops progress today with the question, "Will it make a profit?"

It seems to me almost superfluous to ask whether the future world of mechanized power will belong to those who compete in exploitation of earth's resources for themselves or to those who learn to work together for their common needs and aims to achieve the goals of all of them.

My beloved profession has been learning much about co-operation. We have come to see that we must work *with* people to "achieve their own goals, not the goals of others for them." Our profession has worked where it could and, in a world often hostile to its ideals, has sometimes suffered loss of its relatedness to the progressive movements of the life of its time. It has not willingly, however, accepted a role exploitive of its clients, or a police function to keep people quiet while they starve slowly.

Social work, it seems to me, has least of all to fear from a change from the violent conflicts of today to the new synthesis of forces which will be the co-operative socialist society of tomorrow. Suppose there will not be so many people needing help that all the social work in the wide world cannot begin to reach them. Is that cause for grief? Suppose social work need no longer occupy itself with "fringe benefits" while under-nourishment and disease, hatred and war, dread and futility take their awful toll. Can we bear it? Suppose social work will become a reaching down to individuals on the part of a healthy society, concerned that minor adjustments shall be well made when planning for thousands cannot be exactly right for every single person. Can we not rejoice to be that helping hand? If groups functioning healthily help each other along as naturally as do parents and children, friends and neighbors, must we be exclusive about the privilege of helping?

We began this record of a journey with *social responsibility*. I believe we shall go on to see more of it, not the responsibility of privileged folk for underprivileged but of whole peoples for each other, and responsibility itself a privilege. Fifty years is not too long to spend in learning that individual fulfillment is in relatedness to others in purposes that are greater than any one alone; nor is it too short a time to know that the future is big with promise of a really co-operative society for all of mankind.

NOTES

Chapter 1 EMBARKATION

1. The Monday Evening Club, to which anyone employed in social work was eligible, met at monthly supper meetings for serious discussion of lectures and papers. It was an innovation to allot an evening for a play which was presented by the Papers and Discussions Committee.

2. Mary E. Richmond, "The Term 'Social Case Worker,'" a paper in *The Long View*, papers and addresses (New York: Russell Sage Foundation, 1930), pp. 474-478. "Case worker" was written as two words in the early period.

3. These were: Dr. A. Warren Stearns, later famous as a penologist and author, and Dr. Frankwood E. Williams, later Medical Director of the National Committee for Mental Hygiene and Program Chairman, First International Congress on Mental Hygiene.

4. From St. Paul's letter to the church at Ephesus, Ephesians 4:15.

Chapter 2 SOCIAL RESPONSIBILITY

1. From a chart in *The Long View*, p. 589, comes the following list of national organizations and movements in this period: The Consumers' League, 1899; Children's Courts and Probation, 1899; Housing Reform, 1901; Anti-Tuberculosis Association, 1902; Child Labor Movement, 1904; Association for Labor Legislation, 1905; National Recreation Association, 1905; Child Hygiene, 1909; Mental Hygiene, 1909; Councils of Social Agencies, 1910; Social Hygiene, 1912.

2. *The Long View*, p. 586. See also p. 181.

3. *Ibid.*, pp. 214-221.

4. National Conference of Charities and Correction, *Proceedings,* Thirty-Ninth Annual Session, 1912, p. 376.

5. The members of the Committee and collaborators in the report and the papers appended included Owen R. Lovejoy, Chairman, Dr. Alice Hamilton, Florence Kelley, Paul Kellogg, Samuel McCune Lindsay, Julius Henry Cohen, John B. Andrews, and several others well known for their contribution to labor and social legislation. (From an unpublished manuscript of Miss Mary van Kleeck.)

6. National Conference of Charities and Correction, *op. cit.,* pp. 388-389.

7. Summarized in the manuscript of Miss van Kleeck cited above.

8. In seeking sources of information about the strike, I have tried to secure, whenever possible, reports from observers or participants. This summary is gleaned from: Richard C. Boyer and Dr. Herbert M. Morais, *Labor's Untold Story* (New York: Cameron Associates, 1955); Elizabeth Gurley Flynn, *I Speak My Own Piece* (New York: Masses & Mainstream, 1955); Mary Heaton Vorse, *A Footnote to Folly* (New York: Farrar and Rinehart, 1935).

9. The American Federation of Labor had organized the United Textile Workers of America, a craft union which did nothing for the mass of unskilled workers. In the Lawrence strike, John Golden, its head, ordered the skilled workers to stay on the job, which they could not do alone. Golden repudiated the strike because it was assisted by the Industrial Workers of the World, the I.W.W. See Elizabeth Gurley Flynn, *op. cit.*, p. 123.

10. The I.W.W. was an offshoot of the Western Federation of Miners and represented a demand for industrial unionism (one big union for all workers) which would reach workers hitherto neglected by the A. F. of L.—the "unskilled, foreign-born workers in the mass-production industries of the East and the unorganized, migratory workers of the West, who were largely American born and employed in maritime, lumber, agriculture, mining and construction work." (Elizabeth Gurley Flynn, *op. cit.*, p. 67). The I.W.W. flourished from 1905 until about 1919 and was noted for its militance and its dual unionism which diverted strength from the A.F. of L.

11. I do not know how the social workers of Boston and the vicinity felt about the Lawrence strike or whether the facts about it were ever available to them. Mr. Robert A. Woods, headworker of South End House and widely known for his expert knowledge of labor relations, condemned the strike for its connection with the I.W.W. He deplored the fact that certain groups feel that their business interests are their own and fail to grant concessions through negotiations that strikes eventually compel them to make. He felt that labor organizations should not follow policies that would be destructive of their future growth. While he welcomed the increase in wages in the textile mills of the whole district, he thought: "the amount of gain must depend on how quickly and broadly influences are set at work to make the higher wage standard represent a higher standard of living and of life." Eleanor H. Woods, *Robert A. Woods, Champion of Democracy* (Boston & New York: Houghton Mifflin, 1929), pp. 263-267.

12. Miss Richmond's title of a paper published in *Charities* in 1905. See also *The Long View*, p. 222.

13. Mary E. Richmond, "Charitable Co-operation," *The Long View*, p. 196.

14. Annual Reports of B.C.A.S., 1863-1911.

15. Annual Reports of the Massachusetts General Hospital Social Service from 1905 through 1912.

16. Mary E. Richmond, *The Long View*, pp. 99-104.

17. *Ibid.*, p. 102.

18. Simmons College for women and Harvard University for men.

19. In 1917 the name was changed to School of Social Work. President LeFavour of Simmons College objected to the word "training" in the name because it did not sound academic. Dr. Brackett held out for "social" rather than "philanthropic" which would exclude public agencies. See Alice Channing, "Early Years of a Pioneer School," *Social Service Review*, December, 1954.

20. Simmons College opened its doors in the fall of 1902 as a college founded "to enable women to earn an independent livelihood." It combined a general education with specialization in the fourth year for a vocation in such fields as home economics, secretarial work, science, library work, nursing, retailing, publication, and later social work.

21. Few took the four-year Simmons course for social work, and the School became entirely a graduate school in 1939. In 1916 Harvard University ceased to enroll men for social work at the School, and after 1945 Simmons, by a change in its charter, was authorized to give degrees to men. See Alice Channing, *op. cit.*, Note 19.

22. See *The Long View*, p. 39, for a list of Miss Richmond's papers showing the development of her views on volunteer service.

23. Public relief of need through the Overseers of the Poor was considered a last resort, from which private social agencies hoped to save as many families as possible who were "worthy" cases.

24. Mary E. Richmond, *op. cit.*, "What is Charity Organization?", pp. 131, 133, 141-143, and "Friendly Visiting," pp. 254-261.

25. Mary E. Richmond, *op. cit.*, "Pensions and the Social Worker," pp. 350-364.

Chapter 3 FIRST PRACTICE

1. Boston Children's Aid Society, *48th Annual Report*, p. 9.

2. *Ibid.*, *50th Annual Report*, p. 8.

3. *Ibid.*, *52nd Annual Report*.

4. Mary S. Doran and Bertha C. Reynolds, *The Selection of Foster Homes for Children* (New York: New York School of Social Work, 1919), pp. 23-24.

5. *Ibid.*, p. 26.

6. *Ibid.*, pp. 34-35.

7. Richard C. Cabot, "An Appreciation of Elmer E. Southard," *Bulletin*, Massachusetts Department of Mental Diseases, Vol. IV, No. 1, February, 1920, p. 19.

8. *Ibid.*, pp. 5-29.

9. *Ibid.*, p. 16.

10. *Ibid.*, p. 26.

11. *Ibid.*, p. 20.

12. *Ibid.*, pp. 15-16.

13. *Ibid.*, p. 27.

Chapter 4 EVERYONE IS A LITTLE QUEER

1. The Training School for Psychiatric Social Work, which was a war emergency course, was expanded in the winter of 1919 to a course of two eight-week summer sessions with an intervening period of nine months of field practice. Anticipating a need for trained psychiatric social workers in various fields, the School established courses in psychiatric social work, medical social work, child welfare and community organization. It offered its full course to college graduates working for a diploma in one of the four specialties. All had basic courses in the psychology of behavior, social organization and social casework and also had preparation for the specialties in further academic courses and in field practice. Experienced social workers with sufficient qualifications could complete the work for a specialty in one summer.

By 1921, Professor Everett Kimball became director of what had become a firmly established institution. In 1926 the Trustees of Smith College voted to grant the degree of Master of Social Science to graduates of the School who possessed a Bachelor's degree upon entrance and had completed the course satisfactorily. This degree was made retroactive to previous classes, except the first class, that of March, 1919, which had not had the required length of training.

2. Dr. Elmer E. Southard and Mary C. Jarrett, *The Kingdom of Evils* (New York: Macmillan Co., 1922). For groups of mental diseases see Book III.

3. *Ibid.*, Books I and II.

4. *Ibid.*

5. Dr. George M. Kline became State Commissioner of Mental Diseases.

6. After the first few months, a second worker came for apprentice training, and after that our staff normally consisted of two social workers.

7. For discussion of this method of recording, see Bertha C. Reynolds, *Learning and Teaching in the Practice of Social Work* (New York: Rinehart & Co., 1942), pp. 167 ff.

Chapter 5 THE TWIG IS BENT—THE TREE INCLINED

1. Clifford W. Beers, *A Mind That Found Itself* (New York: Doubleday, Doran & Co., 1908).

2. It is significant that the campaign slogan of President Harding was: "Return to normalcy."

3. Bertha C. Reynolds, "Environmental Handicaps of 400 Habit Clinic Children," read before the National Conference of Social Work, Denver, Colorado, June, 1925. Published in *Hospital Social Service*, Vol. XII (1925), p. 329.

4. One cherished memory is of a vigorous mother who came steaming into the clinic one cold morning followed by a troop of children muffled to the eyes in scarves, which she proceeded to unwind, saying, "Vere is the doctor mit the bad habits?"

5. Bertha C. Reynolds, "The Mental Hygiene of Young Children," *Hospital Social Service,* 1924, pp. 177, 180.

6. *Ibid.,* p. 336, Note 3.

7. Another paper, "Mental Health as Affected by Play," was not given until 1927 and was published in the *Social Service Bulletin,* Massachusetts Department of Mental Diseases, Vol. XVIII, October, 1934.

8. Much later I learned that the School had nearly foundered because of its isolation from social work and because of its association with psychoanalysis, which was then as cordially hated in many influential quarters as it was considered holy in others. It was important that the Smith College School be brought into the orbit of social work as it then existed in the United States.

A further note may make clear the confusion about the position of psychiatric social work which existed for a considerable period. In 1927 Mary C. Jarrett gave a paper on education for psychiatric social work in which she said, "Psychiatric social work is now accepted as a special branch of social casework." She went on to cite differences from this conclusion—that the mental element is so essential that all good casework is necessarily psychiatric or that psychiatric social work is so all-embracing that only the psychiatric social worker is able to qualify as a good caseworker. She saw a special function in adjustment of family and community relationships as they affect the mental health of individuals and would call that the specialty. Mary C. Jarrett, "Present Conditions in Education for Psychiatric Social Work," a paper read at a Round Table of the American Association of Psychiatric Social Workers, Des Moines, 1927. Published in *Hospital Social Service,* Vol. XVII (1928), p. 212.

Chapter 6 DRAWING OUT AND LEADING FORTH

1. Miss Richmond had included a philosophy of life in her definition of a professional standard. See *The Long View,* pp. 99-104.

2. Papers on the interrelationship between religion and mental hygiene were appearing that year in periodicals. For instance: Rabbi Abba Hillel Silver, "Development of Personality Through Religious Experience," *Jewish Social Service Quarterly,* September, 1926; Rev. Pryor McN. Grant, "The Moral and Religious Life of the Individual in the Light of the New Psychology," *Mental Hygiene,* Vol. XII (1928), pp. 449-491.

Chapter 7. CLINICS AND RESEARCH

1. Bertha C. Reynolds, "A Quest for Treatment Processes in Social Work," read before the National Conference of Social Work, Cleveland, Ohio, May, 1926. Published in *Hospital Social Service,* Vol. XVI (1926), p. 454.

2. Virginia P. Robinson, *A Changing Psychology in Social Case Work* (Chapel Hill: University of North Carolina Press, 1931).

3. Bertha C. Reynolds, *op. cit.*

4. *Ibid.*, p. 455.

5. Mary E. Richmond, "Charitable Co-operation," *The Long View,* pp. 186-202.

6. Bertha C. Reynolds, *op. cit.,* p. 457.

7. *Ibid.*, p. 462.

8. *Ibid.*, pp. 462-463.

9. Laughter echoed through the halls when this study, by printer's error, came out with the title, "Maternal Overproduction."

10. For list of publication by the Institute staff, fellows, and students from 1927 to 1933 see Lawson G. Lowrey, M.D. and Geddes Smith, *The Institute for Child Guidance, 1927-1933* (New York: The Commonwealth Fund, 1933), pp. 102-117.

11. Bertha C. Reynolds, "A Way of Understanding; An Approach to Case Work With Negro Families," *The Family,* Vol. XII (1931-32), pp. 203 ff., 240 ff., 287 ff.

12. Bertha C. Reynolds, "An Experiment in Short Contact Interviewing," *Smith College Studies in Social Work,* Vol. III, No. 1, Sept., 1932.

13. It is amusing that statistics, gathered before the Congress, found only one state in the United States with 100% of its psychiatric social workers graduates of professional schools. The state was Montana, and the number was one.

14. The papers were printed in advance in English, French, and German, thanks to a contribution of the Metropolitan Life Insurance Company. They were delivered in abstract and translated without the modern device of earphones. These were later published in *Institute for Child Guidance Studies,* edited by Dr. Lawson G. Lowrey (New York: The Commonwealth Fund, 1931).

15. *Ibid.*, p. 53.

16. *Ibid.*, pp. 68-69.

17. Bertha C. Reynolds, "Can Case Closing Be Planned as a Part of Treatment?" Read at the National Conference of Social Work, Joint Session of Mental Hygiene Division with the American Association of Psychiatric Social Workers, Minneapolis, Minnesota, June 20, 1931. Published in *The Family,* Vol. XII (1931), pp. 135-142.

18. *Ibid.*, p. 142.

19. *Ibid.*

20. Bertha C. Reynolds, "The Church and Individual Security." Read at the Episcopal Conference of Social Work, Philadelphia, May, 1932. Published in *American Journal of Orthopsychiatry,* Vol. III, January, 1933.

Chapter 8 POISED FOR ADVANCE

1. Bertha C. Reynolds, "Can Case Closing be Planned as a Part of Treatment?" *The Family,* Vol. XII, p. 142.

2. Clark E. Moustakas, *Children in Play Therapy* (New York: McGraw-Hill, 1953).

3. Virginia P. Robinson, *A Changing Psychology in Social Case Work* (Chapel Hill: University of North Carolina Press, 1931).

4. Bertha C. Reynolds, Review of the Robinson book (Note 3 above), *The Family*, Vol. XII (1931), p. 111.

5. *Ibid.*, p. 112.

6. *Ibid.*

7. Florence Sytz, Correspondence, *The Family*, Vol. XII (1931), pp. 197-199.

8. *Ibid.*, p. 197.

9. *Ibid.*, p. 198.

10. Bertha C. Reynolds, "A Changing Psychology in Social Case Work—After One Year," *The Family*, Vol. XIII (1932), p. 107.

11. *Ibid.*

12. *Ibid.*

13. In today's speech, there are many variations in the meaning of the term "psychoanalysis," and a wide range of forms of psychoanalytically-oriented therapy. In the 1920's, a psychoanalysis meant something quite definite as described by Freud, and the classic form was only beginning to be modified by the different schools set up by Freud's disciples. If one decided to undergo psychoanalysis in those days, it was a decision to undergo daily sessions for a long period, terminated by formal recommendation. This discussion reflects that period rather than the varied picture in psychotherapy today.

14. In our work with students at the Smith College School, we became familiar with what we called "the November depression"—a reaction to which almost all students were subject in some form. After intense study for eight weeks in summer, accumulating a staggering amount of new and emotionally-charged material, they moved to a strange city and began the test of practice in an agency new to them. At first it was all wonderful, but by November doubts and fears assailed them. Perhaps they lost confidence in themselves, feeling that their former knowledge and skills were all worthless and their personalities probably not adequate to this exacting profession. Some began to complain of the deficiencies of the agency and that the supervision they were getting failed to teach them anything. Whatever truth there was in these allegations, the School knew that this period would pass and a sense of growing mastery of their work would follow. Supervisors were warned not to take all this too seriously and to stand by with encouragement and support.

15. *The Family*, Vol. XIII, April, 1932, pp. 51-54.

16. In the Milford Conference group were represented the following national organizations: Family Welfare Association of America, American Association of Hospital Social Workers, Child Welfare League of America, American Association of Psychiatric Social Workers, International Migration Service, National Association of Travelers Aid Societies, National Committee on Visiting Teachers, and National Probation Association.

17. "Social Case Work, Generic and Specific." A report of the Milford Conference in *Studies in the Practice of Social Work,* No. 2, American Association of Social Workers, 1929, pp. 4, 16, 17.

18. Mary E. Richmond, *What is Social Case Work?* (New York: Russell Sage Foundation, 1922). See definitions in *The Long View,* pp. 374-375, 398-399, 471, 477, 577.

Chapter 9 THE SOLID EARTH IS SHAKEN

1. A famous case publicized the plight of nine teen-age Negro boys who were arrested on a freight train near Scottsboro, Alabama, in March, 1931. They were charged with rape, which carries a death penalty for Negroes in the South. See Earl Conrad and Haywood Patterson, *Scottsboro Boy* (Garden City, N.Y.: Doubleday & Co., 1950).

2. For a description of the Veterans' Bonus March on Washington, June, 1932, see Richard O. Boyer and Dr. Herbert M. Morais, *Labor's Untold Story* (New York: Cameron Associates, 1955).

3. The report of this committee was published for discussion in *The Family,* Vol. XIII, No. 10, February, 1933. Its title was, "Can Social Case Work Be Interpreted to a Community as a Basic Approach to Human Problems?"

4. *Ibid.,* p. 341.

5. *Ibid.,* p. 342.

6. *The Newsletter,* American Association of Psychiatric Social Workers, Vol. II, No. 3, November, 1932.

7. *Ibid.,* pp. 6-7.

8. Published as a monograph, "An Experiment in Short Contact Interviewing," *Smith College Studies in Social Work,* September, 1932. Knowing that this study would be used for teaching, I initiated a method of presentation which I also used later in "Between Client and Community," i.e., the interviews were recorded just as they had been dictated for the agency record, following a form and including a section for *impressions.* Comments were added a week or two later, summing up the worker's thinking about the application for agency use. Finally, this reproduced record material was discussed in the text for the purposes of the study. This was a self-critical and self-exposing method which I could not have used before psychoanalysis.

9. This study was embodied in a paper read at a session of the National Association of Travelers Aid Society at Detroit in June, 1933, entitled "The Social Case Worker's Relationship to Clients When the Community Demands Action of a Definite Sort" and published in 1934 by the N.A.T.A.S. in a pamphlet which included a paper by Madeline L. MacGregor, Executive Secretary, Travelers Aid Society, Chicago. Miss MacGregor showed by case illustrations how a sympathetic and free relationship with clients can be used in T.A.S. work.

10. *Ibid.,* p. 10.

11. Bertha C. Reynolds, "Between Client and Community," *Smith College Studies in Social Work,* September, 1934.

12. David Cushman Coyle, *The Irrepressible Conflict, Business vs. Finance* (New York: privately printed, 1933).

Chapter 10 VITALITY

1. Referred to henceforth as the NRA.

2. The report was published in *The Compass,* magazine of the American Association of Social Workers (AASW) in May, 1933, and reprinted from that issue together with Miss van Kleeck's paper, "A Planned Economy" and a statement by the Executive Committee of the AASW entitled, "A Minimum Standard of Relief."

3. See Note 2 above. Miss van Kleeck was Director of Industrial Studies, Russell Sage Foundation, New York City. She had been President of the Second International Conference of Social Work, held at Frankfurt-am-Main, in 1932.

4. From a statement of purpose included in the first issue of *Social Work Today,* March-April, 1934.

5. The American Association of Social Workers (AASW).

6. This convention met in the Negro Masonic Auditorium, for no other hall would seat Negro and white delegates together. There had been two national demonstrations of the unemployed in Washington before this—in December, 1931, and December, 1932. This time it was a convention. They came on foot, in old trucks, and in boxcars. The California delegation never arrived, being arrested and jailed for vagrancy in Memphis.

7. This letter was signed by Miss Mary van Kleeck, announcing that an informal group of professional workers was discussing the formation of an association of professional workers to co-operate with industrial workers in promoting social insurance. This organization was formally launched on April 29, 1934, as described later, and was known as the Interprofessional Association or IPA.

8. This paper was published in full in the *Mid-Monthly Survey,* June, 1934. Excerpts from it were published in *The Compass,* June, 1934. The quotation is from an introductory note in *The Compass.*

9. Published in abridged form in *Social Work Today,* October, 1934.

10. At that time any organized group associated with social work could register as an Associate Group of the National Conference of Social Work, have meetings announced in the Conference bulletins, and maintain a booth at the exhibit hall.

11. Bertha C. Reynolds, "Between Client and Community," *Smith College Studies in Social Work,* September, 1934.

12. Dr. Frankwood E. Williams, *Russia, Youth and the Present-Day World* (New York: Farrar and Rinehart, 1934).

13. *Ibid.,* Preface, p. xvii.

Chapter 11 RE-THINKING

1. Linton B. Swift, *New Alignments Between Public and Private Agencies in a Community Family Welfare and Relief Program* (New York: Family Welfare Association of America, 1934).

2. It is impossible to know at this distance how much I grasped at the time and how much trickled into my understanding during twenty years of study since then, but the beginnings of a new outlook were undoubtedly there. My references are:
Karl Marx, *Capital*, Vol. I (Chicago: Charles H. Kerr & Co., 1906); *Theories of Surplus Value, Selections* (New York: International Publishers, 1952).
Frederick Engels, *Socialism, Utopian and Scientific* (New York: International Publishers, 1935); *Herr Eugen Dühring's Revolution in Science* (Anti-Dühring) (New York: International Publishers, 1939); Dialectics of Nature (New York: International Publishers, 1940). Applications of dialectical and historical materialism to science were limited, of course, by the stage of development of the sciences in Engel's day. The philosophical outlook is still valid.
Emile Burns, A Handbook of Marxism (New York: International Publishers, 1935). A collection of extracts from writings of Marx, Engels and the greatest of their followers.
T. A. Jackson, *Dialectics: The Logic of Marxism and Its Critics* (New York: International Publishers, 1936).

3. Bertha C. Reynolds, "Between Client and Community," *Smith College Studies in Social Work*, September, 1934, pp. 118-127.

4. "Social Case Work. What Is It? What Is Its Place in the World Today?" *The Quarterly Bulletin*, New York State Conference on Social Work, Vol. VII, No. 1, December, 1935, pp. 95-108. See also Fern Lowry, *Readings in Social Case Work*, 1920-1938 (New York: Columbia University Press, 1939), pp. 136-147.

5. Discussion of paper by Mrs. Lois Meredith French on "The Role of the Visiting Teacher in Group Relationships," *Visiting Teachers Bulletin*, Vol. XI, No. 3, June, 1936, pp. 14-17.

6. *Social Work Today*, April, May, and June, 1938.

7. *Ibid.*, April, 1938, p. 6.

8. *Ibid.*, p. 8.

9. *Ibid.*

10. *Ibid.*

11. *Ibid.*, June, 1938, p. 8.

12. However, many people still insist that they believe in evolution, not revolution. To a Marxist this means that they believe in a chrysalis but not in a butterfly, in gestation but not in birth. Nature does not leave us that choice.

13. It is ironic that while the non-socialist world regards communism as the greatest menace, justifying use of atomic weapons in defence against it, communism actually has never been seen on this earth and is only projected by socialist countries as the goal to be achieved when an age of abundance has been fully realized. It is socialism which exists and which is sometimes confused with fascism when the nature of neither is understood.

14. *Social Work Today*, Vol. VII, No. 2, November, 1940, pp. 9-11.

Chapter 12 NEW DIRECTION

1. Samuel Butler recommended this cure for nervousness as far back as 1867 when he wrote *The Way of All Flesh,* a novel anticipating modern ideas (New York: Modern Library, Random House) pp. 352-354.

2. This discussion refers to general supervision of the students' work throughout the course, not only to the teaching of casework in summer sessions.

Chapter 13 LEADERS AND TEACHERS

1. I used personal interviews with teachers of the arts and books such as: Edward McCurdy, *The Mind of Leonardo da Vinci* (New York: Dodd, Mead & Co., 1928); Robert Henri, *The Art Spirit* (Philadelphia: J. B. Lippincott Co., 1923); Constantin Stanislavski, *An Actor Prepares* (New York Theatre Arts, 1936). In 1941, at a Hobby Show sponsored by *Social Work Today,* I exhibited a collection of statements by teachers of the arts.

2. See under Type-Situation in Index of Bertha C. Reynolds, *Learning and Teaching in the Practice of Social Work* (New York: Rinehart & Co., 1942).

3. See use of "social norms" in "An Experiment in Short Contract Interviewing," *Smith College Studies in Social Work,* September, 1934. See also p. 20 for discussion of, and use in discussion of cases throughout the article.

Chapter 14 TEACHER ON WHEELS

1. An inspiring biography of Rev. Claude Williams, southern preacher and labor leader, was published by Cedric Belfrage under the title, *South of God* (New York: Modern Age Books, 1941). It was reissued with additional chapters by the Peoples Institute of Applied Religion in 1946, under the title, *A Faith to Free the People.*

2. Commonwealth College was wiped out a few years later by certain elements in the region who hated and feared labor organization in any form and used the familiar technique of red-baiting. The mass movement of southern tenant farmers and agricultural laborers into unions, which took place in the 1930's, was a spontaneous protest against intolerable conditions which can never be silenced.

3. I set the fees as low as was consistent with a modest annual income, allowing for some gaps in employment. Time for preparation was included in the charge to sponsors which was based on the number of hours of group discussion or consultation. Looking back, I think I could have set the rates fifty percent higher and would then have earned more than the marginal income which each of the two years of the experiment produced. At the time, I was most interested in being available, even to groups of low-paid workers who had to obtain consultation without subsidy from their agencies.

4. The report which I sent to my sponsors at the end of two years summed up the experience in figures as follows: there had been 80 dif-

ferent groups holding discussions in series; 14 lecture audiences; and 59 people using consultation individually.

Of the discussion groups, 14 met in New York City and 66 in 17 states. The sponsors of discussion groups varied: agency staffs organized 36; professional organizations sponsored 24; councils of social agencies 13; schools of social work accounted for 7; state welfare conferences for 5; state or city units of government for 6; special interest groups for 2; and a social work union for 1 (this was the only appointment with a union for paid work, though I spoke many times before union groups in this period). The members of groups were either public or private agency employees in 39 instances (about equally divided) and were mixed groups in nearly as many instances.

The subject of study was supervision in 26 groups and casework in 44. Some studied the interrelations of casework and group work, administration or community relationships.

5. One piece of research during this period called for study of brief interviews sent me from the New York Bureau of Child Guidance and the Public Assistance Department. The study was reported at a meeting of the American Association of Psychiatric Social Workers at the National Conference of Social Work at Grand Rapids, in May, 1940. It was published in the *Newsletter* of the AAPSW, Vol. X, No. 1, under the title, "Dynamic Possibilities of the Time-Limited Interview."

6. When social workers became affiliated with the Congress of Industrial Organizations (CIO), those employed in private social agencies were in the Social Service Employees Union under the United Office and Professional Workers of America (UOPWA) and those employed by units of government under the United Public Workers of America (UPWA).

Chapter 15 PAUSE IN TRANSIT

1. Bertha C. Reynolds, *Learning and Teaching in the Practice of Social Work* (New York: Rinehart & Co., 1942), Chapter 7.

2. This is not to minimize the skills of social group work which were also held back from full development by the fact that trained group workers became supervisors, and most of the contacts with groups were in the hands of volunteer leaders. Skills in social casework had avoided this pitfall after the early years only to meet the same fate at a later stage, as described in this chapter.

3. This problem was not solely a hangover from an earlier day. The most pressing new problem of the public assistance agencies was the assimilation of new, untrained staff. If agencies could not learn to tolerate, and even welcome and train, workers without adequate professional education, how could they meet the stresses of those pioneer years? The point of view of the survey I have mentioned was to consign all such agencies to the limbo where: "They don't do casework."

4. There were later attempts to start a magazine of fact and opinion in social work. *Staff* was published by the United Office and Professional

Workers of America for four issues in 1947, and *Trends in Social Work* saw five issues from July, 1950, to June, 1952. It was published by an independent committee in co-operation with The Social Welfare Division of the National Council of Arts, Sciences and Professions, New York.

Chapter 16 KEEP 'EM SAILING

1. USO, United Service Organization, provided recreation for members of the armed services.

2. United Seamen's Service (USS) was a co-operative undertaking of the United States Government through the War Shipping Administration, the shipbuilding and ship operating industries, and the seamen represented by their unions, the largest of which was the National Maritime Union affiliated with the CIO. Some of the unions were in the CIO and some were organized by crafts and were in the AF of L. While unions were represented on the Board of USS, they were a minority in number and influential only when they could obviously express widespread sentiment among seamen.

3. The Personal Service Department of the NMU was first organized to take care of individual problems that were consuming too much of the time of union officials. It first functioned with one experienced seaman and a secretary. Early in 1943, a professional social worker, Miss Constance Kyle, was engaged as Director, and the former secretary as Assistant Director. The latter, Miss Toby Fields, formerly a portrait painter, took courses at the New York School of Social Work and contributed her experienced knowledge of the maritime industry.

4. One controversy with the Board, I remember, concerned the giving of loans in cash rather than in orders on restaurants and lodging places. The implication that seamen could not be trusted with money was not only unacceptable to the seamen but the standard of cash relief in public assistance had become a minimal requirement in social work.

5. Many U.S. ships were registered under foreign flags (Panama or Honduras, for example) and took advantage of lower requirements as to wages and working conditions than were mandatory under U.S. registry.

6. The Educational Department of the union set up a school to train seamen for higher ratings under the Coast Guard regulations and was so successful that the Government took it over for the war period. The NMU employed a professional educator to direct that department along with a seaman expert in the industry. The staff of its newspaper, *The Pilot,* was headed by a professional journalist. Its lawyer was an able student of maritime law. When it reorganized its Personal Service, it sought trained and experienced social workers.

7. The United Office and Professional Workers of America (UOPWA) which I had joined, but not without difficulty. When I became convinced during the depression years that a mature working relationship demanded organized association with one's fellow workers, I was the only full-time staff member at the Smith College School. The

Teachers Union (AF of L) which admitted me to membership held no meetings in July and August, which was the only time I was in Northampton. Therefore, I never saw my fellow union members. By 1937, a Social Service Employees Union under the UOPWA (CIO) had been formed in New York, and I transferred to that. However, I did not have a place of employment in New York. The Faculty Chapter of the New York School of Social Work kindly gave me an orphan's home with them, so that I could attend luncheon discussion meetings when I was in the city. I had, therefore, union convictions but little union experience when my coming to the staff of USS made me eligible to belong to a chapter there.

8. The union had its own ways of dealing with a situation in which a man refusing medical care might break down at sea and become a serious danger to others. At one time a plan was organized to send men with "convoy fatigue" to man the ore ships on the Great Lakes for a temporary period. Much as this service was also needed, many could not be persuaded to take what seemed to them a concession to weakness.

9. This fact came alive to Personal Service in the first summer when we were able to offer camp placements to seamen's children of the appropriate ages, ten to fourteen. To our surprise, we found that seamen did not have children that old. They had married after they received better wages after the CIO union was formed in 1937.

10. An able-bodied seaman was a skilled deck worker, above the rank of ordinary seaman and below that of bosun or supervisor. The name, "able-bodied" reflects, as does the term "hands" for factory workers, a lack of respect for a worker's brain power and experience.

11. There did not need to be harangues against prejudice or attempts to change feelings. Economic and wartime necessity and the experience of facing death together on the sea bound the members to one another. If a man could not bear to room with his Negro brother on ship, it was he, not the Negro brother, who had to return his card to the dispatcher and face group disapproval for failure to live up to union standards.

12. An enlightening example came out of the depression years, when for four months, several hundred Baltimore seamen ran their own relief project under the Federal Transient Bureau. Disgusted with bad conditions and inadequate relief which had been administered by The Anchorage, a private seamen's agency, the Waterfront Unemployed Council and the Marine Workers Industrial Union made a collective protest. When after January 1, 1934, a relief program which included seamen was set up under the Transient Division of the Baltimore Emergency Relief Administration and when the seamen made a strong protest against the retention of the former Anchorage staff, the seamen's delegates became an administrative nucleus which elected their own staff and demonstrated to the State Relief Administration that they could administer relief with extraordinary efficiency and economy and with improvement of relief standards. The project was closed when the men, believing that improvement in employment conditions was also essential to lessen the

need for relief, organized a centralized shipping bureau of their own (foreshadowing the union shipping halls of later date) and thereby collided with the shipping companies. The closing of the relief project was on the principle that governmental relief should be administered only by government-paid personnel. It did not undo, however, the demonstration of what client-participation might mean or what citizens might accomplish when they took direct responsibility for a function of their own government. For accounts of this experiment, see *Social Work Today*, Vol. 1, No. 3, July-August, 1934, *When Clients Took Control* by George Hauser, and *The Significance of Baltimore* by Morris Lewis.

13. The social workers in Personal Serice were divided between two employers. The two employed by NMU were affiliated with the Union's office workers in a Chapter of UOPWA. The employees of USS were in the Social Service Employees Union, also under UOPWA, and formed a chapter of USS employees including recreation workers, office workers, and caseworkers.

My position was anomalous, since the USS classed me as an administrator and, as such, excluded from the union contract, while the union accepted me as a member on their definition (and mine) that my position was not administrative. Actually, since the union contract raised all salaries, mine went up correspondingly.

14. For example, a union election took four months, the men voting as they came in from trips and the ballots being deposited with the Honest Ballot Association.

15. The following projects were best known among those undertaken:

a. Detroit, December, 1942 (out of concern about absenteeism in war industries, stemming from acute problems of housing, child care, illness and maladjustments of newcomers from rural areas). A referral service sponsored by unions which had social workers in their membership who volunteered evening time and worked under a local of the United Auto Workers.

b. Cleveland, spring of 1943. Cleveland Welfare Federation joined with the Industrial Union Council to carry referral service to 200,000 union workers from whom social work had traditionally been isolated.

c. Chicago. Social Service Employees Union set up a service with volunteer workers in the hall of the United Packing Workers and later in two locals of United Electrical, Radio and Machine Workers. The service also developed the skills of union officers to whom workers brought many problems.

d. New York. Brooklyn local of United Electrical Workers started a referral service.

e. Willow Run, May, 1944. A Family Counseling Service located in a housing project of 20,000 families was started—an outpost of a family agency but supported by a local of United Auto Workers.

f. Detroit. The UAW placed a counseling service in its Health Institute.

These developments were summarized, with bibliography, in an article I wrote for the *Social Work Year Book*, 1945, under "Labor And Social Work."

16. The key to the new attitudes to labor in wartime was that labor was not superfluous, as in a depression, but a vital part of the nation's life and could command respect.

17. Quoted from an unpublished memorandum for staff discussion.

Chapter 17 THE SMOG THICKENS

1. See "Torpedoing the Good Ship USS," by Tomannie Walker, published in *Staff*, a magazine of the National Social Service Division of UOPWA, March-April, 1947.

2. The Taft-Hartley Act had many complicated provisions, some of which were not enforced immediately, but its main result was to deprive unions of militant leadership through the test of requiring union officers to make affidavit that they were not communists. Penalties of perjury hung over them if, after their denial, a paid informer testified that they were, or, if they had resigned from party membership, gave witness that they did not *really* resign. Some union officials were jailed on such charges.

3. This paper was given at a meeting of the Joint Committee of Trade Unions in Social Work on May 30, 1940. It was published under the title, "Social Workers and Civil Rights," in *Social Work Today*, Vol. VII, No. 9, June-July, 1940.

4. *Ibid.*, pp. 9, 10.

5. For a well-documented history of the treatment of the foreign-born see, Louise Pettibone Smith, *Torch of Liberty* (New York: Dwight-King Publishers, Inc., 1959). In this connection, see especially Chapters 3, "Mass Arrests," and 6, "Legislative Action and Counteraction."

6. A. Delafield Smith, *Community Prerogatives And The Individual* (unpublished, as far as I know, but circulated in mimeographed form).

7. *The Right To Relief* (unpublished).

8. These charges were investigated by the State Board and found to be baseless. For instance, the facts were that the thirty-seven families, housed for a time in cheap hotels, were large families driven out by fires or collapsing buildings or from substandard dwellings they had formerly occupied and were literally unable to find shelter. The capitulation of the DPW to newspaper criticism forced these families either into buildings condemned by the city (and that families lived in these had already been the basis for the charge that children were neglected) or into the Municipal Lodging House. The relief standard of $1.31 per day per person was not luxury by any count and was variously figured to be 14% to 30% below the Budget Council's minimum for health and decency. Yet, even at this rate, a large family could be held up as an example of luxurious income!

9. Although this was the reverse of what he said.

10. The Joint Committee was composed of the United Public Workers, Local 1, New York, and the United Office and Professional

Workers, Local 19, which was the Social Service Employees Union, *The Press Lies About Relief* was published by the Joint Committee as a leaflet in August, 1947.

11. Besides her work as case supervisor, Miss Russell was a lecturer at The New York School of Social Work, Columbia University. Her pamphlet of sixty pages, *Professional Growth On The Job* was published by the Family Service Association of America in 1947.

12. *Confidentiality of Assistance Records,* January, 1952.

13. Accounts of the trials from the point of view of the prosecution filled all the newspapers through 1949. The defendants were literally "tried in the newspapers." For another point of view see, George Marion, *The Communist Trial, An American Crossroads* (New York: Fairplay Publishers). Appendix documents the charges of conspiracy and membership and gives excerpts from the Smith Act and the Supreme Court opinion of 1943 in the case of William Schneiderman. For a later trial of a second group of leaders of the Communist party, see Dr. John Somerville, *The Communist Trials and the American Tradition.*

14. The Subversive Activities Control Act of 1950.

15. I am proud to say that I belonged to most of them. I saw them destroyed one by one, most frequently by the device of requiring their officers to reveal names of members and contributors or be cited for "contempt." Almost without exception this was refused, and a number of men of conscience served prison terms.

16. Documented accounts of this case:

William A. Reuben, *The Atom Spy Hoax,* Book IV (New York: Action Books, 1955).

John Wexley, *The Judgment of Julius and Ethel Rosenberg* (New York: Cameron & Kahn, 1955).

Malcolm P. Sharp, *Was Justice Done?* (New York: Monthly Review Press, 1956).

Morton Sobell, accused with the Rosenbergs and never tried separately, is at this writing serving a thirty-year sentence without a court review of the evidence.

17. After the first eleven Communist party officers were convicted on excerpts taken from books and speeches on the ground that the party advocated "force and violence," thirteen more were put on trial. To meet the criticism that the first group had not been charged with any act, these were charged with attending meetings, mailing letters, etc.

18. See a revealing confession by a professional informer, Harvey Matusow, *False Witness* (New York: Cameron & Kahn, 1955). Mr. Matusow went to jail for perjury for refusing to recant this confession.

19. Bertha C. Reynolds, *Social Work and Social Living* (New York: Citadel Press, 1951).

20. The three papers following were not published, except in mimeographed or leaflet form, and delivered by hand or by mail.

21. Later enlarged and titled, *Focus on Peace.* Distributed by Social Service Volunteers For Peace, New York, 1952.

22. The meeting was sponsored by the Cleveland Council of the Arts,

Sciences and Professions and featured also as speaker, Dr. Edwin A. Brown of the Cleveland Civil Liberties Union. My paper was distributed in mimeographed form.

23. This was at a meeting sponsored by the National Council of the Arts, Sciences and Professions at the time of the National Conference of Social Work at Atlantic City in 1954. Made at the same meeting was a speech by Clifford T. McAvoy, former Deputy Commissioner of Welfare, New York City, and Political Action Director of the New York City CIO Council. *McCarthyism vs Social Work* was printed and sold some 1,500 copies.

24. These were the young sons of Julius and Ethel Rosenberg, who had suffered cruelly in the long imprisonment and final execution of their parents, and were soon to hear of the death by heart attack of their lawyer, "Uncle Manny," to whom their parents had entrusted them. A foster home of superior advantages had just begun to give them love and comfort when, at bedtime, it was entered by police officers, an attorney for the Department of Welfare, and a social worker from a private children's agency, demanding immediate custody of the children on a charge of neglect. The children were sent to an institution away from everyone they knew while the trial of the neglect charge was pending. It took habeas corpus proceedings before the Supreme Court of New York State to release them to the care of their aged grandmother as co-guardian with an eminent social worker. Over 250 courageous social workers signed a petition (in spite of threats of reprisal to some of them if they even discussed the case) and hundreds more wrote letters to the Court. I was one of a delegation to the Mayor, protesting the conduct of the Department of Welfare. We heard at his office wild charges that the foster parents were communists, the children would be spirited away to Canada if not seized at once, the fund raised by "Uncle Manny" for their education proved that they were being exploited for money, etc. All this added up to two suffering children being used as a political football, with the co-operation of social agencies which should have respected such fundamental principles of social work as the right of next of kin to provide for their children. And, if there was just ground for a charge of neglect such that children must be removed from a home, to do so with careful preparation and with less trauma than results from a bedtime raid and a police cordon around the house. I said in my paper: "If we do not take action when professional standards are violated, even in what seem like small matters, we are in no position to resist the decay of everything that makes our profession an honorable calling."

Chapter 18 EDDIES OF CONTROVERSY

1. *Advance or Retreat for Private Family Service?* (New York: United Office and Professional Workers of America, CIO, 1948).

2. The Milford Conference, *Social Case Work, Generic and Specific* (New York: American Association of Social Workers, 1931). See also Bertha C. Reynolds, The Milford Conference Supplementary Report,

"Can Social Case Work be Interpreted to a Community as a Basic Approach to Human Problems?," *The Family*, Vol. 13, February, 1933; Harriet M. Bartlett, *A Study of Current Aims and Methods in Medical Social Work* (Chicago: American Association of Medical Social Workers, 1934); Linton B. Swift, *New Alignments Between Public and Private Agencies in a Community Family Welfare and Relief Program* (New York: Family Welfare Association of America, 1934).

3. *Advance or Retreat for Private Family Service?*, pp. 19-20.

4. *Ibid.*, p. 24.

5. *Ibid.*, p. 25.

6. *Ibid.*, pp. 26, 27, 30.

7. "The Relation of Function to Process in Social Case Work," *The Journal of Social Work Process*, Vol. I, No. 1, November, 1937. Published by the Pennsylvania School of Social Work. Rosa Wessel, "Method and Skill in Public Assistance," *The Journal of Social Work Process*, Vol. II, No. 1, December, 1938. Virginia P. Robinson, *Training for Skill in Social Case Work* (Philadelphia: University of Pennsylvania Press, 1942).

8. "Function and Process in Psychiatric Social Work." Five program papers presented at a meeting of the National Conference of Social Work, Buffalo, New York, June, 1939. Published in *Newsletter* of the American Association of Psychiatric Social Workers, Vol. 8, No. 1.

9. Bertha C. Reynolds, Review in *The Family*, Vol. XXI, No. 1, March, 1940, pp. 31-33.

10. Jessie Taft, "Function as the Basis of Development in Social Work Process."

11. Cora Kasius, *A Comparison of Diagnostic and Functional Casework Concepts*. A report of the Committee to Study Basic Concepts in Casework Practice (New York: Family Service Association of America, 1950).

12. "Digging Deep," *Trends in Social Work*. See Chapter 15, Note 4 regarding *Trends*.

13. These philosophical terms have nothing to do with the popular meanings which make an idealist a person of high ideals and a materialist one who cares for nothing but the things that money can buy. These terms refer to philosophical beliefs about the ultimate nature of reality, whether mind is primary or there exists a material world (including mind) which is independent of what we may think about it. It is the latter philosophy which makes possible scientific study, extending even to such subjects (once forbidden) as the nature of mind itself and the nature of economic systems and human societies.

14. This was done. In June, 1951, *Trends* published another view of the diagnostic-functional controversy. "A Leap to Conclusions," in which Grace Marcus, one of the finest thinkers our profession has ever had, was more critical than I had been of the limitations of the Family Service Study as research. She deplored greatly its conclusion that the differences found were irreconcilable, especially in view of the respon-

sibility of both approaches to serve troubled people. She thought our vested interests in one or the other *way* of serving might be an obstacle to doing so. She closed: "Our various appeals to the scientific . . . may help us eventually to find a better balance between the conviction that must sustain a professional development and the scepticism that is essential to its direction."

15. *Social Breakdown, A Plan for Measurement and Control* (New York: Community Chests and Councils, Inc., 1939).

16. The symposium presented the point of view of a caseworker and a psychiatrist and also appraisals from the fields of research, community organization, and sociology. Along with general approval of better co-ordination of social services and of research, more than one commentator pointed out that, taking as indicator of social breakdown the fact of community recognition of a problem, a community's "rate" would go up the more it paid attention to difficulties. Even preventive work by a social agency might, if it resulted in official steps to commit a mentally sick person or to obtain public assistance, increase the record of social breakdown.

17. "Isolation, by Whom and for What?," *Social Work Today*, March, 1940.

18. A memorandum sent out for discussion by the Community Fund had this to say: "Providing field work for schools of social work can become a much more expensive operation than appears on the surface."

19. Analysis, after the election had continued the Democratic party in power, brought out certain interpretations. One was that the people were responsive to a third party which would represent their interests but not ready, as voters, to risk losing the election to reactionary forces they feared most. While the Progressive party was not a political force in 1952, its campaign for the same issues and for the right to have a third party, kept before the public important matters ignored by the major parties.

20. The statement, with a partial list of signers, was published in *Welfare in Action,* a news sheet of the Joint Committee of Trade Unions in Social Work, for the National Conference, April, 1948.

21. Henry Wallace's speech and the Health and Welfare Program of the New Party were published by the Social Welfare Division of the National Council of Arts, Sciences and Professions, by arrangement with the Joint Committee of Trade Unions in Social Work.

Chapter 19   TIME TO REFLECT

1. However, one of the tragedies of our time is lack of opportunities to enjoy great drama, art collections, the best in "live" music, not only in small town and rural areas but even, for most of the population, in large cities. The hunger for social enjoyment of the arts is not appeased by the television screen, which is too often degraded by commercial interests to exploit sensational scenes of sex and violence. The creative talents, in which America is rich, are stifled by elimination of artists

from employment if they step outside the bounds of approved mediocrity. So there is everywhere impoverishment of the arts which might inspire personal growth.

2. The students at the White Institute were drawn from a wide variety of fields of social work and from the best New York agencies as regards highly trained workers and interest in research to improve methods of practice. It seems fair to conclude, therefore, that my criticism applies to the leading bodies in our profession in that period.

3. Marion K. Sanders, "Social Work: A Profession Chasing its Tail," *Harpers Magazine*, March, 1957.

4. Seeing as I did much waste of time in the practice of casework, I could not wonder too much at the increased demand for cost accounting in the same period.

5. One of the great things J. Prentice Murphy did for the staff at Boston Children's Aid Society was to share his thinking with all of them at staff meetings and to make everyone feel a responsible part of the whole organization. See also page 22.

6. Carl Marzani, *The Open Marxism of Antonio Gramsci* (New York: Cameron Associates, 1957).

Chapter 20 WE HOLD THESE TRUTHS

1. W. E. B. Du Bois, *Souls of Black Folk* (Chicago: A. C. McClurg) Chapters II, IV. Dr. Du Bois has been a leader in the Pan-African Movement.

2. The psychology taught in my college days made reference to Freud's work but had little with which to explore human mental processes beyond the tools of introspection and free association, plus animal experimentation and intelligence tests.

3. Many readers will question this picture of the rise of socialist states and will see them still as centers of cruelty and corruption, a menace to "the free world" of democratic nations. It is not my purpose to claim that all problems of living together are solved for the people of any nation under socialism nor is it possible for me to evaluate the degree of democracy attained in each of the two rival social systems, especially in the circumstance that they face each other under the threat of annihilation in war. All that I can do here is to list verifiable facts true in varied forms of all the socialist systems that now exist—facts of especial interest to my profession. They are: a spectacular rise in the standard of living for the people as a whole; universal health care; education as a corollary of citizenship; and use of natural resources as belonging to the people, not to private interests. The astonishing thing to a social worker (accustomed to: "We cannot afford," when facing human needs) is that the socialist countries can afford whatever they want, and their expenditure of national income seems to point to the values of which a social worker would most approve. If these are facts, we have still to ask *why*. We have still to try to resolve the contradictions between these facts and others which seem to us to need testing.

4. The fascist forces ripening to complete domination of the state in Italy and Germany could not have gained power without the capitulation to them of other countries where fear of socialism was stronger than the threat of fascism with its glorification of aggressive war.

5. This counsel to love and patience on the part of those who suffer wrong may be an unacknowledged willingness that the wrongs continue rather than to disturb the comfort of those who profit by them. Realistically, entrenched wrongs cannot be removed without disturbing somebody. There is, however, a "non-violent resistance" influenced by M. Gandhi which is an active and courageous spiritual force. Whether or not we believe it to be effective under all circumstances, we cannot but admire the courage and self-sacrifice of those who risk their lives in defending their belief that love conquers all.

6. Freudians have tended, nevertheless, to identify aggression with maleness and submission with the role of the female, questioning self-assertion in a woman as evidence of lack of acceptance of femininity. One suspects here some influence from the mores of upper-class Vienna a half century ago.

7. One of the most potent sources of misunderstanding between the nations of "the free world" and those oriented to Marxism is a different valuation of truth in international dealings. We are familiar with diplomatic policies based on: don't rock the boat; don't give your enemies a diplomatic advantage; be sure that propaganda stresses democracy and peace; and war preparations are solely for defense of peace.

The socialist nations are accounted "boorish" in that they call a spade a spade, as they see a spade, even when we think such a word unmentionable. They believe exploitation of the resources of undeveloped countries is economic aggression even when disguised as economic aid. They believe that friendship in words has to be matched by deeds. They believe that what they see as the truth must be spoken, and common people throughout the world will understand, even though their governments may not.

By the "diplomacy" to which the world has been accustomed, this is impermissible boat-rocking, only to be interpreted as menacingly hostile. By the exigencies of modern times, however, if all peoples are to live on the same planet without the total destructiveness of war, they must begin to speak the truth as they see it to each other, no matter how unpleasant it is, and go on to accommodation of differences and to proof in deeds of their sincerity.

8. Of course it is unfair to charge a skit meant for hilarity with failure to express the philosophy of many years later. However, what people pick out to laugh at is a peephole into the thought of their time.

9. Some would define good and bad as cultured people vs. crude and vulgar, superior races vs. inferior, and civilized vs. barbarous. Others would see only exploiters vs. exploited, greedy takers vs. hard-working producers, the rich degenerating from their idleness vs. the potentially creative poor deprived of opportunity.

INDEX

Advance or Retreat for Private Family Service?, 280, 284, 285
All-Philadelphia Child Guidance Clinic, 98
Allen, Cornelia Hopkins, 85, 197
Allen, Frederick H., 98, 99
Alpern, Evelyn, 192, 199
American Association of Hospital Social Workers, 331
American Association of Medical Social Workers, 219, 279
American Association of Psychiatric Social Workers, 142, 285, 331, 336
American Association of Social Workers (AASW), 133, 157, 160, 162, 182, 221, 269-70, 279; Committee on Federal Action on Unemployment, 154; New Jersey Chapter, 165; New York Chapter, 267, 269-70; Providence, R. I., Chapter, 220
American Federation of Labor (A. F. of L.), 26, 138, 326, 337, 338
Andrews, John B., 325
Anti-Tuberculosis Association, 24, 325
"Are Private Agencies Meeting Their Responsibilities?", 279
Associated Charities (Boston), 23, 27-29, 32, 35, 37, 39, 41
Association for Labor Legislation, 325
Association of Public Welfare Employees, 176
Association for Travelers Aid and Transient Service (New York), 147
Atlanta University, 16-17, 311, 312

Baker, Harvey H., 46; Judge Baker Foundation Clinic, 46, 197
Baltimore Emergency Relief Administration (Transient Division), 338
Bancroft, Frank, 175-77, 224
Bech, Elizabeth, 242
Beers, Clifford W., 71
Berger, Victor, 26
Between Client and Community, 165, 174, 332
Beyer, Johanna, 105
Bill of Rights, 263, 264, 265
Binet-Simon tests, 15
Birtwell, Charles W., 31-32, 45

Boston Children's Aid Society (B.C.A.S.), 21, 31, 32, 45, 48, 49, 51, 52, 55, 56, 345; Philanthropic Library, 39
Boston Female Asylum, 41
Boston School for Social Workers, 16, 17, 18, 20-21, 22, 33, 36, 38-40, 42, 44
Boston Social Union, 29
Boston Society for the Care of Girls (B.S.C.G.), 41
Brackett, Jeffrey R., 36-41, 327
Brisley, Mary S., 113
Brockton, Massachusetts, 18, 82
Bronner, Augusta, 46
Brown, Edwin A., 342
Brown, Muriel, 192, 198
Bruno, Frank J., 210, 211, 217
Bureau of Registration, 29

Cabot, Richard C., 33, 34, 53, 54, 77
Cairns, Lucille, 165
Capen, Bessie T., 20, 81
Capen House, 81
Capen School, 20, 81
Casework, *passim;* author's approach to, 88-89, 146-49; use of term, 14, 205, 325
Chapin, F. Stuart, 57, 149
Chapin House, 197
Chappell, Winifred, 215
Charity Organization Movement, 24, 27-28, 29, 35, 43
Charity Organization Society (of Baltimore), 37
Chase, Marie, 101, 108
Chicago, Illinois, 221; Juvenile Court, 46
Child Welfare League of America, 331
Children's Hospital (Philadelphia), 99
Children's Mission, 31
"Church and Individual Security, The," 113
Church Mission of Help, 113
Cincinnati Welfare Department, 176
City Detention Home (Boston), 48
Civil Service Commission (Bureau of Training), 220
Cleveland Civil Liberties Union, 342
Cleveland Council of the Arts, Sciences and Professions, 341-42

Cleveland Welfare Federation, 339
Client, use of word, 14
Cohen, Julius Henry, 325
Committee on Standards of Living and Labor (of the National Conference of Charities and Correction), 24, 325
"Common Goals of Labor and Social Work," 161
Commonwealth College, 215, 233, 235
Commonwealth Fund, 70, 71, 98, 103
Communism, 276, 334
Communist party, 265, 272, 341
Conference on Governmental Objectives for Social Work, 160
Confidential Exchange of Information, 29
Congress of Industrial Organizations (CIO), 154, 217, 235, 245, 250, 263, 273, 336, 337, 338; Health Council, 257; New York City Council of, 342
Consultation Bureau, 232-33
Consumers' League, 39, 325
Council of Social Agencies (Dayton, Ohio), 287
Coyle, David Cushman, 150-51
Curran, Joseph, 261
Curtis, Hannah, 62-64, 67

Danvers (Massachusetts) State Hospital, 53, 62-64, 65, 76, 69, 83, 289
Dawley, Almena, 98, 99, 101
Day, Florence, 197
Dayton, Ohio, Council of Social Agencies, 287
Delta Farm, 213-14
Dietetic Bureau, 48
Dodge Christian Community Center, 234
Doran, Mary S. ("MSD"), 46, 49, 55
Du Bois, W. E. B., 17, 311, 345

Elizabeth Peabody House, 13
Ellis Memorial Camp (Sharon, Massachusetts), 18
Ellis Memorial Neighborhood Centre (Boston), 17
Emergency Home Relief Bureau, 159
Engels, Frederick, 171, 172, 334
"EPD," 45

Episcopal Conference on Social Work (Philadelphia, 1932), 113
Erie (Pennsylvania) Department of Public Welfare, 221
Essex County Hospital (Cedar Grove, New Jersey), 241

Family, The, 120-21, 122, 285, 290
Family Service Association of America, 197, 286
Family Service Society (Utah), 221
Family Service Study, 343
Family Society, The, 101
Family Welfare Association of America, 280, 331
Farm Resettlement Authority, 213
Fascism, 184, 185, 233, 296, 315, 320, 334, 346
"Fear in Our Culture," 275
Feder, Leah, 210
Federal Public Assistance Program, 265, 267
Federal Security Act, 266
Federal Security Agency, 265, 270
Federal Transient Bureau, 338
Federation of Engineers, Architects, Chemists and Technicians, 159
Fields, Toby, 337
"Fireless Cooker, The," 201
First International Congress on Mental Hygiene, 110, 167, 325
Franklin, Sam, 213
Frazier-Lundeen Bill, 159
Freud, Sigmund, 17, 68, 130, 284, 286-87, 331
Freudian psychology, 59, 68, 123-31, 285, 302, 318, 329, 331, 345, 346
Fur Workers' Union of the U.S. and Canada, Int'l., 257

Gain or Loss on the Casework Front, 142
Gandhi, Mohandas K., 346
Garrett, Annette, 197
Gestalt psychology, 120
Girls' High School (Boston), 20
Gluck, Elsie, 192, 198
Golden, John, 326
Gordon, Faith, 90
Gould, Miriam, 90

Habit clinics, 72-74
Hamilton, Alice, 325

Harding, Warren G., 328
Harper's Magazine, 304, 305
Harvard Medical School, 53
Harvard University, 327
Healy, William, 46
Hill, Lewis, 90
Hillhouse, Mississippi, 213
Hodson, William, 159
Home Library Association, 32
Home Relief Bureau (of New York City), 138, 173; Workers Association of, 165
Honest Ballot Association, 339
Hoover, Herbert, 137-38
Hopkins, Harry C., 159

"IGM," 45
Individual Delinquent, The, 46
Industrial Union Council (Cleveland), 339
Industrial Workers of the World (I.W.W.), 26, 326
Institute for Child Guidance, 104-9, 111, 113, 114, 125, 193; publications of staff members, 330
International Migration Service, 331
Interprofessional Association for Social Insurance (IPA), 158, 159, 165, 166, 333
Irrepressible Conflict, Business vs. Finance, The, 150

Jarrett, Mary C., 52, 54, 57, 61, 62, 131, 329
Jenner, William E., 270
Jewish Board of Guardians (JBG), 148, 165
Jewish Service Bureau (Newark, New Jersey), 239-40
Johns Hopkins University, 36-37
Joint Committee of Trade Unions in Social Work, 267, 279, 292
Judge Baker Foundation Clinic, 46, 197
Juvenile Court (Boston), 14

Kelley, Florence, 325
Kellogg, Paul U., 325
Kimball, Everett, 78-79, 83, 84, 85-86, 88, 90-95, 125, 129, 144, 189, 190, 191, 197, 208-9, 328
Kingdom of Evils, The, 60-61
Kline, George M., 64, 328
Kyle, Constance, 242, 244, 337

Lawrence, Massachusetts, 65, 66, 72; strike at, 25-27, 43, 326
Lawyers Guild, 159
League for Preventive Work, 48
Learning and Teaching in the Practice of Social Work, 235
LeFavour, Henry, 327
Lenin, V. I., 171
Levy, David, 106, 193-94, 195
Libbey, Betsey, 101
Liggett, Irene, 101
Lindsay, Samuel McCune, 325
Little Deck House (Sunnyside, New York), 126, 232
Los Angeles, California, 304-6
Louisiana State University School of Public Welfare Administration, 221
Lovejoy, Owen R., 325
Lowell, Massachusetts, 65, 66, 72
Lowrey, Lawson G., 90, 104, 106
Loyalty oaths, 272
Lundeen, Ernest, 159

McAvoy, Clifford T., 342
McCarran-Walter Act, 272
McCarthyism vs. Social Work, 277, 342
McReady, Jane, 17
MacDonald, John B., 64, 65, 67, 70
MacGregor, Madeline L., 332
Marcus, Grace, 343
Marine Workers Industrial Union, 338
Marsh, Marguerite, 113
Marx, Karl, 171, 172
Marxism, 171, 181-85, 308, 317, 322, 334, 346
Massachusetts Commission on Child Labor, 23
Massachusetts General Hospital, 18, 32-34, 62; Out-Patient Department, 32; Visiting Ladies' Committee, 33
Massachusetts Society for the Prevention of Cruelty to Children, 31
Massachusetts State Board of Charity (Division of State Minor Wards), 31
Massachusetts State Department of Mental Diseases, 64; Division of Mental Hygiene, 70, 71
Mena, Arkansas, 214-15

"Mental Hygiene of Young Children, The," 76
Merchant Marine, 243, 251
Methodist Federation for Social Service, 215
Michigan Department of Public Welfare, 232
Michigan Institute for Social Welfare, 221
Milford Conference, The: Milford, Pennsylvania (1928), 132, 331; New York City (1932-33), 140; Reports of, 133, 271
Monday Evening Club, 13, 22, 325
Montclair, New Jersey, Health Department, 242
Murphy, J. Prentice ("JPM"), 21, 22, 32, 45-46, 47-49, 56, 345

National Association for the Advancement of Colored People (NAACP), 17
National Association of Travelers Aid Societies, 331
National Committee for Mental Hygiene, 98, 110, 325
National Committee on Visiting Teachers, 332
National Conference of Charities and Correction, 37; Committee on Standards of Living and Labor, 24, 325; Conference (Cleveland, 1912), 24, 291; Conference (1897), 35; later became National Conference of Social Work, q. v.
National Conference of Social Work, 150, 163, 177; Associate Groups, 333; Conferences: (1922), 70; (Toronto), 76; (Cleveland, 1926), 102; (Detroit, 1933), 150, 155, 157; (Kansas City, 1934), 159-63, 279; (Pittsburgh, 1935), 163; (Cleveland, 1936), 163; (1939), 285; (Grand Rapids, 1940), 221, 263-264, 336; (Atlantic City, 1941), 237; (1946), 265, 267; (Atlantic City, 1948), 279, 291, 292; (Cleveland, 1953), 275; (Atlantic City, 1954), 342
National Convention Against Unemployment, 157
National Council of the Arts, Sciences and Professions, 273, 337, 342

National Maritime Union (NMU), 242, 243-61, 274, 281, 295, 337, 339; Credit Union, 253; Education Department, 337; Personal Service, see under United Seamen's Service
National Probation Association, 332
National Recreation Association, 325
National Recovery Act (NRA), 153, 157, 163, 217
National Unemployed Council of the U.S.A., 157
Nazism, 185, 193, 212, 218, 271, 322
"Need of a Training School in Applied Philanthropy, The," 35
Neilson, William Allan, 144, 209
Neurological Hospital, 220
New Deal, the, 25, 150, 159, 160, 185, 217
"New Forms of Social Workers' Organizations," 162
New Orleans Public Assistance Agency, 221
New York Charity Organization Society, 36, 37, 61-62
New York City: Department of Welfare, 255, 267, 340, 342; Domestic Relations Court, 220; Juvenile Aid Bureau, 220; Juvenile Court, 148; Police Department, 220
New York Psychiatric Institute, 193
New York School of Philanthropy, 36, 37
New York School of Social Work, 49, 104, 255, 337, 341; Faculty Chapter of UOPWA, 338
Northampton, Massachusetts, 20, 81, 90, 91, 388; Northampton State Hospital, 58, 62

Oregon State Department of Welfare, 301
Overseers of the Poor, 42, 48, 327

Passaic, New Jersey, Department of Public Welfare, 219
Peabody, Massachusetts, 19, 66
Pennsylvania Children's Aid, 101
Pennsylvania Hospital, Institute of (Philadelphia), 192
Pennsylvania School of Social Work, 101, 139-40, 284

Peoples Institute of Applied Religion, The, 233, 296
Perkins, Frances, 159
Pilot, The, 337
Plan D, 191-209, 222, 223, 225, 238
Play Night, 13, 14, 22
Poor Laws (English), 40, 43, 271
Presbyterian Hospital, 220
Press Lies About Relief, The, 267
Progressive Party, 272, 291, 344
Psychiatry, psychoanalysis, use of terms, 14-15, 331
Psychology, *see* Freudian psychology
Psychopathic Hospital (Boston), 14, 52, 53
Putnam, James J., 17, 22, 34, 59, 125

Ralph, Georgia, 49
Rank, Otto, 120, 126, 284, 285
Red Cross, 61, 236, 238; Home Service, 49, 178
Re-Thinking Social Case Work, 178, 180-81
Revenue Act of 1951, 270
Reynolds, Bertha C.: analysis experience, 125-31, 332; credo, 186-187, 315-24; education, 16, 20-22, 39-42, 57-63; family, 16, 18-19, 20, 81, 237, 296-97; motto, 22; writings of, 76, 110, 113, 165, 174, 177-178, 180-81, 235, 267, 275, 279, 280, 284, 285 (*see also Notes,* 325 *et seq.*) ; on communism, 276, 334; on Marxism, socialism, 167-68, 181-185, 308-9, 317, 322, 333
Reynolds, Frank, 19, 296-97
Rhode Island State Welfare Department, 220
Richmond, Mary E., 14, 24, 29, 35-36, 37, 43-44, 60, 120, 133, 217; philosophy of life, 329
Robinson, Virginia P., 101, 120-21, 122-3, 284
"Role of the Psychiatric Social Worker in Therapy, The," 110
Roosevelt, Franklin Delano, 25, 140, 185, 274, 291
Roosevelt, Theodore, 24, 291
Rosenberg, Julius and Ethel, 272, 341
Russell, Elizabeth, 268, 341
Russia, Youth and the Present Day World, 166

Schneiderman, William, 341
"SCL," 45
Scottsboro case, 332
Second International Conference of Social Work, 333
Segal, Ida, 239
Service to Transients, 164
"Sex Problems," 33
Simmons College, 22, 37, 38, 327
Simple Simon and the Social Workers, 13-14, 319
Smith, A. Delafield, 265, 267
Smith, Abigail, 98
Smith, Amy, 98
Smith, Ferdinand C., 245
Smith, Zilpha Drew, 18, 37, 39, 42-43
Smith Act, 265, 272, 341
Smith College, 16, 20, 209, 297
Smith College School for Social Work, 54, 55, 57, 59, 61, 68, 69, 76, 78, 79, 80, 82, 84, 85-97, 98, 100, 101, 104, 105, 110, 126, 129, 131, 132, 138, 140, 143-45, 149, 165, 172, 190-93, 197, 198, 200, 201, 205, 208, 210, 211, 242, 284-85, 328, 329, 331, 337; Alumnae Association, 209
Sobell, Morton, 341
"Social Breakdown" plan, 288-89
Social Case Work Generic and Specific, 133
Social Diagnosis, 60, 133, 178; dedication of, 37
Social Security Act, 159, 164, 278
Social Service Employees Union (of the UOPWA), 229, 246, 273, 297, 336, 338, 339, 341
Social Service Index, the, 290
Social Service Volunteers for Peace, 273
Social Syndrome, The, 59
Social Work, 237
Social Work Today, 155-58, 164, 175-177, 224, 226, 290, 335; credos in, 185; Social Work Today Co-operators, 176-77
Socialism, 167-68, 181-85, 308-9, 317, 322, 334, 345, 346
South End House, 30, 326
Southard, Elmer E., 52-54, 58, 60-61
Southern Tenant Farmers' Union, 213
Spaulding, Edith R., 57
Staff, 336

State Hospital for Inebriates (Fox-
  boro, Massachusetts), 30
Stearns, A. Warren, 325
Stoughton, Massachusetts, 16, 19, 80,
  81, 113, 217, 295-98, 301, 307
Subversive Activities Control Act of
  1950, 341
*Supervision and Education in Char-
  ity,* 37
Survey Graphic, 166
Swift, Linton B., 280-83
Sytz, Florence, 121

Taft, Jessie, 101, 285
Taft-Hartley Act, 261, 340
Temple University, 204, 205
Thom, Douglas, 71, 72, 74
Training School for Psychiatric
  Social Work, The, 328
Travelers Aid Society (Chicago),
  332
Trends in Social Work, 286, 337
Tugwell, Rexford D., 159
Tulane University School of Social
  Work, 121
"Type situation," 202, 335

Unemployed Councils, 154, 172
Union of Soviet Socialist Republics,
  166, 171, 172, 185, 218, 271, 272
United Auto Workers, 339; Health
  Institute, 339
United Electrical Workers, 257, 339
United Electrical, Radio and Ma-
  chine Workers, 339
United Nations, 291
United Office and Professional
  Workers of America (UOPWA),
  246, 273, 336, 337, 338, 339, 340-41
United Packing Workers, 339
United Public Workers of America,
  267, 269, 279, 336, 340
United Seamen's Service, 242, 243-
  261, 295, 337, 338; Personal Service
  of, 243-45, 247-48, 250-51, 253-57,
  259-60, 281, 337, 338, 339;
  Women's Auxiliary, 253
United Service Organization (USO),
  243, 337
United States Public Health Serv-
  ice, 251
United Textile Workers of America,
  326

University of California (at Ber-
  keley) School of Social work, 301
University of Chicago School, 145,
  149-50
University of Michigan Institute of
  Public and Social Administration,
  231, 232
University of Minnesota School, 149,
  150
University of Missouri, 164
University of Wisconsin, 192
Utah Department of Public Wel-
  fare, 221

Vaile, Gertrude, 149-50
van Kleeck, Mary, 155, 158, 160-63,
  169, 325, 333
Vassar College, 90
Veterans' Bonus March, 138, 332
Virginia State Welfare Department,
  220

Wallace, Henry, 291-92
War Shipping Administration, 337
Washington University (St. Louis),
  210, 211
Waterfront Unemployed Council,
  338
Wayne University, 232
Welfare in Crisis, 269
Wellesley College, 166
Western Federation of Miners, 326
William Alanson White Institute of
  Psychiatry (New York), 301-2, 345
Williams, Claude, 215, 233-35, 296-
  297, 335
Williams, Frankwood E., 90, 93,
  96-97, 110, 119, 126-27, 159, 325;
  Russian trip, 166-68
Willow Run Family Counseling
  Service, 339
Witmer, Helen, 237
Woods, Robert A., 326
Worcester State Hospital, 93
Workers' Alliance, 154
Workers Social Insurance Bill, 158,
  159, 163
Works Projects Administration, 164
World Federation of Trade Unions,
  261

YWCA, 98, 204, 220
Youth Administration, 164